Published by:

Frommer Media LLC

ISBN: 978-1-62887-501-0 (print); 978-1-62887-502-7 (ebk)

Editorial Director: Pauline Frommer
Editor: Pauline Frommer
Production Editor: Erin Geile
Photo Editor: Meaghan Lamb
Photo Research Interns: Henry Lin-David & Jill Sakowitz
Cartographer: Liz Puhl

Front cover photos, left to right: Humpback whale © Konrad Mostert; Sunset in Maui © Galyna Andrushko; Tiki wood carving in the beautiful Kula Botanical Garden © Sheri Swailes.
Back cover photo: Sunset in Maui © DonLand.

For information on our other products and services, please go to Frommers.com/contactus.

Frommer's also publishes its books in a variety of electronic formats. Some content that appears in print may not be available in electronic formats.

Manufactured in China

5 4 3 2 1

About This Guide

Organizing your time. That's what this guide is all about.

Other guides give you long lists of things to see and do and then expect you to fit the pieces together. The Day by Day guides are different. These guides tell you the best of everything, and then they show you how to see it *in the smartest, most time-efficient way*. Our authors have designed detailed itineraries organized by time, neighborhood, or special interest. And each tour comes with a bulleted map that takes you from stop to stop.

Hoping to sunbathe on a secluded beach or to explore Haleakala National Park? Planning on snorkeling Molokini, driving the winding road to Hana, or relaxing at one of Maui's beachside spas? Whatever your interest or schedule, the Day by Days give you the smartest routes to follow. Not only do we take you to the top attractions, hotels, and restaurants, but we also help you access those special moments that locals get to experience—those "finds" that turn tourists into travelers.

The Day by Days are also your top choice if you're looking for one complete guide for all your travel needs. The best hotels and restaurants for every budget, the greatest shopping values, the wildest nightlife—it's all here.

Why should you trust our judgment? Because our authors personally visit each place they write about. They're an independent lot who say what they think and would never include places they wouldn't recommend to their best friends. They're also open to suggestions from readers. If you'd like to contact them, please send your comments our way at feedback@frommers.com, and we'll pass them on.

Enjoy your Day by Day guide—the most helpful travel companion you can buy. And have the trip of a lifetime.

About the Author

Jeanne Cooper writes frequently about Hawaii for the *San Francisco Chronicle,* where she previously worked as a travel editor, as well as for *Marin* magazine and HawaiiIslander.com. Her stories about the islands have also appeared in the *Houston Chronicle* and other newspapers, plus magazines such as *Southwest, Sunset, Modern Luxury Silicon Valley,* and *Luxury Las Vegas.* Before helping relaunch the Frommer's Hawaii guides, she contributed to guidebooks on San Francisco, Boston, and Washington, D.C., for several different publishers. Now living on *Moku o Keawe,* the Big Island, she was inspired to study hula by her mother, who learned to play ukulele and dance hula in pre-statehood Hawaii.

An Additional Note

Please be advised that travel information is subject to change at any time—and this is especially true of prices. We therefore suggest that you write or call ahead for confirmation when making your travel plans. The authors, editors, and publisher cannot be held responsible for the experiences of readers while traveling. Your safety is important to us, however, so we encourage you to stay alert and be aware of your surroundings.

Star Ratings, Icons & Abbreviations

Every hotel, restaurant, and attraction listing in this guide has been ranked for quality, value, service, amenities, and special features using a **star-rating system.** Hotels, restaurants, attractions, shopping, and nightlife are rated on a scale of zero stars (recommended) to three stars (exceptional). In addition to the star-rating system, we also use a kids **icon** to point out the best bets for families. Within each tour, we recommend cafes, bars, or restaurants where you can take a break. Each of these stops appears in a shaded box marked with a coffee-cup-shaped bullet.

The following **abbreviations** are used for credit cards:

AE	American Express	DISC	Discover	V	Visa
DC	Diners Club	MC	MasterCard		

Frommers.com

Frommer's travel resources don't end with this guide. Frommer's website, **www.frommers.com,** has travel information on more than 4,000 destinations. We update features regularly, giving you access to the most current trip-planning information and the best airfare, lodging, and car-rental bargains. You can also listen to podcasts, connect with other Frommers.com members through our active-reader forums, share your travel photos, read blogs from guidebook editors and fellow travelers, and much more.

A Note on Prices

In the "Take a Break" and "Best Bets" sections of this book, we have used a system of dollar signs to show a range of costs for 1 night in a hotel (the price of a double-occupancy room) or the cost of an entree at a restaurant. Use the following table to decipher the dollar signs:

Cost	Hotels	Restaurants
$	under $150	under $15
$$	$150–$250	$15–$25
$$$	$250–$350	$25–$40
$$$$	$350–$500	$40–$50
$$$$$	over $500	over $50

How to Contact Us

In researching this book, we discovered many wonderful places—hotels, restaurants, shops, and more. We're sure you'll find others. Please tell us about them, so we can share the information with your fellow travelers in upcoming editions. If you were disappointed with a recommendation, we'd love to know that, too. Please write to: Support@FrommerMedia.com

A Note on Hawaiian Words

The Hawaiian language includes the macron (a line over a long vowel) and the ʻokina (a single open quotation mark reflecting a glottal stop, similar to the sound in the middle of "uh-oh.") Most street signs use both marks, but many signs and publications may use only the ʻokina or neither. For typographical reasons, this guidebook only uses the ʻokina except on maps.

16 Favorite **Moments**

16 Favorite Moments

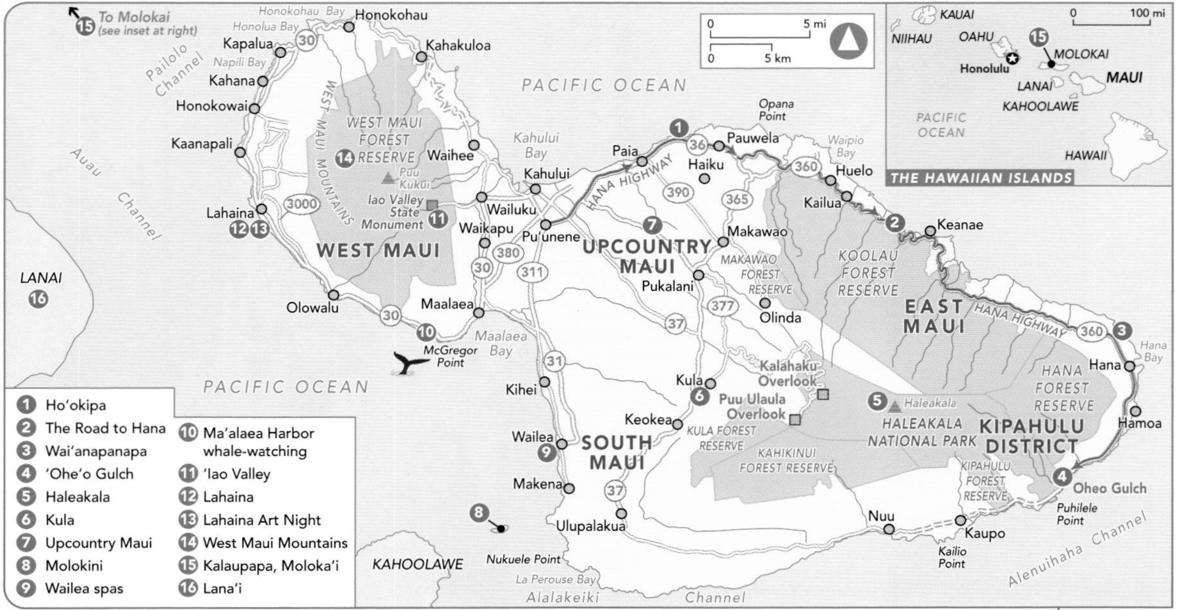
To Molokai (see inset at right)
PACIFIC OCEAN
THE HAWAIIAN ISLANDS
KAUAI
NIIHAU
OAHU
Honolulu
MOLOKAI
MAUI
LANAI
KAHOOLAWE
HAWAII
0 100 mi
0 5 mi
0 5 km
Honokohau Bay
Honokohau
Honolua Bay
Kapalua
Kahakuloa
Napili Bay
Kahana
Pailolo Channel
Honokowai
Kaanapali
Auau Channel
Lahaina
LANAI
WEST MAUI FOREST RESERVE
WEST MAUI MOUNTAINS
Puu Kukui
Iao Valley State Monument
WEST MAUI
Waihee
Wailuku
Waikapu
Kahului Bay
Kahului
Pu'unene
Paia
HANA HIGHWAY
Haiku
Pauwela
Opana Point
Waipio Bay
Huelo
Kailua
Keanae
UPCOUNTRY MAUI
Makawao
Pukalani
MAKAWAO FOREST RESERVE
Olinda
KOOLAU FOREST RESERVE
EAST MAUI
HANA HIGHWAY
Hana Bay
Hana
HANA FOREST RESERVE
Hamoa
Olowalu
Maalaea
Maalaea Bay
McGregor Point
PACIFIC OCEAN
Kihei
Kula
Kalahaku Overlook
Puu Ulaula Overlook
Haleakala
HALEAKALA NATIONAL PARK
KIPAHULU DISTRICT
KIPAHULU FOREST RESERVE
Oheo Gulch
Puhilele Point
Keokea
KULA FOREST RESERVE
KAHIKINUI FOREST RESERVE
Wailea
SOUTH MAUI
Makena
Ulupalakua
Nuu
Kaupo
Kailio Point
Alenuihaha Channel
KAHOOLAWE
Nukuele Point
La Perouse Bay
Alalakeiki Channel
1 Ho'okipa
2 The Road to Hana
3 Wai'anapanapa
4 'Ohe'o Gulch
5 Haleakala
6 Kula
7 Upcountry Maui
8 Molokini
9 Wailea spas
10 Ma'alaea Harbor whale-watching
11 'Iao Valley
12 Lahaina
13 Lahaina Art Night
14 West Maui Mountains
15 Kalaupapa, Moloka'i
16 Lana'i

Previous page: Sun worshippers cavort on Wailea Beach.

To experience the true magic of Maui, just step outside to watch the sun set in a blaze of glorious hues over the ocean, inhale the perfume of delicate ginger blossoms, listen to the clattering of bamboo in the rain forest, or revel in a night sky full of the same stars that guided Polynesians to Hawai'i long ago. A few more of my favorite Maui experiences are described below.

Ho'okipa Beach Park is a top spot for water sports.

❶ **Watch windsurfers ride the waves at Ho'okipa.** This famous beach draws waveriders from around the globe to ride, sail, and pirouette over the waves. Watching them flip into the air while rotating 360 degrees is the best free show in town. *See p 79.*

❷ **Smell the sweet scent of ginger on the road to Hana.** At every twist on this winding road you are greeted by exotic tropical blossoms, thundering waterfalls, breathtaking vistas, and a glimpse at what Maui looked like before it was "discovered." *See p 66.*

❸ **Walk the coast trail at Wai'anapanapa.** This trail will take you back in time, past lava cliffs, mysterious caves, a *hala* forest, an ancient *heiau* (temple), an explosive blowhole, native Hawaiian seabirds, and the ever-changing Pacific. *See p 91.*

❹ **Take a dip in a waterfall at 'Ohe'o Gulch.** Even if conditions don't permit a swim, ogle the fern-shrouded pools spilling seaward at 'Ohe'o Gulch, on the rain-shrouded flanks of Haleakala. *See p 87.*

❺ **Greet the rising sun from atop Haleakala.** Book a permit in advance, dress warmly, and drive the 37 miles (60km) from sea level up to 10,000 feet (3,048m), where you can watch the sunrise. Breathing in the rarefied air and watching the first rays of light streak across the sky is a mystical experience. *See p 86.*

❻ **Head to Kula to bid the sun aloha.** This town perched on the side of Haleakala is the perfect place to watch the sun set over the entire island, with vistas across the isthmus, the West Maui Mountains, and Moloka'i and Lana'i in the distance. *See p 65.*

❼ **Explore Upcountry Maui.** On the slopes of Haleakala, cowboys, farmers, ranchers, and other country people make their serene, neighborly homes, worlds away

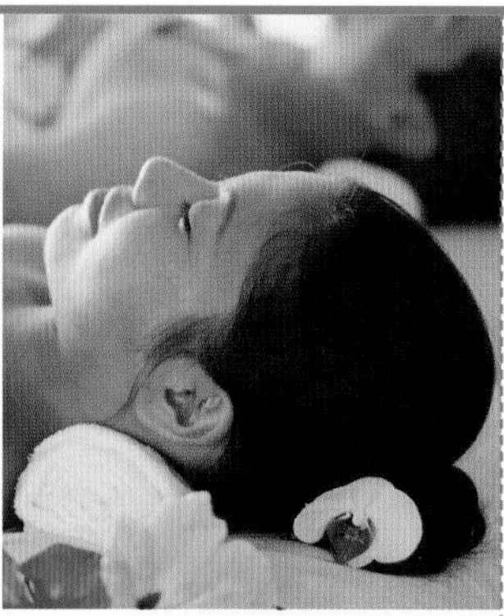

A beachside massage is the perfect way to relax.

from the bustling beach resorts. *See p 64.*

8 **Snorkel off Molokini.** Calm, protected waters in the islet's crater, plus an abundance of marine life, make Molokini one of Hawai'i's best places to snorkel. Paddle with turtles, watch clouds of butterflyfish flitter past, and search for tiny damselfish in the coral. *See p 98.*

9 **Get pampered in paradise.** Maui's spas have raised the art of relaxation and healing to a new level. A massage on the beach will smooth out the kinks, while you bask in the sounds of the ocean, smell the salt air, and feel the caress of a warm breeze. *See p 37.*

10 **Watch for whales.** From mid-December through the end of March, humpback whales can be seen from shore jumping, breaching, and slapping their pectoral fins. *See p 107.*

11 **Explore 'Iao Valley.** When the sun strikes 'Iao Valley in the West Maui Mountains, an almost ethereal light sends rays out in all directions. This really may be Eden. *See p 60.*

12 **Visit a historic port town.** In the 1800s, whalers swarmed into Lahaina and missionaries fought to stem the spread of their sinful influence. Before that, Hawaiian royalty ruled this coast. *See p 50.*

13 **Experience Art Night in Lahaina.** Every Friday, under a canopy of stars, the town's galleries open their doors and serve refreshments. Wander in to see what's going on in Maui's creative community. *See p 116.*

14 **Fly over the remote West Maui Mountains.** The only way to see the inaccessible, prehistoric West Maui Mountains is by helicopter. You'll fly low over razor-thin cliffs and flutter past sparkling waterfalls while descending into canyons and valleys. *See p 101.*

15 **Visit historic Kalaupapa.** Even if you have only 1 day to spend on Moloka'i, walk in the footsteps of St. Damien and St. Marianne Cope in Kalaupapa National Historic Park, accessible only by a steep trail or short flight. *See p 63.*

16 **Take a day trip to Lana'i.** Sailing from Lahaina Harbor, you can admire Maui from offshore, go snorkeling in the clear waters of Lana'i, tour this tiny former plantation island, and still catch the last ferry back. *See p 152.* ●

One of Lahaina's quirky characters.

1 Strategies for Seeing Maui

Strategies for Seeing Maui

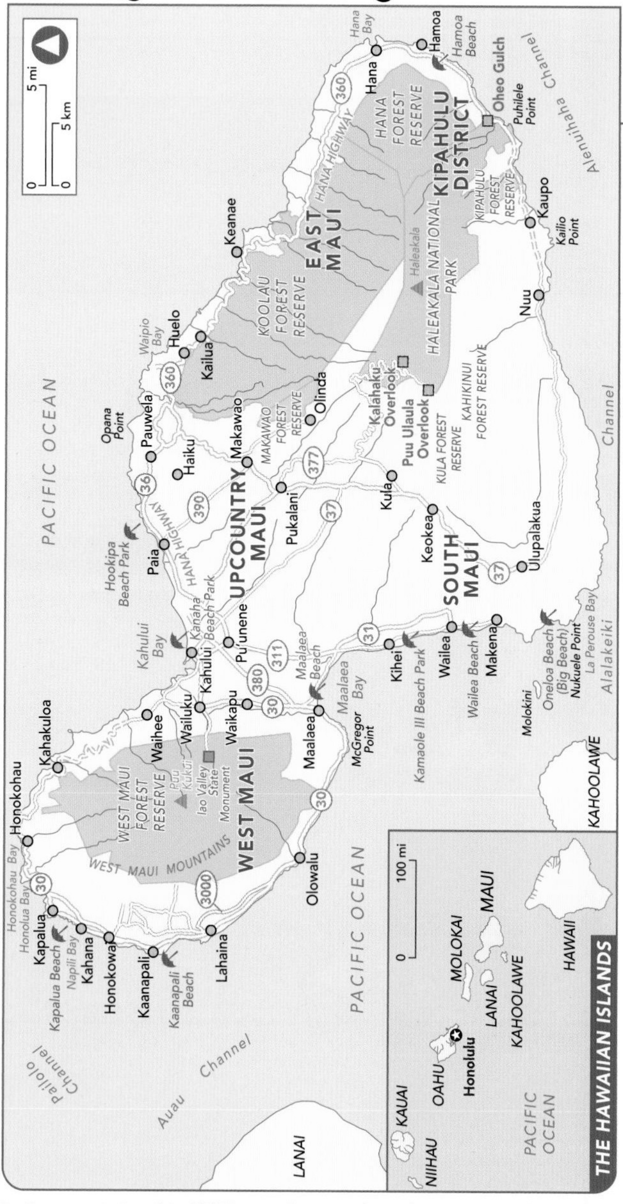
PACIFIC OCEAN
PACIFIC OCEAN
WEST MAUI
WEST MAUI MOUNTAINS
WEST MAUI FOREST RESERVE
UPCOUNTRY MAUI
SOUTH MAUI
EAST MAUI
KIPAHULU DISTRICT
HALEAKALA NATIONAL PARK
Haleakala
KOOLAU FOREST RESERVE
HANA FOREST RESERVE
KIPAHULU FOREST RESERVE
MAKAWAO FOREST RESERVE
KULA FOREST RESERVE
KAHIKINUI FOREST RESERVE
HANA HIGHWAY
Hana
Hana Bay
Hamoa
Hamoa Beach
Oheo Gulch
Puhilele Point
Kaupo
Kailio Point
Nuu
Keanae
Huelo
Kailua
Waipio Bay
Opana Point
Pauwela
Haiku
Makawao
Olinda
Kalahaku Overlook
Puu Ulaula Overlook
Pukalani
Kula
Keokea
Ulupalakua
Paia
Hookipa Beach Park
Kanaha Beach Park
Kahului Bay
Kahului
Pu'unene
Wailuku
Waihee
Waikapu
Kahakuloa
Honokohau
Honokohau Bay
Honolua Bay
Kapalua
Kapalua Beach
Napili Bay
Kahana
Honokowai
Kaanapali
Kaanapali Beach
Lahaina
Olowalu
Maalaea
Maalaea Bay
Maalaea Beach
McGregor Point
Kihei
Kamaole III Beach Park
Wailea
Wailea Beach
Makena
Molokini
Oneloa Beach (Big Beach)
Nukuele Point
La Perouse Bay
Alalakeiki Channel
Alenuihaha Channel
Auau Channel
Pailolo Channel
Iao Valley State Monument
Puu Kukui
LANAI
KAHOOLAWE
0 5 mi
0 5 km
THE HAWAIIAN ISLANDS
NIIHAU
KAUAI
OAHU
Honolulu
MOLOKAI
LANAI
MAUI
KAHOOLAWE
HAWAII
PACIFIC OCEAN
0 100 mi

Previous page: A view of the Cliff House, a champagne bar at the Montage Kapalua Bay Resort.

Maui may be an island, but it's a good-size island and your vacation time is precious. There really is just one cardinal rule: Slow down. Maui is not a place to "see" but a place to experience. If you are too busy rushing to tick things off your to-do list, you won't experience the magic of the island. Here are my suggestions for making the most of your time.

Take some time to stop and smell the plumerias.

Rule #1: Remember you are on vacation

Don't jam your days with activities; allow time to relax, stop and smell the plumerias. That said, if you arrive jet-lagged, use it to your advantage! Get out and watch the sunrise while you're still on East or West Coast time. Book an early morning snorkel trip. Remember: Exposure to sunlight can help reset your internal clock—another good reason to soak up the ambient Vitamin D.

Rule #2: Expect driving to take a lot longer on Maui

Maui lacks adequate public transportation, so you'll need a car to get around. But plan to stretch your legs as much as possible. Don't just rubberneck from your car window; get out and inhale the salty, flower-scented air, revel in the panoramic views, and listen to the sounds of surf crashing or mynah birds arguing over squashed guavas. Sure, you could drive the 50-mile-long (80km) Hana Highway in as few as 2 to 3 hours, but that would miss the point of the journey entirely. One last thing: Maui does have traffic jams. From 7 to 9am and 4 to 6pm the main roads are bumper-to-bumper with commuters. Plan accordingly. Sleep in late and get on the road after the traffic has cleared out, or watch the sunset and then go to dinner.

Rule #3: If your visit is short, stay in one place

Unless you're visiting for a week or longer, try not to hotel hop. With

Maluaka Beach.

An endangered grey-crowned crane, native to Africa, at the Kula Botanical Garden.

the exception of Hana, all the towns on Maui are within easy driving distance. Checking in and out of hotels is inconvenient—there's the schlepping of the luggage (and the corresponding tips to the parking valet, the bellhop, and so on), the waiting in line to check in, and unpacking, only to repeat the entire process a few days later. Your vacation time is too precious.

Rule #4: Pick the key activity of the day and plan accordingly

To maximize your time, decide what you really want to do that day, then plan all other activities in the same geographical area. For example, if you want to go golfing in Kapalua, plan to hit a beach and eat dinner nearby—that way you won't have to trek back and forth across the island.

Rule #5: Remember you are on the island of aloha

Maui residents aren't in a rush and you shouldn't be either. Slow down. Smile. Say "aloha" (hello, goodbye, and I love you all rolled into one) and "mahalo" (thank you). Remember that you are a guest here. Ask questions. Eat unfamiliar fruits. Practice standing up on a surfboard even if it makes you scream. Learn as much as you can about local history—it's fascinating, and knowing even a little will enrich your time here.

Rule #6: Use this book as a reference, not a concrete plan

The best vacations are a mix of careful plans and total spontaneity. Pick and choose the tours you want to take and then let the weather and the new friends you make dictate some diversions. ●

Fly Direct

If possible, fly nonstop and directly to the island of Maui (the airport is in Kahului and the airport code is OGG). Not only is it easier, but it will also save you time. Yes, there are flights from the U.S. mainland through Honolulu and then on to Maui, but the "on to Maui" bit generally means getting off a plane in the big, big Honolulu International Airport and transferring to another terminal. While it's easy to book a connecting flight that doesn't require you to go through security again or recheck your bags, waiting (sometimes up to 2 hours) for your flight to Maui is still no way to begin a vacation.

2 The Best Full-Day Tours

The Best of Maui in Three Days

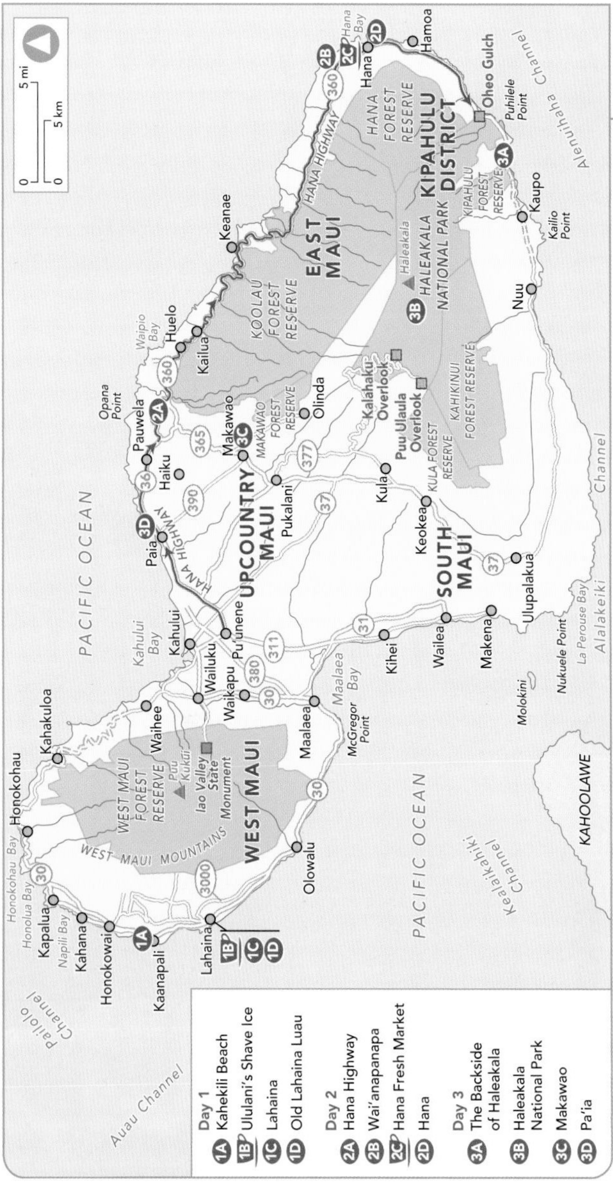
Day 1
1A Kahekili Beach
1B Ululani's Shave Ice
1C Lahaina
1D Old Lahaina Luau
Day 2
2A Hana Highway
2B Wai'anapanapa
2C Hana Fresh Market
2D Hana
Day 3
3A The Backside of Haleakala
3B Haleakala National Park
3C Makawao
3D Pa'ia
0 5 mi
0 5 km
PACIFIC OCEAN
Pailolo Channel
Auau Channel
Kealaikahiki Channel
Alalakeiki Channel
Alenuihaha Channel
KAHOOLAWE
Molokini
WEST MAUI
WEST MAUI MOUNTAINS
WEST MAUI FOREST RESERVE
Puu Kukui
Iao Valley State Monument
UPCOUNTRY MAUI
SOUTH MAUI
EAST MAUI
KOOLAU FOREST RESERVE
MAKAWAO FOREST RESERVE
KULA FOREST RESERVE
KAHIKINUI FOREST RESERVE
HANA FOREST RESERVE
KIPAHULU FOREST RESERVE
KIPAHULU DISTRICT
HALEAKALA NATIONAL PARK
Haleakala
Kalahaku Overlook
Puu Ulaula Overlook
Oheo Gulch
HANA HIGHWAY
Honokohau Bay
Honolua Bay
Napili Bay
Kahului Bay
Maalaea Bay
Waipio Bay
La Perouse Bay
Hana Bay
Honokohau
Kahakuloa
Kapalua
Kahana
Honokowai
Kaanapali
Lahaina
Olowalu
Maalaea
McGregor Point
Waihee
Wailuku
Waikapu
Kahului
Pu'unene
Paia
Haiku
Pauwela
Opana Point
Kailua
Huelo
Keanae
Makawao
Olinda
Pukalani
Kula
Keokea
Kihei
Wailea
Makena
Ulupalakua
Nukuele Point
Nuu
Kaupo
Kailio Point
Puhilele Point
Hana
Hamoa

Previous page: The Garden of Eden botanical garden near Hana.

For a smallish island, Maui has wildly diverse ecosystems and communities—there's a lot to see and experience. If you only have 3 days, concentrate on some of Maui's most quintessential experiences: a beach, a lu'au, the scenic Hana Highway, and the view from the top of Haleakala, a 10,023-foot-high (3,048km) dormant volcano. START: **Kahekili Beach.**

Travel Tip

For detailed descriptions of the beaches in this chapter, see chapter 5. For hotel reviews, see chapter 10. For more on the recommended restaurants, see chapter 8.

To get to Kahekili Beach from Lahaina/Ka'anapali, take Hwy. 30 north toward Kapalua. Turn left on Pu'ukoli'i Street and follow it to the shaded parking lot.

1A ★★★ Kahekili Beach. Check in to your hotel, and then head for Kahekili Beach, named for an ancient Maui king. You'll feel like royalty when you sink your toes into the deep sand here. Don't overdo the sun on your first day. Bring water, sunscreen, and a hat. If you're feeling adventurous, rent snorkel equipment—the reef here is vibrant. Otherwise, simply bask like a turtle on the sand and enjoy the perfect temperature. See p 80.

Retrace your route back to Hwy. 30 and turn right, continuing into Lahaina town.

1B Ululani's Shave Ice. Cool off with this uniquely Hawaiian treat. Snow-fine ice shavings are topped with tropical fruit syrups. Try liliko'i and coconut with ice cream or a "snowcap" (sweet condensed milk). *790 Front St., Lahaina. www.ululanishawaiianshaveice.com. ☎ 808/757-8286. $.*

1C ★★ Lahaina. After an hour or two at the beach, spend a couple of hours walking this historic oceanfront town, which was once the royal capital of Hawai'i, and later a favorite spot for both whalers and missionaries. Today, you can browse its array of unique storefronts, restaurants, and nightlife spots. See the walking tour on p 50 for more information.

1D ★★★ Old Lahaina Lu'au. To really feel as though you are in Hawai'i, immerse yourself in Polynesian culture at this beachfront lu'au. The festivities begin at sunset and feature Tahitian and Hawaiian

The Old Lahaina Lu'au immerses guests in Polynesian culture.

dancing and chanting. The food is a mix of Pacific Rim and traditional Hawaiian, from imu-roasted kalua pig to baked mahi-mahi to teriyaki sirloin steak. *1251 Front St. www.oldlahainaluau.com. ☎ 800/248-5828 or 808/667-1998. $125 adults, $75 children 3 to 12. See p 127.*

From Lahaina take Hwy. 30 south to Hwy. 380 and turn right (east). In Kahului, Hwy. 380 becomes Dairy Road. Turn right (east) on Hwy. 36.

2A ★★★ **Hana Highway.** You'll probably wake up early on Day 2, your first full day in Hawai'i, so take advantage of it and get out as quickly as you can and onto the scenic Hana Highway. Allow at least 3½ to 5 hours for the journey. Pull over often (where it is safe and legal to do so); get out to take photos, smell the flowers, and buy fresh banana bread. Move off the road for those speeding by, and breathe in Hawai'i. For a detailed description of this route, see p 66.

After MM 16, Hwy. 36 becomes Hwy. 360 and starts with MM 0. Just past MM 32 is:

2B **Wai'anapanapa State Park.** Just before reaching Hana town, stop at this state park and hike down to the black-sand beach and cave pool. See p 82.

Back on the Hana highway, a couple of miles down the road between MM 34 and 35 is:

2C **Hana Fresh Market.** This small, outdoor farmer's market and deli (open 11am–3pm every day) sells lunch items made with locally grown produce. I highly recommend the poke bowl and grilled veggie panini. Enjoy a latte made with local coffee before you leave.

About ½ mile (.8km) after MM 35, you come to the outskirts of Hana; veer right at the police and fire station.

2D ★★★ **Hana.** While you're here, make sure to hit three of my favorite spots, the **Hana Cultural Center and Museum,** the **Hasegawa General Store,** and **Hana Coast Gallery.** Spend the night in Hana. For more detailed information on Hana's sights, see p 70. For where to stay in Hana, see p 143.

3A ★★ **The "Backside" of Haleakala.** On Day 3, pack up to leave Hana and head out toward the lush **Kipahulu District of Haleakala National Park.** Bring snacks, water, and a charged camera or phone to capture the stunning vistas you will encounter. Stop at the waterfalls in Kipahulu (save your

The dramatic black sands of Wai'anapanapa State Park.

park receipt for entrance to the summit later). Continue on the cliff-hanging road through the dry, cattle country of **Kaupo.** (The road turns to gravel in a few spots, but it isn't too bad. Drive slowly and watch for cows.) Stop for ice cream at **Kaupo Store.** Proceed on Pi'ilani Hwy. 31 into the rolling green hills of 'Ulupalakua. Take a spin through **MauiWine** and the **'Ulupalakua Ranch Store** (p 65, 5).

Pi'ilani Hwy. 31 becomes Kula Hwy. 37 after 'Ulupalakua. Follow it to Kekaulike Hwy. 377 and turn right. Turn right again onto Haleakala Hwy. 378 to go to the top of Haleakala.

3B ★★★ **Haleakala National Park.** Cruise up to the 10,000-foot (3,048km) dormant volcano, **Haleakala.** You won't have time for a hike, but spend at least an hour gazing into the crater's moonscape. See p 84 for details. *www.nps.gov/hale.* ☎ *808/572-4400. Park open 24 hours daily; main visitor center daily 7am–4pm.*

Retrace your route down Hwy. 378 to Hwy. 377, where you turn right and head north to Hwy. 37. Turn right onto Hwy. 37 and, at the next light, turn right onto Makawao Avenue to drive to the town of Makawao. To get to Pa'ia from Makawao, head downhill on Baldwin Avenue.

MauiWine holds tastings in a former jail.

3C ★★ **Makawao.** Tour the old cowboy town (see p 64 for details), and plan a sunset dinner in 3D ★★ **Pa'ia** (p 32) before heading back to the airport. If you're feeling luxurious, make reservations well in advance for **Mama's Fish House.**

From Hwy. 36 in Pa'ia, drive west to Kahului, turning right on Airport Road.

Maui Driving Tips

Hawai'i residents know the highways by their Hawaiian names; very few know the highway numbers. I've included both the Hawaiian highway name and number on the maps, but the directions in this book mainly refer to the highway number. You'll also see the abbreviation MM, which stands for "mile marker." Below is a quick reference to the names and numbers of Maui's highways.

Hwy. 30: Honoapi'ilani Highway
Hwy. 31: Pi'ilani Highway
Hwy. 36 and Hwy. 360: Hana Highway
Hwy. 37: Haleakala Highway and the Kula Highway
Hwy. 311: Maui Veterans (formerly Mokulele) Highway
Hwy. 377 and Hwy. 378: Haleakala Highway
Hwy. 380: Kuihelani Highway

The Best of Maui in One Week

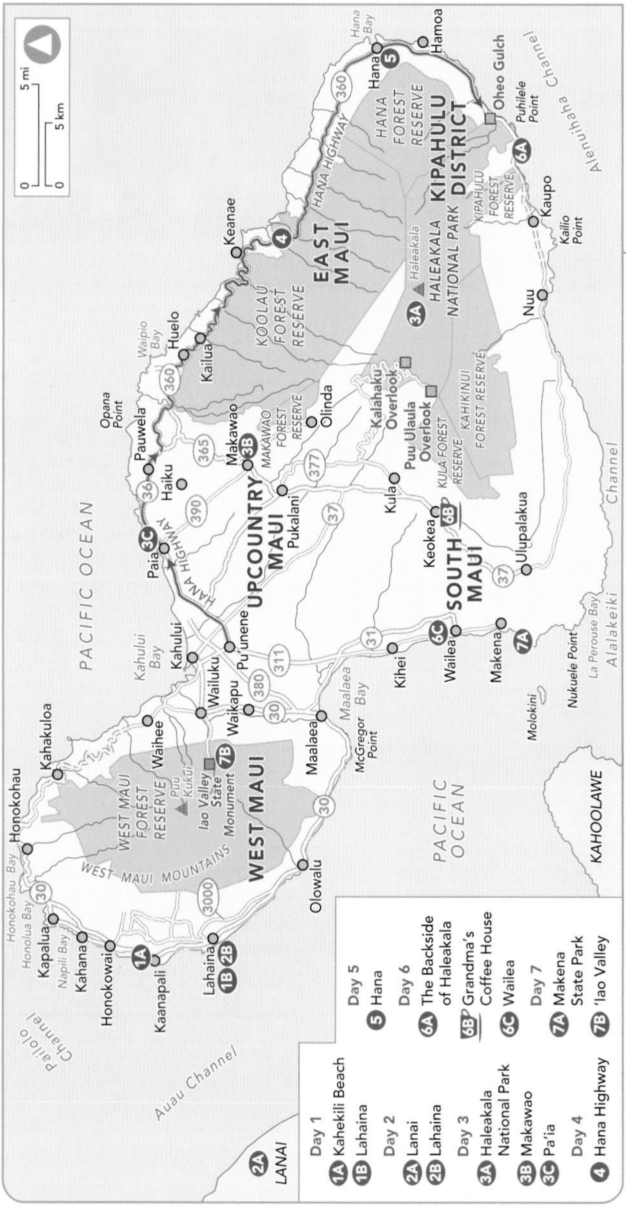
Day 1
1A Kahekili Beach
1B Lahaina
Day 2
2A Lanai
2B Lahaina
Day 3
3A Haleakala National Park
3B Makawao
3C Pa'ia
Day 4
4 Hana Highway
Day 5
5 Hana
Day 6
6A The Backside of Haleakala
6B Grandma's Coffee House
6C Wailea
Day 7
7A Makena State Park
7B 'Iao Valley
0 5 mi
0 5 km
PACIFIC OCEAN
WEST MAUI
UPCOUNTRY MAUI
SOUTH MAUI
EAST MAUI
KAHOOLAWE
LANAI
WEST MAUI MOUNTAINS
WEST MAUI FOREST RESERVE
HALEAKALA NATIONAL PARK
KIPAHULU DISTRICT
HANA FOREST RESERVE
KOOLAU FOREST RESERVE
MAKAWAO FOREST RESERVE
KULA FOREST RESERVE
KAHIKINUI FOREST RESERVE
KIPAHULU FOREST RESERVE
HANA HIGHWAY
Iao Valley State Monument
Puu Ulaula Overlook
Kalahaku Overlook
Oheo Gulch
Lahaina
Kaanapali
Honokowai
Kahana
Kapalua
Honokohau
Kahakuloa
Waihee
Wailuku
Waikapu
Kahului
Pu'unene
Paia
Haiku
Pauwela
Makawao
Pukalani
Olinda
Kula
Keokea
Ulupalakua
Kihei
Wailea
Makena
Maalaea
Olowalu
Huelo
Kailua
Keanae
Hana
Hamoa
Kaupo
Nuu
Molokini
Auau Channel
Pailolo Channel
Alalakeiki Channel
Alenuihaha Channel

I recommend staying at least a week on Maui to take in this sensuous island at a slow, leisurely pace. This weeklong itinerary adds a few new favorites to the 3-day tour: sailing to the island of Lana'i; spending an extra day in Hana; and, depending on your preference, a final day on the beach, at a spa, or shopping for souvenirs. I suggest working your way around the island to avoid unnecessary commuting: spend the first 2 nights in West Maui (Lahaina/Ka'anapali/Kapalua), night 3 in Pa'ia, nights 4 & 5 in Hana, and the last night in South Maui (Kihei/Wailea). If that's too much hotel-hopping for you, pick one home base to drive back and forth from. START: **Kahekili Beach.**

Travel Tip

West Maui is the area from Lahaina north, including Ka'anapali, Honokowai, Kahana, Napili, and Kapalua. South Maui includes Kihei, Wailea, and Makena.

To get to Kahekili Beach from Lahaina/Ka'anapali, take Hwy. 30 north toward Kapalua. Turn left on Pu'ukoli'i Street and follow it to the shaded parking lot.

1A ★★★ Kahekili Beach & 1B ★★ Lahaina. See Day 1 in "The Best in 3 Days," above.

Go south on Hwy. 30 to Lahaina. Turn right at the light on Dickenson Street. Look for the REPUBLIC PARKING sign on the right.

2A ★★★ Lana'i. On your second day, get out on the water early with **Trilogy** (p 99), my favorite sailing-snorkeling trip in Hawai'i. Pack your swimsuit, sunscreen, hat, and plenty of water. You'll spend the morning sailing to the island of Lana'i, snorkeling, and touring the island. Breakfast and lunch are included.

2B ★★ Lahaina. After sailing back to Lahaina, in the afternoon you'll have time to shop for souvenirs or relax in Lahaina. For dinner, I'd book a table on the ocean at sunset at **Mala Ocean Tavern** (p 128)

Sailing to Lana'i offers spectacular views of West Maui.

The Best of Maui in Two Weeks

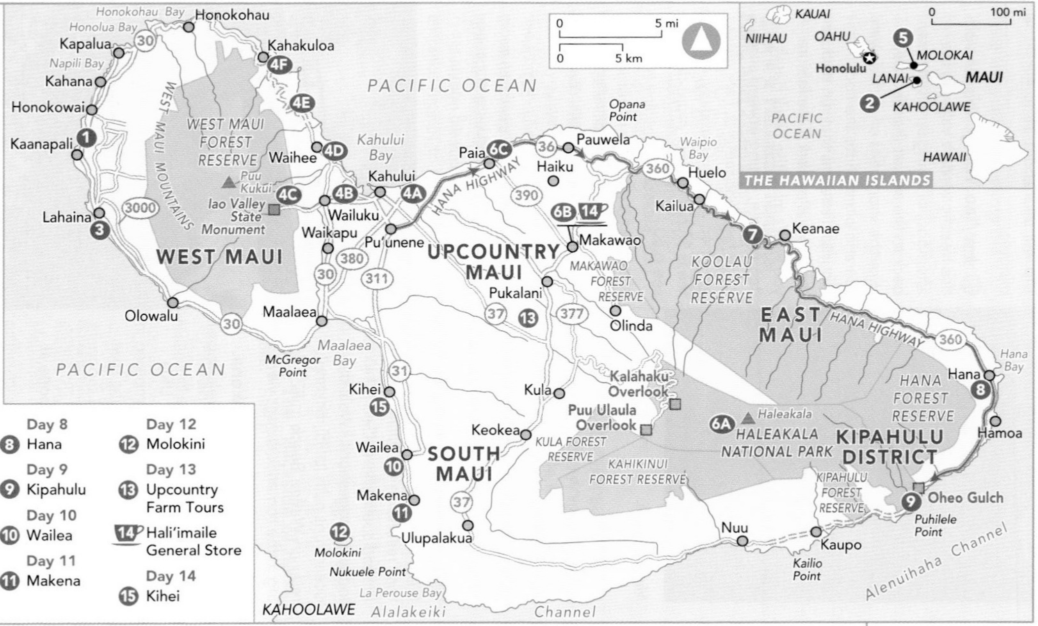

Day 1
1 Kahekili Beach

Day 2
2 Lanai

Day 3
3 Lahaina

Day 4
4A Blue Hawaiian Helicopter
4B Wailuku
4C 'Iao Valley
4D Hale Ki'i and Pihana Heiau
4E Kahekili Highway
4F Kahakuloa

Day 5
5 Kalaupapa National Park, Moloka'i

Day 6
6A Haleakala National Park
6B Makawao
6C Pa'ia

Day 7
7 Hana Highway

Day 8
8 Hana

Day 9
9 Kipahulu

Day 10
10 Wailea

Day 11
11 Makena

Day 12
12 Molokini

Day 13
13 Upcountry Farm Tours
14 Hali'imaile General Store

Day 14
15 Kihei

Two weeks on Maui separates the visitors from the adventurers and gives you time to really get to know this exotic isle. This tour is similar to the 1-week tour above with a few additional stops: flying to Moloka'i and visiting the dramatic Kalaupapa Peninsula; seeing Maui from a helicopter; snorkeling in the old volcanic crater of Molokini; touring Maui's farms; and kayaking off historic Makena. To reduce driving time, plan on spending 6 nights in West Maui, 3 nights in Hana, and 5 nights in South Maui. START: **Kahekili Beach.**

On Day 1, head to the picture-perfect ❶ ★★★ **Kahekili Beach** (see p 80) on the West Maui coast. On Day 2, plan to spend the day on the ocean—well equipped with swimsuit, sunscreen, a hat, and plenty of water—with a boat trip from Lahaina to ❷ ★★★ **Lana'i** (see p 154).

Turn right on Hwy. 30 to Lahaina town.

❸ ★★ **Lahaina.** After a day on the remote island of Lana'i, head for the bustling town of Lahaina. Plan to arrive in this historic town early, before the crowds. I recommend a big breakfast—at **Mala Ocean Tavern** (p 128) or **Lahaina Coolers** (p 128)—then put on your walking shoes and take the self-guided **historic walking tour** of the old town (p 50), do some browsing in the quaint stores (p 112), and watch the surfers skim the waves in front of the library.

Up-close with a waterfall on the Blue Hawaiian helicopter tour.

Travel Tip—Rush Hour

Plan ahead to avoid Maui's rush hour, which lasts from 7 to 9am and from 4 to 6pm. Roads can be packed bumper-to-bumper—not a fun way to spend your vacation!

From the West Maui coast, take Honoapi'ilani Hwy. 30 through Ma'alaea and then branch northeast on Kuihelani Hwy. 380, which becomes Airport Road. Follow the signs toward the heliport, turning right on Kala Road. Make a left on Leleipio Place.

4A ★★★ **Maui from above.** Day 4 gets you a bird's-eye view of the island. Flying over Maui in a helicopter will give you an entirely different perspective of the island, from canyons and lush rainforests to plunging waterfalls and mountain peaks. Of all the helicopter companies, I think **Blue Hawaiian Helicopter** (p 102) offers the most comfortable, informative, and thrilling tours.

After your flight, head to Wailuku. Return to Airport Road. Turn right (northwest) on Hana Hwy. 36. Follow Hwy. 36 until it merges with Hwy. 32 (Ka'ahumanu Ave.), which will take you into Wailuku (the street name changes to Main St. in Wailuku).

Meander around the old town of 4B ★★ **Wailuku** (see the walking tour on p 44). Visit **Native Intelligence** (p 118) and stop at **Hale Ho'ike'ike** (formerly the Bailey House Museum, p 44). Continue up Main Street, which becomes 'Iao Valley Road, to the end, where you will be in 4C ★★ **'Iao Valley** (p 45). Hike the trails or pack a swimsuit and plunge into the cool mountain streams that run through the 'Iao Valley park.

From here, retrace your route back to Main Street in Wailuku. From there, make a left on N. Market Street, then a right on Mill Street, which ends at Lower Main Street. Turn left and, as you near the coast, go left again onto Waiehu Beach Road (Hwy. 340). Take the second left onto Kuhio Place and then take your first left on Hea Place.

At the end of the street are the ancient temples of 4D **Hale Ki'i and Pihana Heiau** (see p 44). If you aren't too tired or fearful, take the long route back to West Maui via the 4E **Kahekili Highway** (see p 44 for its storied history): Return to Waiehu Beach Road (Hwy. 340), turn left, and when the road ends, make a right onto Kahekili Highway

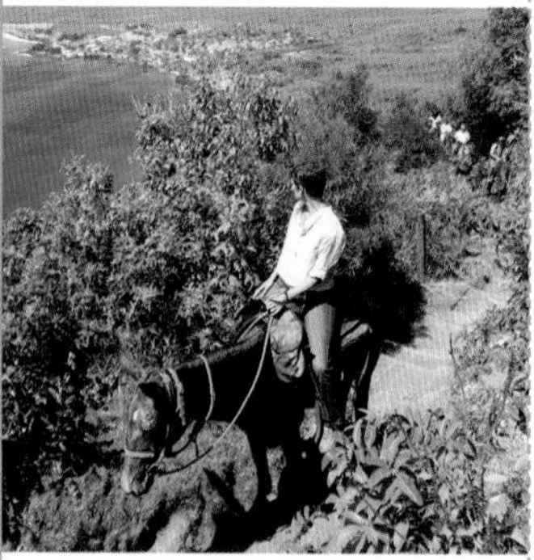

Molokai's famed mule ride up the world's steepest sea cliffs.

(also Hwy. 340), a winding, narrow road with blind curves. Follow Hwy. 340 about 12 miles (19km) to visit the ancient Hawaiian village of 4F **Kahakuloa** (see p 44). From there it is another 21 miles (34km) on Hwy. 340, then Hwy. 30, to return to Lahaina.

To fly to Moloka'i for the day, go to Kahului Airport. From West Maui, take Hwy. 30 to just past Ma'alaea and veer right onto Kuihelani Hwy. 380, which becomes Airport Road.

5 ★★★ **Kalaupapa National Park.** For an unforgettable all-day adventure, hop over to Moloka'i to visit the beautiful, haunting **Kalaupapa Peninsula.** Meet up with **Damien Tours** to explore this extraordinary area, now a National Historical Park. You can fly or, depending on trail conditions, hike or ride a mule down the world's tallest sea cliffs and then take a bus tour of historic sites, most relating to its 19th-century role as a compulsory "home" to sufferers of Hansen's Disease, also known as leprosy. See p 62 for more details.

From West Maui, take Hwy. 30 south, pick up Hwy. 380 just past Ma'alaea, and turn right on to Hwy. 36. Take another right on Hwy. 37 and follow it southeast through Pukalani. Turn left on Hwy. 377, then right at the sign to the Haleakala National Park on Hwy. 378 and take it to the top. The summit is 40 to 50 miles (64–80km) from West Maui. Allow at least 2 hours.

6A ★★★ **Haleakala National Park.** Cool off and dress warmly for Day 6 at the summit of this 10,000-foot volcano. For details on exploring this volcano, see p 84; if you have time, you'll want to add on the rural towns of 6B ★★ **Makawao** (p 64) and 6C ★★ **Pa'ia** (p 67).

To reach Hana Highway from Lahaina/Ka'anapali, take Hwy. 30

Pool at the Four Seasons Wailea.

south to Hwy. 380 and turn right (northeast). In Kahului Hwy. 380 becomes Dairy Road. Turn right (east) on Hwy. 36, otherwise known as the Hana Highway.

7 ★★★ **Hana Highway.** On Day 7, pack your bags and head out to heavenly Hana along the famous Hana Highway (see p 66 for a complete driving tour). Stop in **Pa'ia** for snacks at **Mana Foods** (p 67). Visit the napping sea turtles at **Ho'okipa Beach Park** (p 79). From here on out, cell service is iffy or nil. You'll spend the next few days unplugged and blissed out in East Maui's rainforested hinterlands.

8 ★★★ **Hana** and 9 ★★★ **Kipahulu.** In addition to the activities in Hana listed on p 67 5, visit the **Kipahulu District of Haleakala National Park** (see p 87 for full information). Pack a picnic lunch and hike to **Waimoku Falls,** above 'Ohe'o Gulch (see p 74).

After 'Ulapalakua, Hwy. 31 becomes Hwy. 37. Follow it across the island to Hana Hwy. 36 and turn left. Take the next left onto Hansen Road and follow it until it ends at Maui Veterans Hwy. (Hwy. 311). Turn left and head south. Hwy. 311 becomes Hwy. 31, Pi'ilani Hwy., which ends at Wailea. The drive will take a little more than an hour.

10 ★★ **Wailea.** Spend a day relaxing in this tony resort area: Indulge yourself at a **spa** (p 37), lounge on **Wailea Beach** (p 82), or browse the **Shops at Wailea** (p 120).

To get to Makena Beach from Wailea, take Hwy. 31 south, which ends at Wailea 'Ike Drive. Turn left at the intersection onto Wailea Alanui Road, which becomes Makena Alanui Road. Turn right on Makena Road to Makena Bay. From there to La Pérouse Bay, continue on Makena Road until it ends, then take off on foot for a couple of miles to reach the bay.

11 ★★★ **Makena.** Take things easy on Day 11 by venturing out to wild, untamed Makena and beyond. Consider exploring this scenic coast by kayak—the water is calm and clear enough that you can see the fish, and you are protected from the wind (see "Kayak Tours," p 106). After a couple of hours of kayaking and snorkeling at **Makena**

Kids love visiting the Surfing Goat Dairy.

Upcountry, the Ali'i Kula Lavender Farm welcomes visitors.

Landing, break for a picnic lunch. If you have energy to spare, hike over to **La Pérouse Bay,** along the rugged shoreline, and see the **'Ahihi-Kina'u Natural Area Reserve** (p 97). Return for dinner at **Ka'ana Kitchen** (p 128) or **Lineage** (p 128).

Many boat trips to Molokini depart from Ma'alaea Harbor. Travel on Hwy. 31 north, turn left on Hwy. 30. The left-turn exit to Ma'alaea comes up within a mile.

⓬ ★★★ **Molokini.** On Day 12, the deep sea beckons. Board a boat to Molokini Crater, that tiny crescent on the horizon. You'll see dazzling corals and schools of fish in 100 feet of crystal-clear water. If it's whale season, you'll be treated to a show on the way over or back. I recommend taking one of **Trilogy's** tours (p 99) or **Kai Kanani** (p 99); the latter departs from Wailea's **Maluaka Beach.**

From Wailea, take Hwy. 31 north, which becomes Hwy. 311. Turn right on Hansen Road in Pu'unene, turn right at Hwy. 36, and in a half-mile turn right onto Kula Hwy. 37, the main Upcountry Maui road.

⓭ ★★ **Upcountry farm tours.** Return to the slopes of Haleakala on Day 13 for a tour through Maui's verdant farmlands. (See the driving tour on p 38 for fuller details.) Book a multi-farm trip with **Maui Country Farm Tours** (p 39), a luncheon at **O'o Farm** (p 40), or investigate a few farms on your own. Cheese aficionados will love sampling fromage at the **Surfing Goat Dairy Tour** (p 39). The **Ali'i Kula Lavender Farm** (p 40), will revive your senses with its fragrant herb gardens.

14 Heading down the mountain, stop for dinner in the middle of the pineapple fields at **Hali'imaile General Store.** See p 127.

Head south on Hwy. 31, South Kihei Road.

⓯ **Kihei.** After 13 days of exploring Maui, spend your last full day doing whatever you love best in the laidback town of Kihei, whether it's shopping, beach-hopping the 5 miles (8km) of white-sand beaches (see p 80), visiting the wildlife preserve (see p 57), or taking a whale-watch tour (p 99). Don't forget one last rainbow shave ice. ●

Kihei Kalama Village shopping center.

3 The Best Special-Interest Tours

Maui with Kids

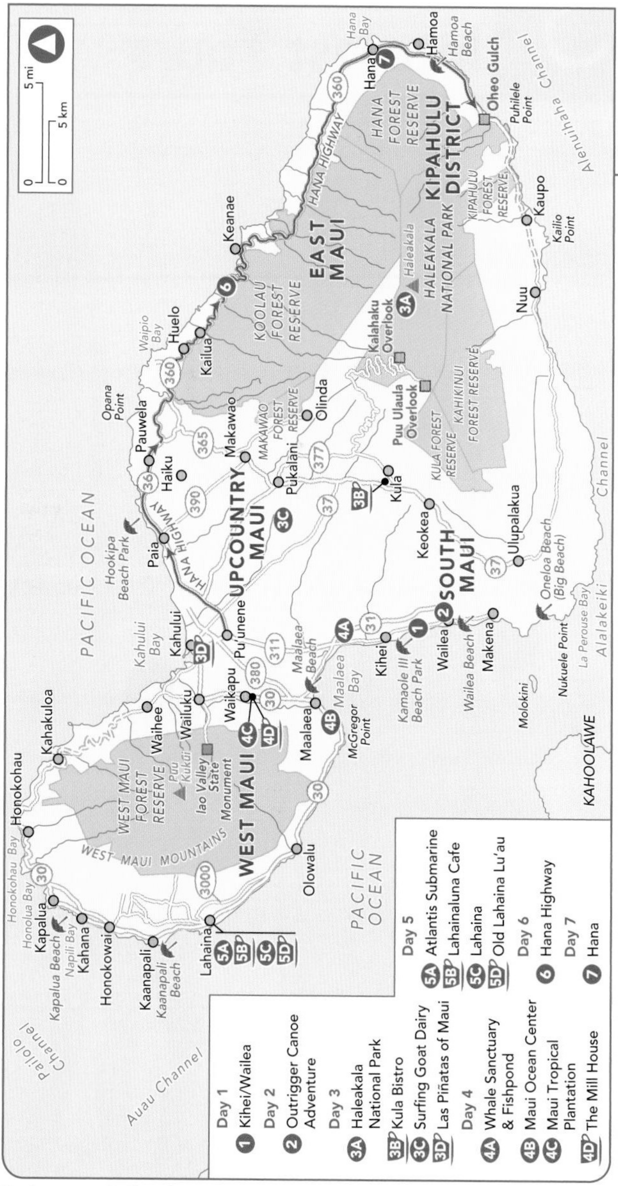
Day 1
1 Kihei/Wailea
Day 2
2 Outrigger Canoe Adventure
Day 3
3A Haleakala National Park
3B Kula Bistro
3C Surfing Goat Dairy
3D Las Piñatas of Maui
Day 4
4A Whale Sanctuary & Fishpond
4B Maui Ocean Center
4C Maui Tropical Plantation
4D The Mill House
Day 5
5A Atlantis Submarine
5B Lahainaluna Cafe
5C Lahaina
5D Old Lahaina Lu'au
Day 6
6 Hana Highway
Day 7
7 Hana
PACIFIC OCEAN
WEST MAUI
UPCOUNTRY MAUI
SOUTH MAUI
EAST MAUI
KIPAHULU DISTRICT
HALEAKALA NATIONAL PARK
KAHOOLAWE
Alalakeiki Channel
Alenuihaha Channel
Auau Channel
Pailolo Channel
Lahaina
Kaanapali
Kapalua
Kihei
Wailea
Makena
Kahului
Wailuku
Paia
Haiku
Makawao
Pukalani
Kula
Hana
Kaupo
Keanae
Maalaea
Olowalu
Oheo Gulch
5 mi
5 km

Previous page: Surfboards on Ka'anapali Beach.

The number-one rule of family travel is don't plan too much, especially with young children, who will be fighting jet lag, trying to get adjusted to a new bed (and most likely new food), and may be hyped up to the point of exhaustion. The 7-day itinerary below is a guide to the various family-friendly activities available on Maui; I suggest staying in a convenient South Maui (Kihei or Wailea) condo or resort for the first 5 nights. Then venture out to Hana for an unforgettable last 2 nights. START: **Kihei/Wailea.**

Travel Tip

See chapter 10 for hotel recommendations and chapter 8 for detailed reviews of the restaurants mentioned in this chapter.

1 Kihei/Wailea Beach & Pool. The first thing kids will want to do is hit the water. In Wailea, **Wailea Beach** (p 82) is a safe place to start; in Kihei, head to one of three **Kama'ole Beach Parks** (p 80). If your youngsters aren't used to the waves, consider sticking to the hotel swimming pool. (If you're staying at the Grand Wailea, with its fantasy water park, they'll be ecstatic with this choice.) You'll probably want an early dinner with food your kids are used to. My family-friendly picks in Kihei: **Nalu's South Shore Grill** (p 131) or **Peggy Sue's** (p 131). Get to bed early.

Canoe trips may leave from Polo or Wailea Beach, or from Olowalu, halfway to Lahaina on Honoapi'ilani Hwy. 30.

Outrigger canoe paddling.

2 ★★★ Outrigger Canoe Adventure. Day 2 is the prime time to build upon your family's cooperation and teamwork. Climb into a six-person outrigger canoe and learn how to paddle in sync while you explore the South Maui coastline amid surfacing sea turtles, curious manta rays, and, in winter months, humpback whales. Several resorts, such as the Fairmont Kea Lani, have their own canoes and guides. My favorite company to paddle with is **Hawaiian Ocean Sports** (p 105). After a few hours on the water, reward your brave ocean explorers with shave ice at **Ululani's** (p 131) and sushi at **Sansei** (p 132)—maybe even with a little karaoke fun.

Allow 1 hour and 45 minutes to reach the Haleakala summit from South Maui. Go north on Pi'ilani Hwy. 31 to Maui Veterans Hwy. 311. Turn right on Hansen Road, merge onto Hana Hwy. 36, then turn right onto Haleakala Hwy. 37. Turn left onto Hwy. 377 and left again onto Hwy. 378.

3A ★★★ Haleakala National Park. Today is the day to tackle the 10,000-foot (3,048m) dormant volcano at Maui's heart. Depending on the age of your children, you can either hike in the crater, speed down the mountain on a bicycle, or just wander about the park. See p 84 in chapter 6 for details. *www.nps.gov/hale. ☎ 808/572-4400. Open daily 24 hours a day.*

Goats at the Surfing Goat Dairy.

3B Kula Bistro. Either on the way to or from Haleakala, stop off at this upcountry fave for delish pastries, breakfast, or lunch. See p 128.

From the summit, retrace Hwy. 378 to Hwy. 377 to Hwy. 37 and turn left onto Oma'opio Road. Look for the SURFING GOAT DAIRY sign on the left about 4 miles (6.4km) down. Allow 1 hour and 10 minutes.

3C Surfing Goat Dairy. Your kids will love petting and playing with the four-legged kids of the goat variety. If you time it right, you can help with the evening chores and milking—at 3:30pm Monday through Saturday. *See p 39.*

Continue down the mountain on Oma'opio Road, which after MM 5 joins Pulehu Road (Hwy. 370). When the road ends, turn right on Ho'okele Street, left on Hana Hwy, then right on Dairy Road to Las Piñatas of Maui.

3D Las Piñatas of Maui. Kids can stick to the comfort zone with cheese quesadillas while the grown-ups can go nuts over cilantro-jalapeño-battered fish tacos. *395 Dairy Rd., Kahului. www.pinatasmaui.com. ☎ 808/877-8707. $.*

4A Whale Sanctuary & Fishpond. Today's the day to study Maui's rich marine life. Head up coastal S. Kihei Road, which parallels Hwy. 31, and stop by the **Hawaiian Humpback Whale Sanctuary Visitor Center** (726 S. Kihei Rd.; hawaiihumpbackwhale.noaa.gov; ☎ 808/879-2818) to learn about the giants of the sea. Next door, the **Ko'ie'ie Fishpond** is a prime example of ancient Hawaiian aquaculture.

Head north on S. Kihei Rd., which merges into N. Kihei Rd. Turn left onto Honoapi'ilani Hwy. 30.

4B Maui Ocean Center. On your way north, the kids may enjoy stretching their legs along the **Kealia Boardwalk** (just north of MM 2 on North Kihei Rd.) in a wetland wildlife refuge. Then continue to the **Maui Ocean Center** to spend a couple of hours exploring marine life in this impressive aquarium. *See box below.*

Shark tanks enthrall youngsters at the Maui Ocean Center.

Ziplining at the Maui Tropical Plantation.

Return to Honoapi'ilani Hwy. 30 and head north to the Maui Tropical Plantation in Waikapu.

4C Maui Tropical Plantation. Explore the plantation's verdant grounds, take a 40-minute tram ride through exotic flora and fruit, and soar on a speedy zipline that will amuse even jaded teenagers. *(1670 Honoapi'ilani Hwy.; www.mauitropicalplantation.com; ☎ 808/244-7643)*

4D The Mill House. The menu might be a little adventurous for youngsters, but they'll love the train engines, gears, and fantasy fountains decorating this eclectic restaurant. Adults will love the refined cuisine and handcrafted cocktails. *At Maui Tropical Plantation, 1670 Honoapi'ilani Hwy., Waikapu. www.millhousemaui.com. ☎ 808/270-0333. $$$.*

Head north on Pi'ilani Hwy. 31. Turn left onto North Kihei Road, then left onto Honoapi'ilani Hwy. 30. Turn left onto Prison Street, right onto Front Street, and find parking.

5A Atlantis Submarine. In Lahaina you can take the kids underwater in a Jules Verne–type fantasy, the

A Great Way to Spend a Rainy Day

If it rains during your vacation, take the kids to **Maui Ocean Center** (www.mauioceancenter.com; ☎ 808/270-7000), located at 192 Ma'alaea Rd. in Ma'alaea. Introduce the *keiki* (children) to the underwater world, without getting wet. This terrific aquarium starts with the reef world, where you can see the animals living in the reefs surrounding Maui. Then the exhibits go deep—very deep—to feature big pelagic fish like 100-pound tunas and sleek barracudas. But most kids' favorite exhibit has to be the shark tanks, where you can watch these kings of the deep prowl through the water. *Daily 9am–5pm. $30 adults, $20 ages 4–12.*

The Atlantis Submarine.

Atlantis Submarine. You'll plunge 100 feet (30m) under the sea in a state-of-the-art, high-tech submarine and meet swarms of vibrant tropical fish up close as they flutter through the deep blue waters. Atlantis offers trips out of Lahaina Harbor hourly from 9am to 2pm. *658 Front St. www.atlantisadventures.com. ☎ 800/548-6262 or 808/667-2224. $124 adults, $48 children 11 and under (children must be at least 3 ft./.9m tall). Book online for free child (maximum age 12) fare with paying adult.*

5B **Lahainaluna Cafe.** Grab fancy grilled cheese sandwiches, hot dogs, and soba noodle salads from this casual courtyard restaurant, and then reward yourself with shave ice from Ululani's (p 131) next door. *790 Front St., Lahaina. www.lahainaluna cafe.com. ☎ 808/757-8286. $.*

5C **Lahaina.** In the afternoon, wander around Lahaina (see walking tour p 50). Even if you don't visit all the attractions, be sure to hit the kid-friendly highlights, including the giant **Banyan Tree**, the **Old Lahaina Courthouse**, and the **Old Prison**. Then pick a nearby beach—gentle **Launiupoko Beach Park** (p 81) for younger children to paddle around, or long **Ka'anapali Beach** (p 80) for teenagers to swim or snorkel.

5D **Old Lahaina Lu'au.** Book seats far in advance for the Old Lahaina Lu'au (p 140) in the evening. Your drive back to the hotel will take about 30 minutes to Kihei, or 45 minutes to Wailea-Makena.

Head north on Pi'ilani Hwy. 31 to Maui Veterans Hwy. 311. Turn right on Hansen Road, then right on Hana Hwy. With stops, this drive will take the whole day.

Participants in the Maui Whale Festival.

❻ ★★★ **Hana Highway.** Get an early start, pack your bags, and head out to heavenly Hana. (see detailed driving tour p 70). Stop in **Pa'ia** for snacks at **Mana Foods** (p 67). Visit the napping sea turtles at **Ho'okipa Beach Park** (p 79). Pull over wherever allowed to take photos, smell the flowers, and dip in the mountain-stream pools. Stop for ice cream at **Coconut Glen's** (see p 69) and dig your toes into the black sand at **Wai'anapanapa State Park** (p 82). Spend the night in Hana (see tour p 32).

❼ ★★★ **Hana & Environs.** Make the most of your last full day on Maui. Depending on your children's ages and interests: Go bodysurfing at **Hamoa Beach** (p 79), hiking to waterfalls in the **Kipahulu District of Haleakala National Park** (p 87), or spelunking in **Ka'eleku Cavern,** below a ti-leaf botanical maze (205 Ula'ino Rd.; www.mauicave.com; ☎ 808/248-7308). Rise early the next day to return to Kahului Airport on Hana Highway.

Family-Friendly Events

Your trip may be more exciting with the added attraction of attending a celebration, festival, or party on Maui. Check out the following events:

- **Chinese New Year,** Lahaina (www.visitlahaina.com; ☎ 888/310-1117). In 2020, lion dancers will be snaking their way around Maui towns, celebrating the Chinese Year of the Rat. Lahaina rolls out the red carpet with a traditional lion dance, accompanied by fireworks, food booths, and a host of activities.
- **Maui Whale Festival,** Kalama Park, Kihei (www.mauiwhalefestival.org; ☎ 808/249-8811). This monthlong celebration in February features a parade, film festival, entertainment, whale count, and running events.
- **Whale & Ocean Arts Festival,** Lahaina (www.visitlahaina.com; ☎ 888/310-1117). Kids love this early to mid-March event with marine-related activities, games, and a touch-pool exhibit.
- **Annual Lei Day Celebration,** islandwide (www.gohawaii.com/maui; ☎ 808/875-4100). May Day (May 1) is Lei Day in Hawai'i, celebrated with lei-making contests, pageantry, arts and crafts, and concerts.
- **King Kamehameha Celebration,** islandwide (www.visitlahaina.com; ☎ 888/310-1117). June 11 is a state holiday with a massive floral parade, a *ho'olaulea* (party), and much more.
- **Fourth of July Parade & Rodeo,** Makawao. (www.makawaorodeo.net; ☎ 808/757-3347). Hawaiian-style cowboys ride up Baldwin Avenue on the first Saturday in July, on their way to an exciting rodeo.
- **Maui County Fair,** War Memorial Complex, Wailuku (www.mauifair.com; ☎ 808/242-2721). At the end of September or early October, this traditional county fair features a parade, amusement rides, live entertainment, and exhibits.

Romantic Maui

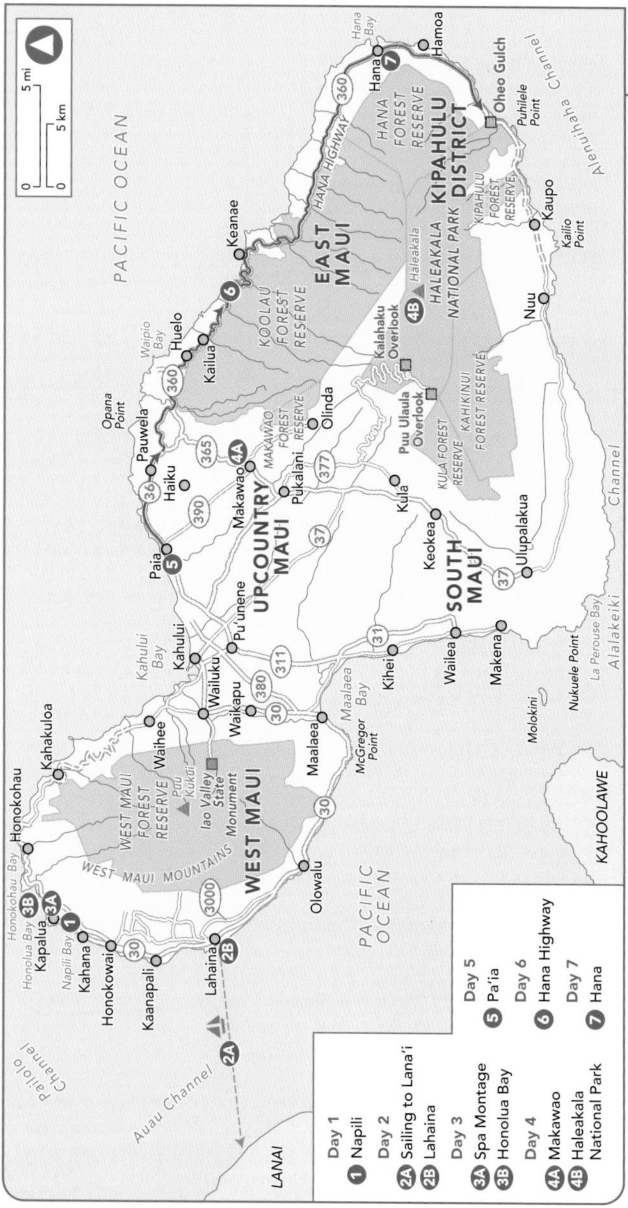
Day 1
1 Napili
Day 2
2A Sailing to Lana'i
2B Lahaina
Day 3
3A Spa Montage
3B Honolua Bay
Day 4
4A Makawao
4B Haleakala National Park
Day 5
5 Pa'ia
Day 6
6 Hana Highway
Day 7
7 Hana
PACIFIC OCEAN
WEST MAUI
UPCOUNTRY MAUI
SOUTH MAUI
EAST MAUI
KIPAHULU DISTRICT
HALEAKALA NATIONAL PARK
WEST MAUI MOUNTAINS
WEST MAUI FOREST RESERVE
KOOLAU FOREST RESERVE
HANA FOREST RESERVE
HANA HIGHWAY
LANAI
KAHOOLAWE
Lahaina
Kaanapali
Honokowai
Kahana
Kapalua
Wailuku
Kahului
Paia
Makawao
Pukalani
Kula
Kihei
Wailea
Makena
Keanae
Hana
Kaupo
Oheo Gulch
Alenuihaha Channel
Alalakeiki Channel
Auau Channel
Pailolo Channel
5 mi
5 km

Maui's sensual landscape makes it the perfect place to fall in love. The scent of flowers, the sound of tumbling waves, and the island's intoxicating beauty beckon lovers. If you're discovering Maui as a twosome for a week, I suggest spending the first 3 nights in Napili, 2 nights in Pa'ia, and the final 2 in Hana. START: **Napili.**

❶ ★★★ **Napili.** Check into the **Napili Kai Resort** (p 148) and revive with a swim in the turquoise bay. Enjoy an early ocean-view dinner (perhaps at happy hour) at its **Sea House Restaurant.**

Head south on Honoapi'ilani Hwy. 30 to Dickenson Street and find parking near Lahaina Harbor. It's a 22-minute drive. Allow extra time for traffic.

2A ★★★ **Sailing to Lana'i.** Climb aboard **Trilogy** (p 99), my favorite sailing outfit, and chase the horizon to the island of Lana'i. On the half-day excursion, the crew hands you hot cinnamon rolls and coffee as soon as you step on board, and after the 9-mile (14km) trip to Lana'i, you'll snorkel in the island's protected waters and land for a barbecue lunch. Upon your return, spend the remainder of the day strolling through 2B historic **Lahaina** (see tour p 50). Dine at **Gerard's** (p 127) or **Lahaina Grill** (p 128).

Head north on Lower Honoapi'ilani Rd., turning left onto Bay Dr. to get to Spa Montage.

3A ★★★ **Kapalua Spa Morning.** A visit to any of the island's spas would be a treat, but **Spa Montage** (1 Bay Dr., Kapalua; ☎ 800/548-6262 or 808/665-8282) has a few perks for couples: a co-ed spa pool and gorgeous garden *hale* (huts) with romantic rock tubs. Plus, it's only 2 minutes up the road. After indulging in luxurious massages or body treatments, take a walk along the **Kapalua Coastal Trail** (accessed from multiple points along the coast, between the Merriman's Maui parking lot and D.T. Fleming Beach).

Take Office Road inland to connect with Honoapi'ilani Hwy. 30. Turn left and continue on to Honolua Bay at MM 32 and Nakalele Blowhole at MM 38.5. Return the same way.

3B **Honolua Bay.** At MM 32, leave the highway to explore this jeweled bay. Linger a little on the forest path; snorkel in the bay (or watch surfers if the waves are up). Then continue on to see the **Nakalele Blowhole**. (The cars crowding the roadside at MM 38.5 are the tip-off.) Stay a safe distance from the explosive saltwater geyser. Turn around and look at the lava rock walls facing the blowhole. You'll see a perfect photo-op: a **heart-shaped rock.** It's actually a heart-shaped window in the rock that frames the dramatic coast—a perfect place to document your love. Dine at one of Kapalua's fine restaurants such as **Merriman's** (p 130; see chapter 8 for more ideas.)

Head south on Hwy. 30, then go right on Hwy. 380, right on Hwy. 36, and right on Hwy. 37 for 7.3 miles to a left on Makawao Ave. In 1.8 miles it intersects Baldwin Ave. in the heart of Makawao.

Find the heart-shaped hole in the rock by the Nakalele Blowhole.

A tiki torch–lit dinner at Merriman's.

★★★ Sunset atop Haleakala. You've probably heard about watching sunrise from atop Maui's highest mountain. Hot tip: It's unique, but not that romantic if you're cold and sleepy after a 2-hour-plus winding drive in the dark. Treat yourself instead to a leisurely daytime drive that ends with a captivating sunset—no reservations required. After pausing for lunch en route in the cowboy town of 4A **Makawao** (see p 64), you'll slowly make your way up the mountain via Hwy. 377 and 378, heading into 4B **Haleakala National Park** (see p 84). Stop in **Hosmer Grove** to listen for birdsong on a short nature trail, check out the visitor center (open 'til 4pm) and drive to the spectacular summit to look for rare blooming silverswords before watching the sun descend into the ocean or a vast sea of clouds, spreading gold as it goes. It turns cold quickly here, so you'll soon head back down to spend the night at a boutique inn in Pa'ia, where lots of casual, colorful dining options also await (p 123).

Watching the sunset on Haleakala.

Retrace your route down Hwy. 378, turn right onto Hwy. 377, and go north to Hanamu Rd. and turn right. At the end of Hanamu Rd., turn left onto Olinda Rd. Follow Olinda into Makawao town, where it becomes Baldwin Ave. Take Baldwin 6 miles down to Pa'ia.

5 A Play Day in Pa'ia. Perk up at Pa'ia Bay Coffee (115 Hana Hwy., Pa'ia; www.paiabaycoffee.com; ☎ 808/579-3111), which serves great espresso and breakfast in a garden setting, starting at 7am. Follow the signs in the Nalu Place alley. Cruise the cute boutiques or go for a dip at beautiful H. A. Baldwin Park (p 79). Drive out to Ho'okipa Beach Park (p 79) to watch the windsurfers and see the napping sea turtles. In the evening, you'll appreciate having made reservations far in advance for Mama's Fish House (p 129), overlooking a gorgeous secluded cove just outside Pa'ia. Book an early table, since you'll want to linger over the beautifully prepared, island-inspired cuisine and enjoy the relaxed hospitality—as well as get an early start the next day.

Head east on Hwy. 36 toward Hana. With stops, this 44.5-mile (72km) drive will take a whole day.

6 Hana Highway. Keep your swimsuit handy, put the top down, and turn the radio up. Plan on spending the entire day cruising the curves of Maui's most famous road. Stop at waterfalls, go for a swim in

Getting Maui'd

Maui weddings are magic. Not only does the entire island exude natural beauty and romance, it also has an experienced industry in place to help you with every detail.

Most Maui resorts and hotels have wedding coordinators who can plan everything from a simple, relatively low-cost wedding to an extravaganza that people will talk about for years. Remember that resorts can be pricey—be frank with your planner if you want to keep costs down. Independent companies such as **White Orchid Wedding** (1961 E. Vineyard St., Wailuku; www.whiteorchidwedding.com; ☎ 800/240-9336) and Sugar Beach Events (85 N. Kihei Rd., Kihei; www.sugarbeachevents.com; ☎ 808/856-6151) have exclusive access to stunning venues and can help you select photographers, caterers, and florists.

You can plan your own island wedding, even from afar, without spending a fortune. The chef/owner of CJ's Deli & Diner in Kaanapali offers useful tips for DIY couples on his blog: www.cjsmaui.com/blog. For a marriage license, both parties will need to appear in person before a license agent, but should first apply online at https://emrs.ehawaii.gov/emrs/public/home.html. A license (with online fee) costs $65 and is good for 30 days.

tranquil pools, buy five passionfruit for a dollar at a roadside stand, share a picnic, and enjoy every spontaneous moment. Lush, tropical Hana is the perfect place for romance, and it's well worth spending a couple of nights here. *See p 70.*

7 Hana. Ready for some relaxing beach time? On your last full day, choose between swimming in the perfect crescent bay at **Hamoa Beach** (p 79), watching surfers from your perch on the dark red sand of **Koki Beach** (p 81), or exploring the freshwater pools at **'Ohe'o Gulch** (p 87), where (if conditions permit) you can sit and soak while watching the waves rolling ashore. Around sunset, walk the ancient coastal trail in **Wai'anapanapa State Park** (p 91). For more detailed information on Hana's sights, see the tour on p 70. Splurge for dinner at the **Preserve Kitchen & Bar** at Travaasa Hana (p 131).

Start the day with topnotch java at Paia Bay Coffee.

Relax & Rejuvenate on Maui

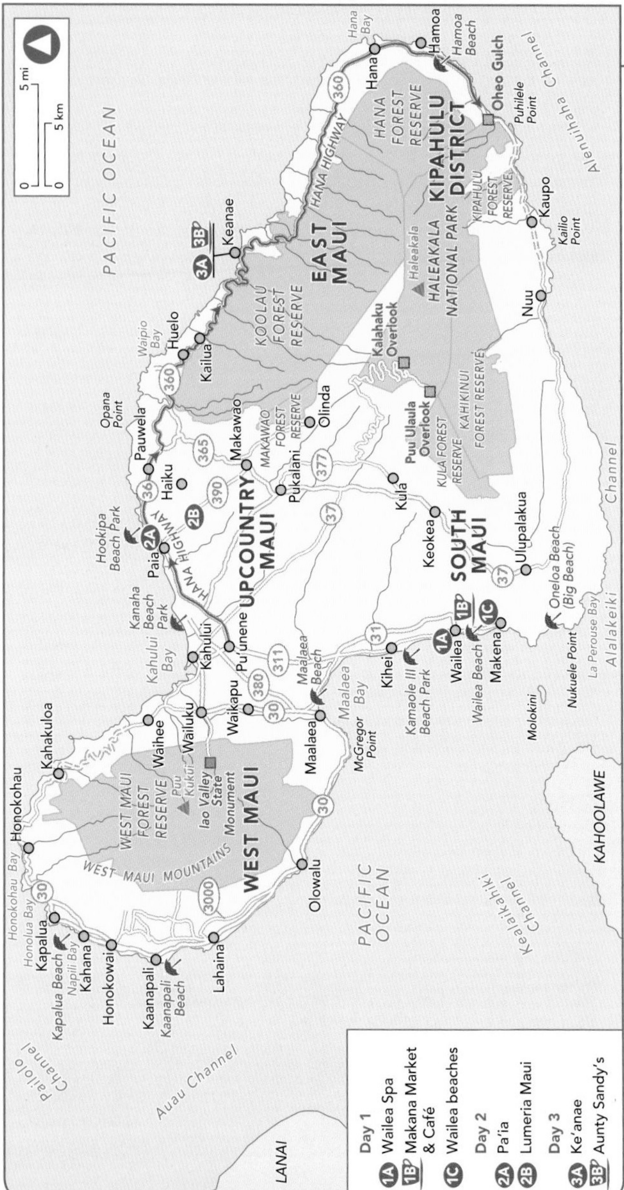
PACIFIC OCEAN
PACIFIC OCEAN
0 5 mi
0 5 km
Honokohau Bay
Honokohau
Honolua Bay
Kapalua
Kapalua Beach
Napili Bay
Kahana
Honokowai
Kaanapali
Kaanapali Beach
Lahaina
Olowalu
Kahakuloa
WEST MAUI FOREST RESERVE
WEST MAUI MOUNTAINS
Puu Kukui
Iao Valley State Monument
WEST MAUI
Waihee
Wailuku
Waikapu
Maalaea
McGregor Point
Maalaea Bay
Maalaea Beach
Kahului Bay
Kahului
Kanaha Beach Park
Pu'unene
Hookipa Beach Park
Paia
HANA HIGHWAY
Haiku
Pauwela
Opana Point
UPCOUNTRY MAUI
Makawao
MAKAWAO FOREST RESERVE
Pukalani
Olinda
Waipio Bay
Huelo
Kailua
KOOLAU FOREST RESERVE
Keanae
EAST MAUI
HANA HIGHWAY
Hana Bay
Hana
HANA FOREST RESERVE
Hamoa
Hamoa Beach
KIPAHULU DISTRICT
Oheo Gulch
Puhilele Point
KIPAHULU FOREST RESERVE
Kaupo
Kailio Point
Alenuihaha Channel
Nuu
Haleakala
HALEAKALA NATIONAL PARK
Kalahaku Overlook
Puu Ulaula Overlook
KULA FOREST RESERVE
KAHIKINUI FOREST RESERVE
Kula
Keokea
SOUTH MAUI
Ulupalakua
Kihei
Kamaole III Beach Park
Wailea
Wailea Beach
Makena
Molokini
Oneloa Beach (Big Beach)
Nukuele Point
La Perouse Bay
Alalakeiki Channel
Kealaikahiki Channel
KAHOOLAWE
LANAI
Auau Channel
Pailolo Channel
30
3000
380
311
31
37
36
390
365
377
360
Day 1
1A Wailea Spa
1B Makana Market & Café
1C Wailea beaches
Day 2
2A Pa'ia
2B Lumeria Maui
Day 3
3A Ke'anae
3B Aunty Sandy's

Maui's near-perfect weather, unspoiled beaches, lush tropical vegetation, and invigorating trade winds are just the recipe to soothe your body, mind, and spirit. Below are some of my favorite ways to relax over a 3-day weekend. START: **Wailea.**

Yoga on the garden terrace at Lumeria.

1A Wailea Spa Day. There are wonderful spas to choose from at several resorts all over Maui (see box p 37), but in my opinion, the best place to start is in Wailea, by booking a massage, either at the opulent **Spa Grande at the Grand Wailea Resort** or in a thatched *hale* (hut) at the **Four Seasons Resort Maui** (p 146). The Four Seasons spa is wonderful, but I love the smell of salt in the air and the gentle whisper of the wind while experiencing Hawaiian *lomilomi* (massage).

1B Makana Market & Cafe (in the Fairmont Kea Lani, 4100 Wailea Alanui Dr., Wailea; www.fairmont.com/kea-lani-maui; ☎ 808/875-4100) is one of my favorite South Maui spots for a casual lunch to go. The deli and bakery at the Kea Lani resort serves wonderful poke and açai bowls, and pastries almost too pretty to eat.

1C Wailea beaches. After grabbing your picnic lunch, walk along the beach path, looking for whales and inhaling the fragrance of the native flowers growing on the rocky coastline. Float in the warm, tropical waters at one of several beaches nearby (see chapter 5 for more details). For an elegant finish, dine at **Morimoto Maui** (p 130).

Take Wailea 'Ike Dr. up to Pi'ilani Hwy. 31. Continue on Maui Veterans Hwy. 311 toward Kahului. Turn right on Hansen Road, and merge onto on Hana Hwy. 36. Continue to Pa'ia.

2A Pa'ia. On Day 2, head out to Pa'ia, the plantation-town-turned-hippy-haven on Maui's North Shore (see shopping map, p 114). A dilapidated sugar mill looms over Baldwin Avenue like a steam punk sculpture, evidence of the industry that built this town 100-plus years ago. In the 1960s hippies dropped out here, and in the '80s windsurfers moved in, having discovered nearby **Ho'okipa** (p 79), one of the world's best places to catch air from the sea. Today you'll find eclectic cafes, yoga studios, and bikini shops crowding the

Hikers explore the Keanai Arboretum.

intersection of Baldwin and Hana Highway. Willie Nelson sometimes drops by to play a surprise set with his son Lukas Nelson at **Charley's** (p 137). The Dalai Lama himself visited Pa'ia, to bless the gleaming white and gold stupa at the **Maui Dharma Center** (81 Baldwin Ave; ☎ 808/579-8076). Pop in and give the prayer wheel a reverent spin.

Head up Baldwin Ave. to Lumeria, 3.4 miles (5.5km) up on the left.

2B Lumeria Maui. Check into this retreat center (p 148) and try out one of the many complimentary classes: yin yoga, Tibetan bowl sound bath, Kundalini meditation, or 5 Rhythms dance. For dinner, return to Pa'ia for savory crepes or deep-flavored curries at **Café Des Amis** (p 126).

From Lumeria Maui, take Baldwin Ave. back to Pa'ia and turn right onto Hana Hwy. 36. Park on the roadside just after MM 16 and before the turnoff to Ke'anae Rd.

3A Ke'anae. Enjoy a delicious organic breakfast at Lumeria Maui's onsite restaurant **Wooden Crate** (complimentary with your room rate), then head out on the Hana Highway for a rainforest tour. Park at the **Ke'anae Arboretum** and pass through the turnstile. This easy 2-mile (3.2km) stroll through a rainforest is a wonderful way to relax and commune with nature. I'd allow at least 2 hours here, longer if you bring your swimsuit and plunge into the swimming hole near the end of the trail. You start off on a flat trail where you can see the plants that have been introduced to Hawai'i (all with identification tags). The rainbow eucalyptus,

A spa treatment room at Montage Kapalua Bay Resort.

Relax, Breathe Deep & Say "Sp-Ahh"

Hawai'i's spas are airy, open facilities that embrace the tropics. Here are your best options on Maui, in alphabetical order:

- **'Awili Spa and Salon at Andaz Maui at Wailea Resort** (maui.andaz.hyatt.com; ☎ 808/573-1234): Inspired by Japanese spas, 'Awili treatments all begin with a customized, apothecary-style blend of natural ingredients.
- **The Spa and Wellness Center at Four Seasons Resort Maui** (www.fourseasons.com/maui; ☎ 808/874-2925): Imagine the sounds of the waves rolling on Wailea Beach as you are soothingly massaged in the privacy of your cabana, tucked into the beachside foliage. Come here to be absolutely spoiled.
- **The Spa at Travaasa Hana** (www.travaasa.com/hana; ☎ 888/820-1043): Hana is relaxing in its own right, but when you add a lava rock hot tub and expert *lomilomi* (Hawaiian massage) therapists to the equation, it's next level.
- **Spa Grande at Grand Wailea** (www.grandwailea.com; ☎ 808/875-1234, ext 4949): Maui's most elaborate spa combines Japanese-style furo baths and Swiss-jet showers with traditional Hawaiian treatments and island-inspired products. You can easily spend half a day luxuriating in the two-story marble bathhouse and toning muscles in the top-tier fitness center. The roomy facilities make it great for bachelorette parties.
- **Spa Montage Kapalua Bay** (www.montagehotels.com/spamontage; ☎ 808/665-8282): This freestanding spa facility in Kapalua has perks for couples: a co-ed spa pool, a huge yoga/fitness studio with an ocean view, and private treatment *hale* (huts) with romantic rock tubs. Day passes are available.
- **Waihua Spa at Ritz-Carlton, Kapalua** (www.ritzcarlton.com/kapalua; ☎ 800/262-8440 or 808/669-6200): *Waihua* translates as "healing waters." The treatments at this serene 17,500-square-foot (1,626 sq. m) spa with private cabanas are rooted in ancient Hawaiian techniques and theories on healing.
- **Willow Stream Spa at the Fairmont Kea Lani Maui** (www.fairmont.com/kea-lani-maui; ☎ 808/875-2229): This intimate spa offers a mud bar, Hawaiian rain showers, and unique treatments such as the Volcanic Foot Experience. The fitness center next door has a personal trainer on duty.

while not native to these Islands, is downright magical. After your hike, drive down **Ke'anae Road** to explore the peninsula. Let the salty breeze tousle your hair at the shore.

3B Visit **Aunty Sandy's** shack (210 Ke'anae Rd., Ke'anae; ☎ 808/248-7448) for shave ice and some homemade still-warm banana bread. Buy two loaves, since the first won't make it home.

Maui's Farmlands

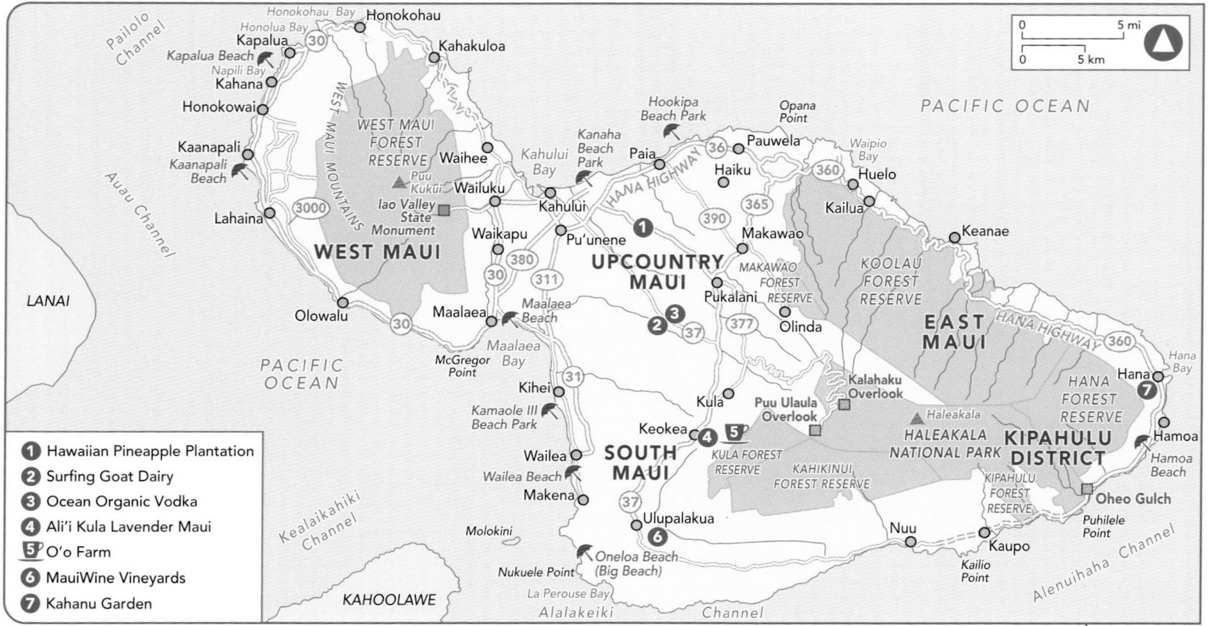
1 Hawaiian Pineapple Plantation
2 Surfing Goat Dairy
3 Ocean Organic Vodka
4 Ali'i Kula Lavender Maui
5 O'o Farm
6 MauiWine Vineyards
7 Kahanu Garden
PACIFIC OCEAN
WEST MAUI
UPCOUNTRY MAUI
SOUTH MAUI
EAST MAUI
KIPAHULU DISTRICT
HALEAKALA NATIONAL PARK
WEST MAUI FOREST RESERVE
WEST MAUI MOUNTAINS
KOOLAU FOREST RESERVE
MAKAWAO FOREST RESERVE
HANA FOREST RESERVE
KULA FOREST RESERVE
KAHIKINUI FOREST RESERVE
KIPAHULU FOREST RESERVE
HANA HIGHWAY
Honokohau Bay
Honokohau
Honolua Bay
Kapalua
Kapalua Beach
Napili Bay
Kahana
Kahakuloa
Honokowai
Kaanapali
Kaanapali Beach
Lahaina
Olowalu
Waihee
Puu Kukui
Wailuku
Iao Valley State Monument
Waikapu
Maalaea
Maalaea Beach
Maalaea Bay
McGregor Point
Kahului
Kahului Bay
Kanaha Beach Park
Pu'unene
Paia
Hookipa Beach Park
Haiku
Pauwela
Opana Point
Waipio Bay
Huelo
Kailua
Keanae
Makawao
Pukalani
Olinda
Kula
Keokea
Kihei
Kamaole III Beach Park
Wailea
Wailea Beach
Makena
Molokini
Ulupalakua
Oneloa Beach (Big Beach)
Nukuele Point
La Perouse Bay
Alalakeiki Channel
Kalahaku Overlook
Puu Ulaula Overlook
Haleakala
Nuu
Kaupo
Kailio Point
Puhilele Point
Oheo Gulch
Hamoa
Hamoa Beach
Hana
Hana Bay
Alenuihaha Channel
Pailolo Channel
Auau Channel
Kealaikahiki Channel
LANAI
KAHOOLAWE
0 5 mi
0 5 km

When people think of Maui, flowers or pineapple often come to mind, but Maui's fertile soil grows lush fields of everything from sweet onions to lavender, coffee, chocolate, and every tropical fruit you can imagine, including dragonfruit. The island even has its own vodka farm! Below is a 1- or 2-day tour of Maui's bounty. START: **Hali'imaile.**

Taste of Maui

To visit the farms listed here, as well as others, book a guided bus tour with Maui Country Farm Tours (www.mauicountryfarmtours.com; ☎ 808/283-9131). Marilyn Jansen Lopes and her husband, Rick, share their rich knowledge of the history of Maui's sugar mills, coffee plantations, family farms, and vineyards. Tours start at $175 and include lunch.

❶ Hawaiian Pineapple Plantation. Start with Hawai'i's golden fruit by taking the 1½-hour Maui Pineapple Company tour. Learn about the prickly fruit's history and how to grow, harvest, and pack it. Sample sweet slices along the way; tours with lunch or a distillery visit are also options. ⏲ *1½ hr. Across from the Hali'imaile General Store, Hali'imaile Rd., Hali'imaile. mauipineappletour.com. ☎ 808/665-5491. Daily tram tours starting at 9:30am, 11:45am or 1:30pm. Adults $65, child $55.*

From Hali'imaile, head west to Haleakala Hwy. 37. Turn right at the light and continue to 'Oma'opio Road. Turn left and drive 4 miles to Ikena Kai Place. Watch for Surfing Goat Dairy signs nailed to trees.

❷ kids Surfing Goat Dairy. In Kula, just beyond the sugar-cane fields and on the slopes of Haleakala, lies this dairy, where some 140 dairy goats blissfully graze the 42 acres (17ha) and contribute the milk for the 24 different cheeses that are made every day. Choose from the 2-hour **Grand Dairy Tour** ($49 adults, $39 children ages 3 to 12), where you can learn how to milk a goat, make cheese, and sample the different varieties; or drop by for the 30-minute casual dairy tour ($12, children $8). ⏲ *30–120 min. 3651 Oma'opio Rd., Kula. www.surfinggoatdairy.com. ☎ 808/878-2870. Open Mon–Sat 9am–5pm, Sun 9am–2pm.*

Return to Oma'opio Road and turn left. Ocean Organic Vodka is less than 1 mile down.

❸ Ocean Organic Vodka. Never heard of a vodka farm? Neither had I until this one opened just below Surfing Goat Dairy, halfway up Haleakala. (The views alone are worth the

The Maui Pineapple Tour explores the history of Maui's famous fruit.

Wow! Look at the Size of That Fish

Enormous fish swim around the island of Maui. The largest caught in Maui waters, a Pacific blue marlin, tipped the scale at 1,200 pounds. To see some of these giants, wander down to the docks at Lahaina or Ma'alaea just after noon or around 5pm when sportfishing boats return with their catch. In October or early November, some 75 teams compete in the island's largest fishing tournament, the **Lahaina Jackpot Fishing Tournament;** nightly fish weigh-ins at the Lahaina Harbor start at 4pm. For more information contact the **Lahaina Yacht Club** (835 Front St., Lahaina; www.lyc.us; ☎ 808/661-0191).

price of admission.) Sustainably harvested sugarcane is blended with deep ocean mineral water to make fine-quality liquor at this solar-powered distillery. Those 21 and over get to sample various spirits (and vodka-filled truffles!) and take home a souvenir shot glass. ⏲ *20–120 min. 4051 Oma'opio Rd., Kula. oceanvodka.com. ☎ 808/877-0009. Open daily 9:30am–5pm. Tours $15 for ages 21 and older; free for children with adult. Lunch $15 extra (24-hr. notice needed).*

Return up Oma'opio Road to Hwy. 37 and turn right. Take the second left after Rice Park onto Kekaulike Hwy. 377, drive about ¼ mile around a bend, and take a quick right up Waipoli Road.

4 Ali'i Kula Lavender Maui. Here, a choice of terrific tours take you to see the varieties of lavender that bloom year-round. I enjoy the daily 50-minute Walking Tour, which explores the grounds. You can add a Lavender Gourmet Lunch Basket ($26, book 24 hours in advance) that includes a lavender-infused dessert. Walking tour $10 in advance or $12 on site; cart tours $25 with 48-hour advance notice. General admission is $3. ⏲ *30 min. for self-guided tour, 50 min. for guided. 1100 Waipoli Rd., Kula. www.aliikulalavender.com. ☎ 808/878-3004.*

5 O'o Farm. About ⅓ mile west of the lavender farm on Waipoli Rd., this bucolic orchard and biodynamic farm hosts scrumptious breakfast coffee tours and gourmet lunches. O'o Farm supplies its sister restaurants in West Maui: Pacifico, Feast at Lele (p 140), and 'Aina Gourmet Market. Pluck your own coffee cherries, learn how beans are roasted, and then sit under a vine-covered canopy for a feast by chef Daniel Eskelsen; $74 adults, $37 ages 5 to 12. ⏲ *2½ hours. 651 Waipoli Rd., Kula. www.oofarm.com. ☎ 808/667-4341. Tours Mon–Fri, breakfast 8:30am–11:30am, lunch 10:30am–1:30pm.*

A catch of fresh fish.

From Kula take Hwy. 378 to Hwy. 377, then make a left turn on Hwy. 37. The winery is 9 miles (14.5km) down the road.

❻ **MauiWine Vineyards.** Plan to arrive in time for a free tour (10:30am and 1:30pm) of Maui's only winery. Not only will you get to see the historic grounds, including the tasting room—once a guest cottage built for King Kalakaua in 1874—but you'll also learn about the six different varietals grown on the slopes of Haleakala. ⏱ *1 hr. 14815 Pi'ilani Hwy., 'Ulupalakua. www.mauiwine.com. ☎ 877/878-6058. Tasting room open daily 10am–5pm; $12–$16 to taste flight of four wines.*

Vineyards at MauiWine.

Take Hwy. 31 east to Hana. Just before MM 31, turn down Ula'ino Road toward the ocean. Allow about 2 hours driving time.

❼ **Kahanu Garden.** The world's largest collection of breadfruit trees—a staple food for Pacific islanders—thrives here. The garden has some 130 distinct varieties gathered from 20 tropical island groups. You'll also view a Canoe Garden, filled with the many useful plants that the early Polynesian settlers brought to Hawai'i: sugar cane, banana, sweet potato, taro, and paper mulberry (used to make *kapa* cloth). The 3-acre stone *heiau* (temple) behind the garden radiates spiritual power. ⏱ *1–2 hr. 650 Ula'ino Rd., Hana. www.ntbg.org/gardens/kahanu. ☎ 808/248-8912. Mon–Sat 9am–2pm. Self-guided tours $10; guided tours by reservation $25; children 12 and under free.*

Maui's Farmers' Markets

For the freshest Maui fruits, flowers, and produce (at budget prices), bring your reusable bag to the closest farmers' market.

The best by far is the **Upcountry Farmers Market** ★★★ (55 Kiopa'a St., Pukalani, in the Kulamalu Town Center parking lot; www.upcountryfarmersmarket.com). Every Saturday from 7 to 11am you'll find local honey, fresh-shucked coconuts, pickled veggies, and heaps of bright Maui-grown produce, plus ready-to-eat foods, flower bouquets, and gorgeous hand-carved cutting boards. Also on Saturday, in Kahului the **Maui Swap Meet** ★★ (see p 120) rewards shoppers with produce from Ono Farms and other local growers.

In South Maui, the **Farmer's Market of Maui-Kihei** is open from 8am to 4pm weekdays at 61 S. Kihei Rd. On the West Side, try the **Honokowai Farmers' Market,** on Lower Honoapi'ilani Rd., across from the Honokowai Park. It's open Monday, Wednesday, and Friday, from 7 to 11am.

Maui's History & Culture

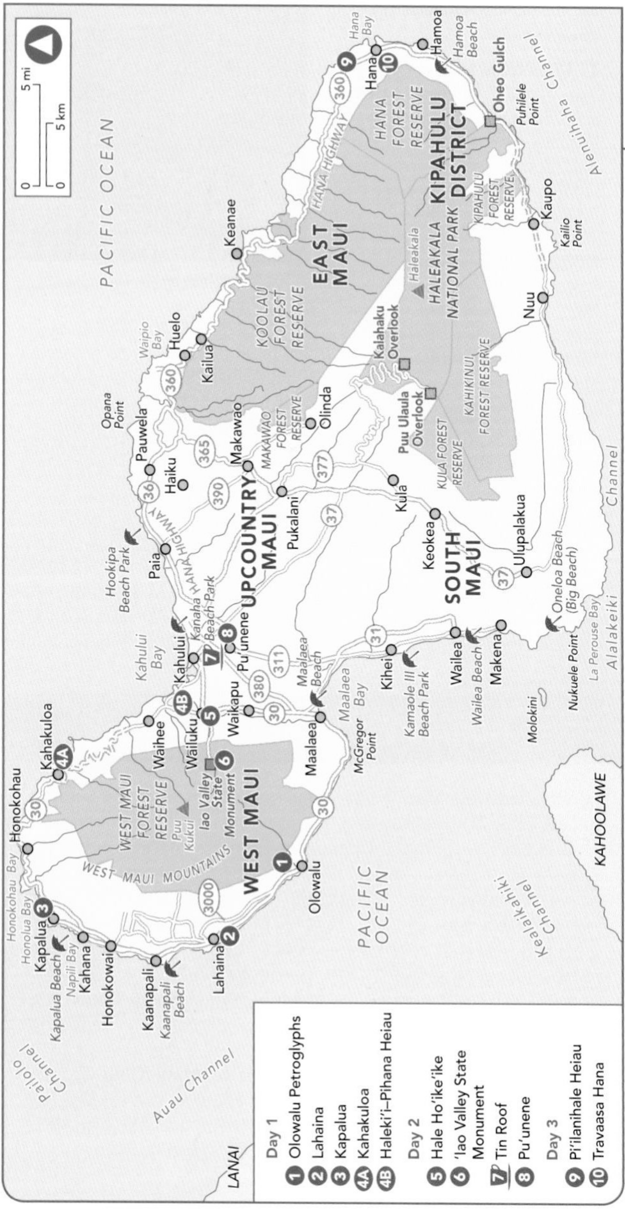
PACIFIC OCEAN
0 5 mi
0 5 km
Day 1
1 Olowalu Petroglyphs
2 Lahaina
3 Kapalua
4A Kahakuloa
4B Haleki'i–Pihana Heiau
Day 2
5 Hale Ho'ike'ike
6 'Iao Valley State Monument
7 Tin Roof
8 Pu'unene
Day 3
9 Pi'ilanihale Heiau
10 Travaasa Hana
WEST MAUI
WEST MAUI MOUNTAINS
WEST MAUI FOREST RESERVE
Puu Kukui
Iao Valley State Monument
UPCOUNTRY MAUI
EAST MAUI
SOUTH MAUI
KOOLAU FOREST RESERVE
MAKAWAO FOREST RESERVE
HANA FOREST RESERVE
KIPAHULU DISTRICT
KIPAHULU FOREST RESERVE
HALEAKALA NATIONAL PARK
Haleakala
KULA FOREST RESERVE
KAHIKINUI FOREST RESERVE
Kalahaku Overlook
Puu Ulaula Overlook
Oheo Gulch
HANA HIGHWAY
Lahaina
Kaanapali
Kaanapali Beach
Honokowai
Kahana
Napili Bay
Kapalua
Kapalua Beach
Honolua Bay
Honokohau Bay
Honokohau
Kahakuloa
Waihee
Wailuku
Waikapu
Kahului
Kahului Bay
Kanaha Beach Park
Pu'unene
Paia
Hookipa Beach Park
Haiku
Pauwela
Opana Point
Makawao
Pukalani
Olinda
Kula
Keokea
Ulupalakua
Huelo
Kailua
Waipio Bay
Keanae
Hana
Hana Bay
Hamoa
Hamoa Beach
Puhilele Point
Kaupo
Kailio Point
Nuu
Maalaea
Maalaea Bay
Maalaea Beach
McGregor Point
Olowalu
Kihei
Kamaole III Beach Park
Wailea
Wailea Beach
Makena
Oneloa Beach (Big Beach)
La Perouse Bay
Nukuele Point
Molokini
KAHOOLAWE
LANAI
Auau Channel
Pailolo Channel
Kealaikahiki Channel
Alalakeiki Channel
Alenuihaha Channel

Walk back in time on Maui, to when Polynesian wayfinders first settled the island more than 1,000 years ago, to when whiskey-soaked whalers and earnest missionaries arrived in the 1800s, and to the hardscrabble days of sugar plantations and cattle ranches in the 1900s. This 3-day itinerary moves from West Maui to Central Maui to Hana. Wailuku is a convenient home base for all three, or you can hotel-hop as you go (see chapter 10). START: **Olowalu.**

On Honoapi'ilani Hwy. 30 near MM 15, turn north on Luawai St. Drive .7 miles (1.1km). Follow signs to petroglyphs.

❶ ★ Olowalu Petroglyphs (Pu'u Kilea). Start your voyage into Hawaiian history at this off-the-beaten-path archeological site. A cliff-face in the small village of Olowalu holds clues to the past: the shapes of people, animals, and sailing canoes chiseled into the rocks. Observe the ancient artwork in silence; let the grandeur of the West Maui Mountains overtake you. ***Note:*** Don't touch the petroglyphs or climb onto the rocks.

Continue north on Honoapi'ilani Hwy. 30, a 15-minute drive.

❷ ★★★ Lahaina. This storied town, whose name translates as "merciless sun," dates back to at least A.D. 700. Head over to the **Baldwin Home Museum** to begin the Lahaina walking tour (p 50), which covers the days of the whalers and missionaries and their effect on Lahaina. At night, immerse yourself in Hawaiian culture by attending the **Feast at Lele** (p 140) or the **Old Lahaina Lu'au** (p 127).

Take Hwy. 30 north to Kapalua, a 20-minute drive.

❸ Kapalua. Travel further back in time at the **Ritz-Carlton, Kapalua,** where the remains of hundreds of ancient Hawaiians were discovered

Baldwin Home Museum.

during the resort's construction. This discovery sparked a cultural resurgence within the Native Hawaiian community. People came together to re-inter the sacred *'iwi* (bones) and the hotel was relocated inland. You'll find a plaque here detailing the history. *Admission free; see p 149 for resort details.*

Continue north, past Kapalua, on winding, narrow Kahekili Hwy. 30 (which becomes Hwy. 340). As the road bends, turn left on Waiehu Beach Road (Hwy. 3400). Turn right on Kuhio Place (into a subdivision) and then take the first left on Hea Place, following it to the end. Allow 45 minutes to 1 hour to reach Wailuku.

4 ★★ Kahekili Highway (Hwy. 340). Along this highway (named for the great chief Kahekili, who built houses from the skulls of his enemies), nestled in a crevice between two steep hills, is the picturesque village of **4A Kahakuloa**

A church in Kahakuloa Village.

with its red-roofed church and vivid green taro patches. Life here has not changed much during the past few decades. Continue into **4B Wailuku** to see an ancient site built in 1240 from stones carried up from the 'Iao Stream below. **Haleki'i-Pihana Heiau State Monument** sits forgotten atop a suburban hillside. Chief Kahekili lived here, as did the most sacred princess, Keopuolani. When Kamehameha the Great came to wage war, 8-year-old Keopuolani fled across the mountains to Lahaina. Kamehameha chased her all the way to the island of Moloka'i, where he married her to absorb her *mana* (power). Haleki'i ("house of images") has stacked rock walls and a thatched top, whereas Pihana Heiau ("gathering place of supernatural beings") is a pyramid-shaped mound of stones. If you sit quietly nearby (never climb on any *heiau*), you'll see that the view alone explains why this spot was chosen.

Return to Waiehu Beach Rd (Hwy. 3400) and turn left. At Kahekili Hwy. intersection, turn left and follow 1.7 miles to slight left on N. Market St. Turn right on E. Vineyard St., left on N. High St. and immediate right onto Main St.; Hale Ho'ike'ike is .2 miles ahead on the left.

5 ★★ Hale Ho'ike'ike. Explore Central Maui on Day 2, starting with this museum in Bailey House, the 1833 home of missionary and sugar planter Edward Bailey. Its trove of Hawaiiana offers everything from foreboding *ki'i* (temple images) and rare collections of tree-snail shells, to latter-day relics like Duke Kahanamoku's 1919 redwood surfboard. ⏲ *30–45 min. 2375-A Main St. www.mauimuseum.org.*

A display at the Alexander & Baldwin Sugar Museum.

☎ 808/244-3326. Admission $7 adults, $5 seniors, $2 children 7–12 (younger free). Mon–Sat 10am–4pm.

Continue west on Main Street, which becomes 'Iao Valley Road, to the end.

6 ★★ 'Iao Valley State Monument. It's hard to imagine that peaceful 'Iao Stream was the site of one of Maui's worst battles. In 1790 King Kamehameha and his men fought here to conquer the island. When the battle ended, so many bodies blocked the stream that the battle site was named Kepaniwai, or "damming of the waters." The park and stream get their names from the 'Iao Needle, a phallic rock that juts an impressive 1,200 feet (366m) above the valley floor. *'Iao* in Hawaiian means "supreme cloud." *30–45 min. end of 'Iao Valley Rd. Entry fee $5 per car. Daily 7am–6pm.*

7 Tin Roof. Pop into this local lunchtime favorite for a taste of plantation-era cuisine. (See p 132) *360 Papa Pl., Kahului. www.tinroofmaui.com. ☎ 808/868-0753.*

Retrace your route to Main Street and continue straight through Wailuku and Kahului. Turn right at the light onto South Pu'unene Avenue, and continue until Hansen Road. Museum is on the left.

8 ★ Pu'unene. In the center of Maui, the town of Pu'unene ("goose hill") has essentially disappeared. Once a thriving sugar plantation with numerous homes, churches, a school, and a hospital, Pu'unene is now just a post office, a shuttered sugar mill, and the **Alexander & Baldwin Sugar Museum** (Pu'unene Ave./Hwy. 350 and Hansen Rd.; www.sugarmuseum.com; ☎ 808/871-8058). Inside the humble museum, you'll learn how sugar was grown, harvested, and milled, and the inside story of how Samuel Alexander and Henry Baldwin (founders of Hawai'i's largest and last sugar plantation, HC&S) managed to acquire huge chunks of land from the Kingdom of Hawai'i, then ruthlessly fought to gain access to water on the other side of the island, making sugar cane an economically viable crop. *30 min. Admission $7 adults, $5 seniors, $2 children 6–12, free for children 5 and younger. Daily 9:30am–4:30pm.*

Head east on Hansen Road. Merge onto Hana Hwy. 36. Continue east 45 miles (72.4km) to Ula'ino Rd. Turn left, drive 1.7 miles (2.7km) to Kahanu Garden.

The ancient Pi'ilanihale Heiau in Kahanu Garden.

9 ★★★ Pi'ilanihale Heiau. Stroll through **Kahanu Garden** (p 71) to stand in awe of the largest and one of the most important *heiau* (temples) in all of Polynesia, named after the great Pi'ilani dynasty. If the terraced 3-acre platform doesn't immediately impress you, imagine hand-carrying each basalt rock from Hana Bay 5 miles away, as the Hawaiians did during construction 800 years ago. Tour the lush grounds, sit in the shade of the thatched canoe house, and imagine the lives of seafaring chiefs.

Return to Hana Hwy. (now Hwy. 360), turn left and head 3.5 miles (5.6km) east into the town of Hana, to Travaasa Hana.

10 Travaasa Hana. In the hotel lobby, you'll find rare Hawaiian artifacts: chiefly necklaces made of braided human hair with whale-tooth pendants, carved koa bowls, and dog-tooth anklets. During lunch at the onsite Preserve Kitchen+Bar, gaze at **Kau'iki Hill,** the birthplace of King Kamehameha the Great's powerful Queen Ka'ahumanu. If you ask nicely, your server might share *mo'olelo* (stories) of the area. *5031 Hana Hwy., Hana. www.travaasa.com/hana.* ☎ *808/359-2401.* ●

4 The Best Regional & Town Tours

West Maui

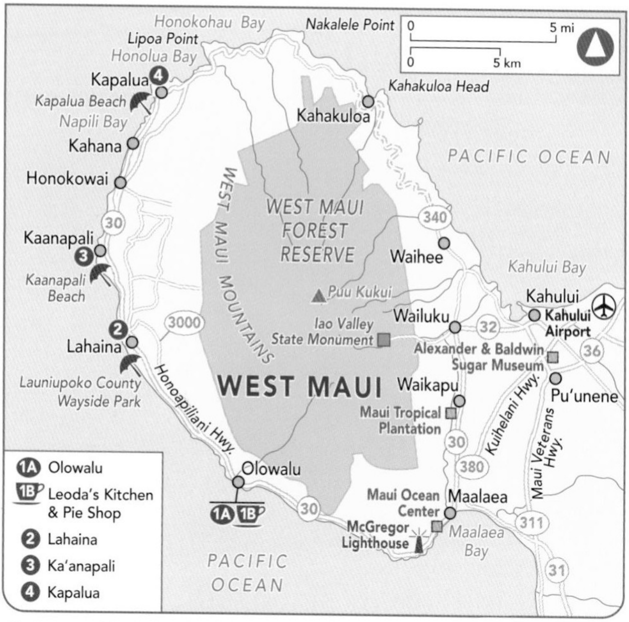

West Maui has it all: rain-carved mountains, sandy beaches, fish-filled reefs, and plenty of action on shore. The stretch of coastline from the historic port of Lahaina to Kapalua is the island's busiest resort area (with South Maui a close second). Traffic jams frequently clog Honoapi'ilani Hwy., although the new Lahaina Bypass has helped some. START: **Olowalu.**

Travel Tip

I've used the highway number, not the name of the highway, when detailing how to get around on Maui. The abbreviation MM stands for "mile marker." For more information, see "Maui Driving Tips" on p 13.

1A kids **Olowalu.** Most visitors drive right past this tiny hamlet, halfway to Lahaina. Stop at MM 14 for one of my favorite snorkeling spots—over a turtle-cleaning station about 150 to 225 feet (46–69m) out from shore, where turtles line up to have cleaner wrasses (small fish) pick parasites off their shells. Further offshore, manta rays are known to congregate. Take care not to step on live coral; do wear reef-friendly sunscreen. After exploring the underwater world, head across the street to view the **Pu'u Kilea** petroglyphs—ancient rock carvings of sailors, canoes, and animals. See p 98 for directions. Fuel up at **Leoda's.**

Previous page: The Kapalua region is one of the swankiest enclaves on Maui.

1B Leoda's Kitchen & Pie Shop. The gourmet sandwiches, hot dogs, and burgers are sinfully delicious, but save room for a pint-sized pie! The banana cream is divine. *820 Olowalu Village Rd. www.leodas.com. ☎ 808/662-3600. $.*

Take Hwy. 30 north 2¼ miles (3.5km) to Hwy. 3000 bypass, turn left at Kai Hele Ku until it ends at Hwy. 30, turn right and head 3 miles north.

2 ★★★ kids Lahaina. Spend half a day exploring Lahaina's surf boutiques, museums, and shave ice shops. Kids might take special interest in the fossils, dinosaur eggs, and sharks' teeth at the **Whaler's Locker** shop (780 Front St.; ☎ 808/661-3775). See p 50 for a full walking tour of the town.

Take Hwy. 30 for 3 miles (4.8km) north of Lahaina.

3 Ka'anapali. Hawai'i's first master-planned resort consists of pricey midrise hotels and condos lining nearly 3 miles (4.8km) of gold sandy beach. Golf greens wrap around the slope between beachfront and hillside properties. You can't miss the huge (almost life-size) metal sculpture of a mother whale and two calves that greets you at **Whalers Village,** a seaside mall that will open a wildlife discovery center in 2020. For information on its stores, see p 120. As you stroll down the beach path, at the **Hyatt Regency Maui** (p 147) you can spy on South American penguins playing in the lobby.

Continue north on Hwy. 30 for 7 miles (11km) and turn onto Office Rd.

4 ★★ Kapalua. Follow Highway 30 through the small seaside villages of Honokowai, Kahana, and Napili, and then head for the ocean shore along Office Road, bordered by elegant Cook pines. This is the domain of the luxurious **Ritz-Carlton, Kapalua** (p 149). Kapalua Resort has a long list of amenities: a golf school, two golf courses (p 94), multiple swanky condos and restaurants, a collection of perfect beaches, and a rainforest preserve with hiking trails and a zipline tour—and all are open to the general public.

Whalers Village.

Lahaina

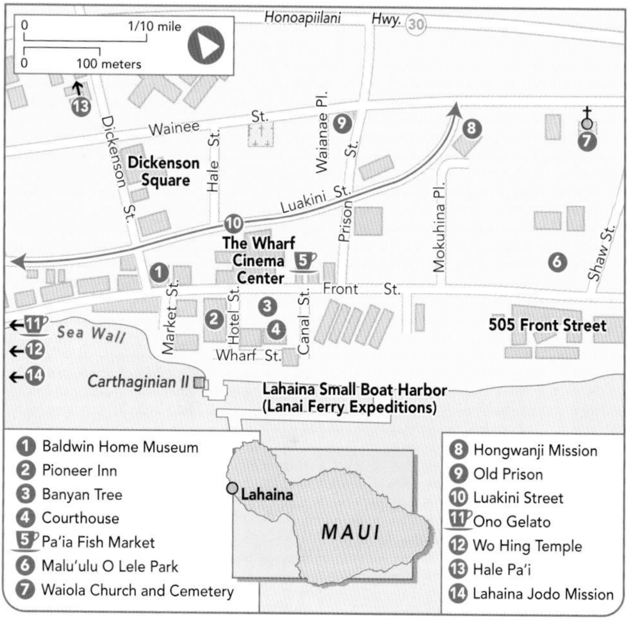

Between the West Maui Mountains and the deep azure ocean, Lahaina has managed to preserve its 19th-century heritage while still accommodating 21st-century guests. It has been at various times the royal capital of Hawai'i, the rowdy center of the whaling industry, the home of austere missionaries who founded churches and schools, and the site of sugar and pineapple plantations. Today, it's one of the most popular towns in Maui for visitors to explore. START: **Baldwin Home Museum on Front Street.**

Travel Tip

Purchase a $12 Passport to the Past for entry to four popular museums: Baldwin Home, Wo Hing, A&B Sugar, and Hale Ho'ike'ike. Buy the Passport at any of these museums.

1 kids Baldwin Home Museum. Step into this coral-and-rock house and travel back in time. Built in 1835, it belonged to Rev. Dwight Baldwin, a missionary, naturalist, and self-trained physician who saved many Native Hawaiians from influenza and smallpox. Baldwin's rudimentary medical tools (on display here) bear witness to the steep odds he faced. He was rewarded with 2,600 acres in Kapalua, where he grew pineapple, which was then an experimental crop. On Friday night, docents dressed in period attire offer candlelit tours. Pick up a Lahaina walking map here, then visit the gift shop in the **Masters' Reading Room** next door. *30 min.*

Pioneer Inn.

120 Dickenson St. (at Front St.). lahainarestoration.org. ☎ 808/661-3262. Admission $7 adults, $5 seniors, kids ages 12 and under free. Admission also grants access to Wo Hing Museum (p 52). Daily 10am–4pm (Fri until 8:30pm).

2 Pioneer Inn. Lahaina's first hotel looks much as it did when it was built in 1901 by George Freeland, of the Royal Canadian Mounted Police, who tracked a criminal to Lahaina and then fell in love with the town. The scene of some pretty wild parties at the turn of the 20th century, the Pioneer is still open for business. Get a cold drink at the old bar or sit outside and watch the goings-on at the harbor. *30 min. 658 Wharf St. www.pioneerinnmaui.com. ☎ 800/457-5457.*

3 kids Banyan Tree. With octopus-like limbs, this enormous tree is so big that you can't fit it in your camera's viewfinder. It was only 8 feet (2.4m) tall in 1873, when Maui sheriff William O. Smith planted it. Now it's the largest banyan in the U.S., more than 60 feet (18m) tall, with 46 major trunks, and it shades ⅔ of an acre (.3ha) in Courthouse Square. *15 min. At the Courthouse Bldg., 649 Wharf St.*

4 Courthouse. This 1860 building has served as a courthouse, customs house, post office, tax collector's office, and jail. On August 12, 1898, locals somberly watched the Hawaiian flag come down and the American flag rise in its place, marking annexation to the U.S. Visit the **Lahaina Heritage Museum** upstairs to see fine exhibits on the history of Lahaina and whaling. The basement jail is now an art gallery. *20 min. 648 Wharf St., Lahaina. lahainarestoration.org. ☎ 808/661-3262. Free admission. Daily 9am–5pm. Free guided tours Tues–Thurs hourly 10am–noon*

5 kids Paia Fish Market. Across from the Banyan Tree, this counter-service cafe serves fresh-catch plates and fish tacos, but also tasty burgers, fajitas, quesadillas, and salads, just in case you don't have an aquatic appetite. *632 Front St. www.paiafishmarket.com. ☎ 808/662-3456. $.*

6 Malu'ulu O Lele Park. Not much to look at now, this ball field sits atop one of the most significant archeological sites in all of Hawai'i: **Moku'ula**, a former island where the highest-ranking *ali'i* (chiefs) took refuge. Beneath the grass, the royal residence and a glittering fishpond—home to a powerful *mo'o* (lizard deity)—await excavation and restoration. *5–10 min. Front/Shaw sts.*

7 Waiola Church and Cemetery. Hawai'i's first stone church,

A gravestone in Waiola Cemetery.

built in 1828, was razed twice by hurricane winds and twice by fire—and rebuilt from the ground up each time. In the cemetery beside the church are the graves of two powerful women: Princess Keopuolani—considered the highest-born, most sacred of all the Hawaiian *ali'i* (royals)—and Queen Ka'ahumanu, the two most influential wives of King Kamehameha I. Both women converted to Christianity and broke the ancient system of *kapu* (restrictions) by sitting down to eat with men, an act that signified the end of the old ways. ⏲ *10–15 min. 535 Waine'e St.*

❽ **Hongwanji Mission.** Originally built in 1910 by Lahaina's Buddhist residents, this temple hosts a marvelous Obon festival in the summer. The reverend, who lives next door, takes time to talk to visitors, and will give tours of the church to those interested. ⏲ *5 min., longer if you get a tour inside. Waine'e/Luakini sts.*

❾ **Old Prison.** Stuck-in-Irons, or Hale Pa'ahao, is the Hawaiian name for this humble penitentiary. Drunken sailors were sent here, along with reckless horse riders. Wander inside and see the cells, complete with shackles. ⏲ *5 min. Waine'e/Prison sts. Daily 10am–4pm.*

❿ **Luakini Street.** Sometimes to experience Hawai'i you have to feel with your heart, and not look with your eyes. That is true of this place. Back in 1837 this street was the route for the funeral procession of Princess Nahi'ena'ena, sister of kings Kamehameha II and III. A convert to Protestantism, she fell in love with her brother at an early age. Just 20 years earlier, their relationship would have been encouraged as a way to preserve the purity of the royal bloodlines. The missionaries, however, condemned it as incest. In August 1836 the couple had a son, who lived only a few hours; Nahi'ena'ena never recovered and died in December of that same year. Her funeral route became known as Luakini—meaning a *heiau* (temple) where chiefs prayed and human sacrifices were made—in reference to the gods "sacrificing" the beloved princess. Originally at Moku'ula (p 51), her mausoleum is now at Waiola Church (p 51). Stop on this street in the shade of one of the big breadfruit trees, and try to imagine the sorrow and fear of a population in transition. The old ways were dying—and the new ways seemed foreign and frightening.

11 **Ono Gelato Co. and Espresso Bar.** This is a great place for tropical ice cream (including dairy-free options) and sorbet, plus smooth-roasted espresso drinks and delicious chocolates. Enjoy the view from the oceanfront dock, plus free Wi-Fi. *815 Front St.* ☎ *808/495-0203. $.*

⓬ **Wo Hing Temple.** I adore this temple and museum; it's small but filled with unexpected treasures. Starting in 1852, sugar planters began drafting Chinese contract laborers to work in the sugarcane

Wo Hing Temple.

fields. Their growing community built this temple and social hall in 1912. Today it hosts a lovely altar, gift shop, and rustic old cookhouse. Duck inside to view some of the first movies ever made—Thomas Edison's footage of Hawai'i shot in 1898 and 1903! Check the calendar for Chinese New Year and kite-flying festival dates. ⏲ *20 min. 858 Front St.* ☎ *808/661-3262. Admission $7 adults, $5 seniors, free for children ages 12 and under. Daily 10am–4pm.*

⓭ **Hale Pa'i.** Little known fact: Lahaina was home to the first secondary school and first newspaper west of the Rockies. Even more remarkably, after the missionaries introduced the alphabet in the mid-1800s, Hawaiians became the most literate population of the time, with 90% able to read and write. Hawaiian-language newspapers became the rage, spreading news from distant continents to the most remote Hawaiian valleys. It all started at this tiny print house, an off-the-beaten-track museum on the edge of Lahainaluna High School campus. Note the limited hours. ⏲ *25 min. 980 Lahainaluna Rd.* ☎ *808/662-0560. Free admission. Open Mon–Wed 10am to 4pm and by appointment.*

⓮ **Lahaina Jodo Mission.** An enormous Buddha statue (some 12-ft./3.7m high and weighing 3½ tons) beams over this temple garden. It came here from Japan in 1968, to commemorate the 100th anniversary of the Japanese arrival in Hawai'i. On the first weekend in July, this temple hosts a beautiful lantern ceremony and Obon dance—not to be missed. ⏲ *10–15 min. 12 Ala Moana St. (off Front St., near the Mala Wharf).* ☎ *808/661-4304. Free admission. Daily during daylight hours.*

The Lahaina Jodo Mission temple.

South Maui

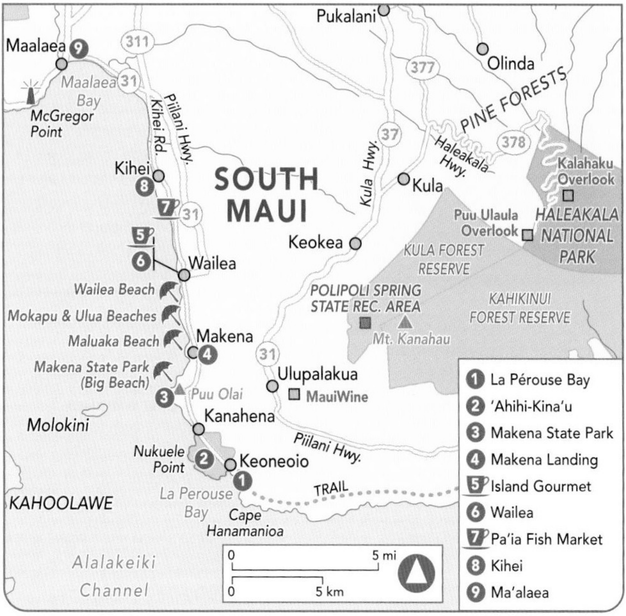

To experience South Maui's treasures, you have to get wet: Strap on a snorkel, climb into a kayak, or just dip in a toe. You won't appreciate this hot, dry coastline by merely looking out the window as you drive by. Once home to small Hawaiian fishing villages, the south shore now includes four distinct communities: windy Ma'alaea, traffic-swollen Kihei, glitzy Wailea, and wild, serene Makena—a paradise locals fight to keep pristine. START: **'Ahihi-Kina'u Natural Area Reserve.**

Travel Tip

Your South Maui adventure begins at the untamed end of the road, then wends its way back to civilization. Pack a swimsuit, towel, hat, hiking shoes, plenty of water, reef-safe sunscreen, and (depending on what you want to do) snorkel gear and/or a kayak (see chapter 6 for rental recommendations). Get going early to avoid the hot sun; start off before 7am in the winter and 6am in the summer for the best weather conditions.

Drive south on Makena Road to 'Ahihi Bay, where the road turns to gravel. Go another 2 miles (3.2km) along the coast to La Pérouse Bay.

1 ★ La Pérouse Bay & Monument. At the road's end in South Maui, a pyramid of lava rocks marks the spot where the first Westerner to "discover" the island, French explorer Admiral Comte de La Pérouse, set foot on Maui in 1786.

Park here, and if you're up for it, start hiking. Bring plenty of water and sun protection, and wear shoes that can withstand walking on loose, prickly lava rocks. From La Pérouse Bay, you can pick up **Hoapili Trail,** the old king's highway that once circled the island. The trail crosses a beach and shadeless lava plains, winding down to the lighthouse at the tip of Cape Hanamanioa, about a .75-mile (1.2km) round trip. Give yourself an hour or two to soak in the solitude of this wilderness.

Return north on Makena Road 1.6 miles (2.6km) to park in gravel lot on left.

❷ ★ 'Ahihi-Kina'u Natural Area Reserve. This stark, seemingly barren 1,238-acre preserve protects dynamic marine ecosystems and lava fields from Haleakala's last eruption of 200–500 years ago. 'Ahihi Bay is a favorite snorkel spot for experienced waterfolk. Park at the gravel lot and walk 5 minutes north to enter at Kanahena Cove. Portions of the preserve are temporarily restricted, to allow fragile marine resources to recover from overuse. For current information on what's open and what's not, visit http://dlnr.hawaii.gov/ecosystems/nars/maui/ahihi-kinau-2 or call ☎ 808/984-8100.

Continue north on Makena Road to Makena State Park. Choose from three entrances: The southernmost is unpaved with street parking, while the other two have large paved lots and portable toilets.

❸ ★★★ Makena State Park (Big Beach). This gorgeous stretch of sand is stunning at all hours of the day, particularly in the early morning when dolphins like to visit. Beware the strong shorebreak. See p 78.

Head north on Makena Rd. (which becomes Makena Alanui), turn left on Hono'iki St., and then right on Makena Rd.

❹ ★ Makena Landing. This beach park with boat-launching facilities, showers, toilets, and picnic tables has generally calm waters teeming with colorful tropical fish.

The Hoapili Trail overlooking La Pérouse Bay.

The waters off Makena Beach.

It's the perfect place for beginner kayakers and snorkelers. **Makena Kayak & Tours** (p 106) specializes in teaching first-time kayakers. Or if history is more to your taste, go south on Makena Road from the landing; on the right is **Keawalai Congregational Church ★** (☎ 808/879-5557), built in 1855. Surrounded by *ti* leaves (planted for spiritual protection) and built of 3-foot (.9m) thick lava rock with coral for mortar, this Protestant church sits on its own cove. On Sundays, voices soar in song during the 10am Hawaiian-language service.

Travel north on Makena Alanui, which becomes Wailea Alanui. Turn left into the parking lot past the Four Seasons Resort Wailea.

5 Island Gourmet Markets. This well-stocked grocery and deli dishes out everything from eggs and hash-browns to French macarons. Choose from a rainbow of varieties of poke (raw, seasoned fish). *Shops at Wailea, 3750 Wailea Alanui Dr., Wailea. ☎ 808/874-5055. $*

6 ★ Wailea. From serene Makena, proceed into multimillion-dollar luxury. Wailea's resorts line the palm-fringed gold coast. For an up-close look, park in the public beach access lot between the **Four Seasons Resort Maui** and the **Grand Wailea** and walk the 3-mile (4.8km) round-trip beach path. It has terrific views of Kaho'olawe and Molokini (plus whales in winter) and the ocean side of the path is planted with rare native coastal flowers and trees. The Four Seasons and the Grand Wailea both have **museum-quality art collections** and offer self-guided tours. Allow about an hour, longer if you want to linger with the art.

Go left on Wailea Alanui Road and left again at stop sign to Okolani Drive, which becomes Kihei Road.

7 kids Pa'ia Fish Market. This North Shore favorite has a south shore counter as well as one in Lahaina (see p 51). Get your mahimahi burger to go and eat it across the street at Kalama Beach Park. *1913 S. Kihei Rd. ☎ 808/874-8888. $*

Maui's Early History

The first Hawaiian settlers arrived by canoe. Unsurpassed navigators, early Polynesians used the stars, birds, clouds, and currents to guide them across thousands of miles. They packed their canoes with food, plants, medicine, tools, and animals: everything necessary for building a new life on a distant shore. No one is sure exactly when they arrived on Maui, but artifacts at the **Malu'ulu O Lele Park** in Lahaina (see p 51) date back to between A.D. 700 and 900.

Over the ensuing centuries, a distinctly Hawaiian culture arose. Sailors became farmers and fishermen. They built highly productive fishponds, terraced *kalo lo'i* (taro patches), and massive rock *heiau* (temples). They also cultivated more than 400 varieties of *kalo,* their staple food; 300 types of sweet potato; and 40 different bananas. Hawaiian women fashioned intricately patterned *kapa* (barkcloth)—some of the finest in all of Polynesia.

Each of the Hawaiian Islands was its own realm, governed by *ali'i* (high-ranking chiefs) who drew their authority from an established *kapu* (taboo) and caste system. Those who broke the *kapu* could be sacrificed. In the early years, Maui was divided into three chiefdoms: Hana, Wailuku, and Lahaina. Pi'ilani, a 15th-century ruler from Hana, became the first to unite Maui. His rule was a time of peace; he built fishponds and began the highway that encircled the island.

The ancient Hawaiian creation chant, the *Kumulipo,* depicts a universe that began when heat and light emerged out of darkness, followed by the first life form: a coral polyp. The 2,000-line epic poem is a grand genealogy, describing how all species are interrelated, from gently waving seaweeds to mighty human warriors. It is the basis for the Hawaiian concept of *kuleana,* a word that simultaneously refers to privilege and responsibility. To this day, Native Hawaiians view the care of their natural resources as a family duty and honor.

8 Kihei. Kihei consists of unimaginative condos and mini-malls—crowded up against a string of golden beaches, each one near perfect. At the north end of town, the **Hawaiian Islands Humpback Whale National Marine Sanctuary** (725 Kihei Rd.; www.hawaiihumpbackwhale.noaa.gov; ☎ 808/879-2818) offers some background on the mighty whales that visit Hawai'i from December through March. Next door, the **Ko'ie'ie Fishpond** is a prime example of ancient Hawaiian aquaculture. Continue north on Kihei Road to **Kealia Pond National Wildlife Preserve** (☎ 808/875-1582), a 700-

The habitat viewing boardwalk at Kealia Pond National Wildlife Preserve.

acre (283ha) U.S. Fish and Wildlife wetland preserve that's a fantastic place to see many endangered Hawaiian species, like the black-crowned herons and Hawaiian stilts, coots, and ducks. From July to December, hawksbill turtles come ashore here to lay eggs. Stroll along the preserve's boardwalk, dotted with interpretive signs and shade shelters, through sand dunes, and around ponds. The boardwalk starts at the outlet of Kealia Pond on the ocean side of North Kihei Road (near MM 2 on Hwy. 31).

Continue north on Hwy. 31, then go left on Hwy. 30 to the Ma'alaea turn off. It's about 3 miles (4.8km).

9 ★★★ kids **Ma'alaea.** The star of this wind-blasted harborside village is the **Maui Ocean Center,** Hawai'i's largest aquarium. This 5-acre (2ha) facility houses numerous family-friendly exhibits, including a 100-foot-long (30m), 750,000-gallon tank featuring sharks, rays, and dazzling schools of fish. The aquarium is designed to usher you from the beach to the

A touch pool at Maui Ocean Center.

Ocean Safety

The range of watersports available in Maui is astounding—this is a prime water playground with conditions for every age and ability. But the ocean is also an untamed wilderness; don't expect a calm swimming pool.

Many people who visit Hawai'i underestimate the power of the ocean. But with just a few precautions, your Pacific experience can be a safe and happy one.

Before jumping in, **familiarize yourself with your equipment.** If you're snorkeling, make sure you feel at ease breathing and clearing water from the snorkel.

Take a moment to **watch where others are swimming.** Observe weather conditions, swells, and possible riptides. If caught in a riptide, stay calm and swim parallel to the shore until you can head inland. If you get caught in big surf, dive underneath each wave until the swell subsides. Never turn your back to the ocean; rogue waves catch even experienced swimmers unaware.

Be realistic about your fitness—more than one visitor has ended his or her vacation with a heart attack in the water.

Don't go out alone, or during a storm.

Note that **sharks** are not a big problem in Hawai'i; in fact, local divers look forward to seeing them. Only 2 of the 40 shark species present in Hawaiian waters are known to bite humans, and then it's usually by accident. But here are the general rules for avoiding sharks: **Don't swim at dusk or in murky water**—sharks may mistake you for one of their usual meals. And, while it should be obvious, it bears repeating: **Don't swim where there are bloody fish** in the water, as sharks become aggressive around blood.

depths of the ocean. A see-through tunnel goes right through the tank, so you're surrounded by marine creatures on all sides. If you're a certified scuba diver, you can participate in the **Shark Dive Maui Program,** which allows you (for a fee of $199) to plunge into the aquarium and swim with the sharks, stingrays, and tropical fish. ⏲ *2 hr. or more. Ma'alaea Harbor Village, 192 Ma'alaea Rd. (the triangle btw. Honoapi'ilani Hwy. and Ma'alaea Rd.) www.mauioceancenter.com.* ☎ *808/270-7000. Buy tickets online to avoid long lines. Admission $30 adults, $27 seniors, $20 children 4–12. Daily 9am–5pm.*

Central Maui

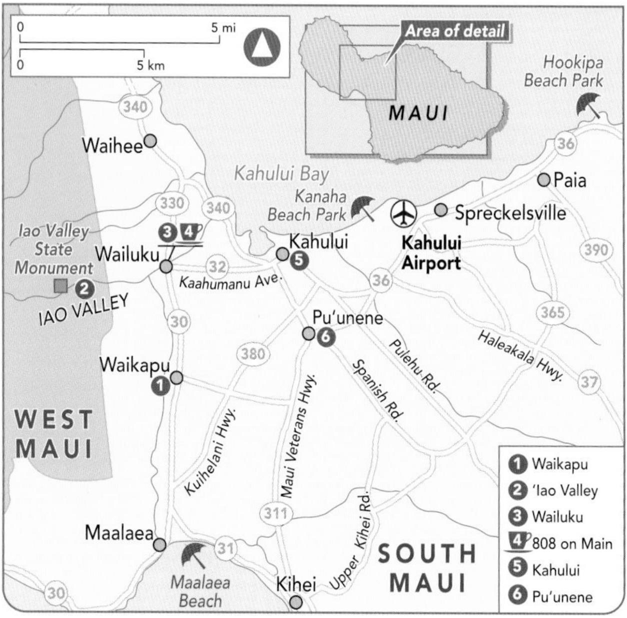

The central plain between Maui's two volcanoes is the site of the main airport, where you'll probably arrive. Distinctly un-touristy, it's home to the majority of the island's population, the heart of the business community, and the center of the local government. START: **Waikapu.**

❶ kids **Waikapu.** Tucked up against the verdant West Maui mountains, you'll find the **Maui Tropical Plantation** (p 27). Spend an hour here riding the 40-minute narrated tram ride through fields of pineapple, vegetables, and plumeria trees, or soaring overhead on a zipline. Check out its **Mill House** restaurant, country store and farm stand before you leave.

Turn left on Honoapi'ilani Hwy. 30, then left on Main Street. In ½ mile (.8km) take a slight right onto 'Iao Valley Road. Follow it to the end, about 2 miles (3.2km).

❷ ★★ kids **'Iao Valley.** This peaceful valley, full of tropical plants, rainbows, waterfalls, swimming holes, and hiking trails (two of them paved and easy), offers cool rejuvenation. The park and stream get their names from the **'Iao Needle,** a phallic rock that juts an impressive 2,250 feet (686m) above sea level; ancient Hawaiians called it unflatteringly "broken dung." Pack a picnic, take your swimsuit, and spend a couple of hours in the shady rainforest. **Kepaniwai Park** has streamside picnic tables and charming memorial buildings that celebrate each of Hawai'i's diverse ethnic

The buildings at the Kepaniwai Heritage Gardens honor the many cultures that have populated Maui.

cultures: a Hawaiian thatched *hale* (house), a Filipino farmer's hut, a Chinese pavilion, and a Portuguese villa. *'Iao Valley State Monument, 54 S. High St., Wailuku. ☎ 808/984-8109. Open daily 7am–6pm.*

Return via Main Street into the town of Wailuku.

3 ★ Wailuku. With its faded wooden storefronts, old plantation homes, and shops straight out of the 1940s, quaint little Wailuku is worth exploring. Stop at the **Hale Ho'ike'ike** Hawaiian museum (see p 44), then continue northeast of the town center to see the ancient sites of the **Haleki'i-Pihana Heiau State Monument** (p 44.)

4 808 on Main. Pop into this bustling restaurant (open Mon–Sat) for hearty sandwiches, soups, and salads. The lamb lettuce cups and "Squealer" (pulled pork and coleslaw on a hoagie) are both tasty. *2051 Main St., Wailuku. www.808onmain.com. ☎ 808/242-1111. $$.*

Head east on Main St., which becomes Ka'ahumanu Ave., leading into the town of Kahului.

5 Kahului. Aside from picking up supplies at Costco or Whole Foods, this industrial town is not the place to spend your vacation. There are few attractions worth noting, however. The first is **Maui Nui Botanical Gardens** (150 Kanaloa Ave; www.mnbg.org; ☎ 808/249-2798). Once the site of a sad little zoo, the gardens are now a rich, living library of rare native Hawaiian plants. Ask to see the *hapai* (pregnant) banana trees that produce fruit inside their trunk. Then head to the **Maui Arts & Cultural Center** (1 Cameron Way; www.mauiarts.org; ☎ 808/242-7469) where the Schaefer International Gallery hosts top-quality art exhibits. From here, head over to **Kanaha Beach Park,** where kiters and windsurfers catch air and twirl above the surf like fluorescent butterflies. Across the street, peek into the **Kanaha Pond** wildlife sanctuary (Haleakala Hwy. Ext. and Hana Hwy; ☎ 808/984-8100). See if you can spot an endangered Hawaiian stilt—a tuxedoed bird with skinny pink legs.

From Ka'ahumanu Ave., turn south on Pu'unene Ave. Follow it through town to Hansen Rd. Turn left and the Sugar Museum is on your left.

6 Pu'unene. Soak up a little more colorful history in this Central Maui ghost town. Once a thriving sugar-plantation town, Pu'unene today consists of a post office, a shuttered sugar mill, and the **Alexander & Baldwin Sugar Museum** (p 45).

Kalaupapa, Moloka'i

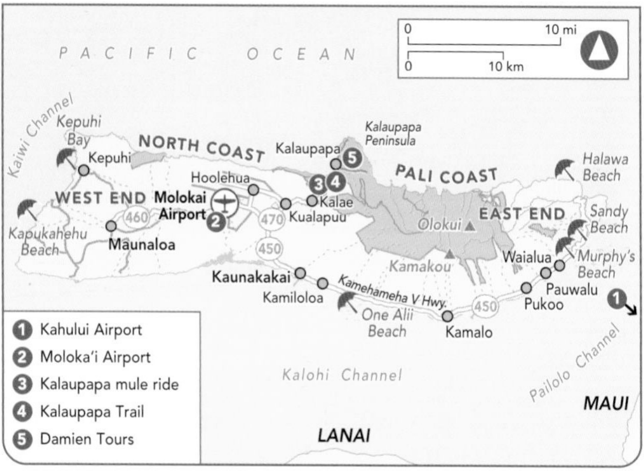

A visit to remote Kalaupapa on the island of Moloka'i is a once-in-a-lifetime experience. This isolated peninsula at the base of the world's tallest sea cliffs is a simply stunning locale. You must travel here on foot or by mule, or by plane—there's no road, and access by water is not allowed—but the trek is worth the effort. Kalaupapa's lush valleys once supported several Native Hawaiian communities; they were evicted in 1865 when King Kamehameha V signed the Act to Prevent the Spread of Leprosy, which ultimately sent some 8,000 people with the disease (now called Hansen's disease) to this natural prison. The exiles' suffering was eased somewhat by the arrival of Father Damien, a Belgian priest who served them tirelessly, along with other helpers. Patients were finally freed to come and go in the 1960s, but a handful of elderly folks still live here. To protect their privacy, visitation is restricted to 100 people a day, age 16 and older. START: **Kahului Airport on Maui.**

Travel Tip

One alternative to the mule ride is to hike down the Kalaupapa Trail. To do that, you'll need to book the first flight to Ho'olehua, arrange airport transfer to the trailhead in Kualapu'u, and start hiking by 7:30am in order to meet Damien Tours at the base of the sea cliffs by 9am. (You'll also want to get onto the trail early to avoid being overtaken by the mule trains!) The knee-pounding descent takes 60 to 90 minutes; it's 90 to 120 minutes back up.

1 Kahului Airport, Maui. Plan to fly out *early*—it's only a half-hour flight to Moloka'i, but you must get there in time to meet your mule tour by 7:30am, so you can meet the bus tour by 9am. If you're worried about logistics, consider flying to Moloka'i the day before your tour and spending the night.

2 Moloka'i Airport. If you've signed up for the mule ride (see 3), fly into Ho'olehua airport, where guides will meet you to transport you

to the mule barn. A quicker, equally scenic option is to fly directly into Kalaupapa by booking a tour package with **Mokulele Airlines** (www.mokulele.com; ☎ 808/495-4188). It's a 15-min. flight from Ho'olehua.

❸ ★★★ **Kalaupapa Rare Adventures mule tour.** The surefooted animals step down the narrow, muddy trail, rain or shine, pausing often to calculate their next move—and always, it seems to me, veering a little too close to the edge. The first switchback may make you gasp, but the mules have safely tromped up and down the trail for years. Settle into your saddle and enjoy the scenic view of the majestic cliffs, the green peninsula, and the dramatic ocean below. ***Note:*** If the trail is closed due to landslides, as it was in early 2019, the company can arrange access by plane. ⏲ *7½ hr. round trip. 100 Kalae Hwy., on Hwy. 470, 5 mi (8km) north of Hwy. 460. www.muleride.com.* ☎ *800/567-6088. $209 per person. Riders must be at least 16 years old and physically fit.*

❹ ★★★ **Kalaupapa Trail.** The trail is only 3 miles long, but it zig-zags down a knuckle-whitening 1,700-foot cliff, via a series of 26 switchbacks. Whether you ride it or hike it (permit required, see #5 below), take time to savor the views—and keep an eye out for trailside shrines and flowering *wiliwili* trees.

❺ ★★★ **Touring Kalaupapa.** To explore this beautiful and haunting place, you must go with permitted guides. **Kekaula Tours** (www.muleride.com; ☎ 808/567-6088) and **Saint Damien and Mother Marianne Cope Molokai Tours** (☎ 808/895-1673) offer 3-hour tours of the peninsula's most fascinating sites as part of hiking, mule ride or plane ride packages. Buses or minivans retrieve passengers first at the tiny airstrip near the lighthouse, then pick up riders and hikers at the trail's end. Climb aboard for a journey along the steep, craggy cliffs to **Father Damien's grave.** Born to wealth in Belgium in 1840, Father Damien arrived on Moloka'i in 1873 and devoted his life to caring for the sufferers of Hansen's disease, building houses, schools, and churches for his patients. He himself died of the disease in 1889 and was canonized in 2009. Other tour stops include **St. Philomena Church,** built by patients in 1872, and **Kalaupapa Book Store,** filled with a wealth of information on the history and people of this place. You can't help but be profoundly moved by the tragic circumstances of those who lived here, and their remarkable resilience.

A Night on Moloka'i

If the simplicity of Moloka'i appeals to you, consider spending the night and taking a day or two to explore the island. There is only one hotel on the island, **Hotel Molokai**, Kamehameha V Hwy., Kaunakakai (www.hotelmolokai.com; ☎ 877/553-5347 or 808/553-5347). Rates here start at $170. If you'd prefer a condo or vacation rental, contact **Molokai Vacation Properties** (www.molokaivacationrental.com; ☎ 800/367-2984 or 808/553-8334). The agents represent an assortment of rentals, most of them oceanfront.

Upcountry Maui

A 10,023-foot tall volcano lords over Maui. The fertile slopes of Haleakala, or House of the Sun, are home to cowboys, farmers, and easygoing folk. Crisp air, rolling green pastures, and flower farms are the highlights of the area known as "Upcountry." Bring a jacket; as locals like to joke, "It's cooler in Kula." START: **Makawao.**

❶ ★ **Makawao.** Maui has a longstanding tradition of ranchers and rodeo masters, and this cool, misty upcountry town is its epicenter. Modern-day *paniolo* (cowboys) come here to fuel up on cream puffs and stick donuts from **T. Komoda Store & Bakery,** 3674 Baldwin Ave. (☎ 808/572-7261), founded in 1916 and seemingly frozen in time. The neighboring businesses offer chic clothing, fine art, and decent snacks. Five minutes down Baldwin Avenue, you'll find the gracious **Hui No'eau Visual Arts Center** (p 116).

Take Makawao Avenue to the light at Kula Hwy. 37, turn left and drive 4.5 miles (7.2km). Turn left onto Lower Kula Rd.

❷ **La Provence.** Every item in this French bakery is exquisite. Arrive before noon or risk watching the mango blueberry scone walk out the door without you. Enjoy an addictively good crepe in the garden. *3158 Lower Kula Rd. ☎ 808/878-1313. $$.*

Return to Kula Hwy. 37. It's a 20-minute detour down 'Omaopio Rd. to Surfing Goat Dairy and

Makawao Rodeo.

about a 20-minute detour up Waipoli Rd. to Ali'i Kula Lavender Farm. (You can also hit Surfing Goat Dairy at the end, on your way back down the mountain.)

❸ ★ **Kula.** Continue south through the bucolic rolling hills of this upland community, past old flower farms, humble cottages, and new suburban ranch houses with million-dollar views that take in the ocean, isthmus, West Maui Mountains, Lana'i, and Kaho'olawe in the distance. Kula sits at a cool 3,000 feet (914m), just below the cloud line, and from here a winding road snakes its way up to **Haleakala National Park** (see p 84). Everyone in this area grows something—Maui onions, carnations, persimmons, and proteas, those strange-looking blossoms that look like "Star Trek" props. Must stops: **Surfing Goat Dairy** (p 26) and **Ali'i Kula Lavender Farm** (p 40).

Continue on Hwy. 37 for 11 miles (17.7km).

❹ ★ **Keokea.** Fill up your gas tank in this charming blink-and-you'll-miss-it town. Grab a hot dog or a snack at the quaint, family-run **Fong Store** (9226 Kula Hwy., ☎ 808/878-1525) or sip a cup of joe at **Grandma's Coffee House** (p 16).

Continue on Hwy. 37 for 17 miles (27km).

❺ ★ **'Ulupalakua.** The final stop on the Upcountry tour is **'Ulupalakua Ranch,** a 20,000-acre (8,094ha) spread once owned by legendary sea captain James Makee. The ranch is now home to Maui's only **winery,** established in 1974 by Napa vintner Emil Tedeschi. Stop in the tasting room and sample a few vintages, which have truly improved with age. Across from the winery are the remains of the three smokestacks of the **Makee Sugar Mill,** built in 1878. This is home to Maui artist Reems Mitchell, who carved the mannequins on the front porch of the **'Ulupalakua Ranch Store:** a Filipino with his fighting cock, a cowboy, a farmhand, and a sea captain, each representing a piece of Maui history. *MauiWine, 14815 Pi'ilani Hwy. 31, Kula. www.mauiwine.com. ☎ 808/878-6058. Daily 10am–5pm. Free tours given 10:30am and 1:30pm; tasting flights $12–$16.*

The Road to Hana

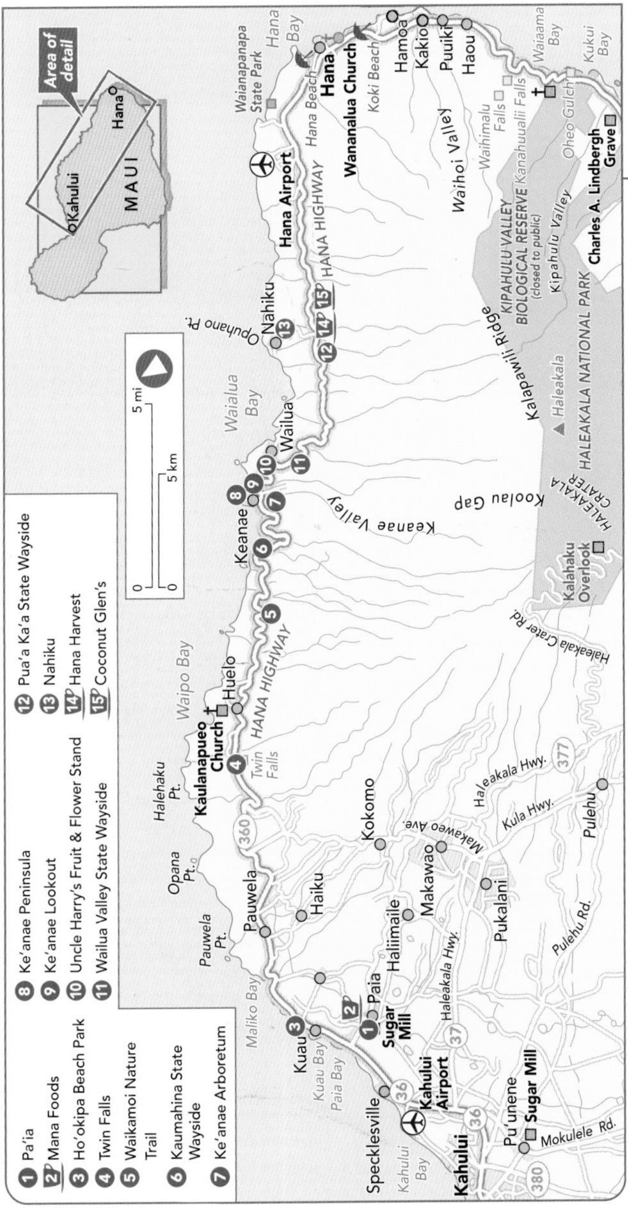

Top down, sunscreen on, swimsuit handy, and radio tuned to a Hawaiian music station: It's time to explore the Hana Highway (Hwy. 36). This wiggle of a road winds for 45 miles (72km) along Maui's northeastern shore, passing taro patches, magnificent seascapes, waterfalls, botanical gardens, and verdant rainforests. Bring water, snacks, beach towels, and a fully charged camera or smartphone. The drive itself should take only about 2 hours, but plan to spend a full day to enjoy all the sights along the way. START: **Pa'ia.**

❶ **Pa'ia.** Fuel up on gas and groceries. There are several options for breakfast, if you'd like a hearty meal before you go. See p 123 for more details.

2 Mana Foods. Stock up on sandwiches, drinks, and ginger candies to stave off potential road sickness. *49 Baldwin Ave., Pa'ia.* ☎ *808/579-8078. $*

Drive east on the Hana Highway (Hwy. 36) until just before MM 9.

❸ ★ kids **Ho'okipa Beach Park.** See p 79.

After MM 16, the road is still called Hana Highway, but the number changes from Hwy. 36 to Hwy. 360, and mile markers go back to 0. Park in the dirt lot at the fruit stand just past MM 2; if full, park in the lot past the fruit stand across a bridge.

❹ **Twin Falls.** Pull over on the mountainside and park; the waterfall and pool are a 3- to 5-minute walk. The mountain stream water is a bit chilly when you first get in, but it's good for swimming. If it's crowded, keep going; other waterfalls are coming up on this next stretch of the road, which gets narrower and extra-curvy from here on. Try counting every fern-draped bridge you cross—at least 59 of them before you get to Hana, including many beautiful, one-lane arches built 100 years ago.

Continue to MM 9.

❺ kids **Waikamoi Nature Trail.** Stretch your legs here with an easy .75-mile (1.2km) loop-trail hike.

The Road to Hana.

Ke'anae Congregational Church.

Look for the Quiet Trees at Work sign and follow the path.

Just past MM 12, you'll find:

6 kids Kaumahina State Wayside. This is a good pit stop, with actual restrooms (though no drinking water) and a great view of the rugged coastline all the way to the jutting Ke'anae Peninsula.

Between MM 16 and MM 17, take right-hand turn-off to reach:

7 ★★ kids Ke'anae Arboretum. Maui's botany is represented here in three parts: native forest; introduced forest; and traditional Hawaiian food and medicine plants. You can swim in the refreshing pools of Pi'ina'au Stream or walk a mile-long (1.6km) trail into Ke'anae Valley's lush tropical rainforest.

Return to Hana Hwy. Just past MM 17, turn left (north) onto Ke'anae Rd., which leads down to the Ke'anae Peninsula.

8 ★★★ Ke'anae Peninsula. The old Hawaiian village of **Ke'anae** stands out against the Pacific like a place time forgot. For untold generations, Native Hawaiians have lived off the land here, diverting fresh stream water into their *kalo lo'i* (taro patches). Take a reverent stroll through the **Ke'anae Congregational Church** (☎ 808/248-8040), built in 1860 of lava rocks and coral mortar; it stands in stark contrast to the surrounding green fields. Stop by **Aunty Sandy's** (210 Ke'anae Rd.; ☎ 808/248-7448) for warm banana bread.

Return to Hana Highway and continue east for about ¼ mile. Look for a turnout on your left (ocean side).

9 Ke'anae Lookout. Stop here to take in a postcard-worthy panorama of the entire Ke'anae Peninsula, from its checkerboard pattern of green taro fields to its salt-kissed coast etched in black lava.

Around MM 18 look for:

10 Uncle Harry's Fruit & Flower Stand. On this stretch of the road, you'll start to see numerous small stands selling fruit or flowers. Uncle Harry sells a variety of fruits and juices plus kalua pig tacos.

end

Just before MM 19.

11 ★★ Wailua Valley State Wayside. Climb the stairs beneath an archway of *hau* (tree hibiscus) for jaw-dropping views in both directions: the taro patches of Wailua village on side and the waterfalls of Ko'olau Gap on the other. Imagine

An overview of the Ke'anae Peninsula.

the massive erosional forces that carved this valley.

Between MM 22 and MM 23.

⓬ Pua'a Ka'a State Wayside. Waterfalls provide background music for this small park area with a shaded picnic area and restrooms. Cross the stream to take a quick dip in the falls. Ginger plants are everywhere: Pick a few blossoms for your car so that you can travel with their sweet smell.

Just after MM 25, turn left onto narrow Nahiku Rd., which leads 3 miles (4.8km) from the highway, at about 1,000 feet (305m) elevation, down to sea level.

⓭ Nahiku. This remote, wildly beautiful area was once a thriving village of thousands; today the population has dwindled to fewer than a hundred—including a few Hawaiian families, but mostly extremely wealthy mainland residents who jet in for a few weeks at a time. At the end of the road, you can see the remains of the old wharf from the town's rubber-plantation days. There's a small picnic area off to the side. Dolphins are frequently seen in the bay.

Continue south on Hwy. 360. You'll have your choice of refreshment stops, one at MM 26.5, the other at MM 27.5.

14 Hana Harvest. The drinks may be pricey but the kiawe wood-fired pizza at this roadside stand is well worth the $6–$7 a slice. Or try the breadfruit-based vegetarian chili or chips and guacamole made from local avocados. There's also free Wi-Fi. *800 Hana Hwy., at Waione Bridge Rd. hanaharvest.us.* ☎ *808/248-8228. $.*

15 Coconut Glen's. When you see Coconut Glen's rainbow-splashed sign, pull over and indulge in some truly splendid ice cream—dairy-free and made with organic coconut milk. Scoops of chocolate chili, liliko'i, and honey macadamia nut ice cream are served in coconut bowls. This whimsical stand oozes aloha. From here, you're only 20 minutes away from Hana town. *Hana Hwy., at MM 27.5. www.coconutglens.com.* ☎ *808/248-4876.*

Ice cream from Coconut Glen's stand.

Hana

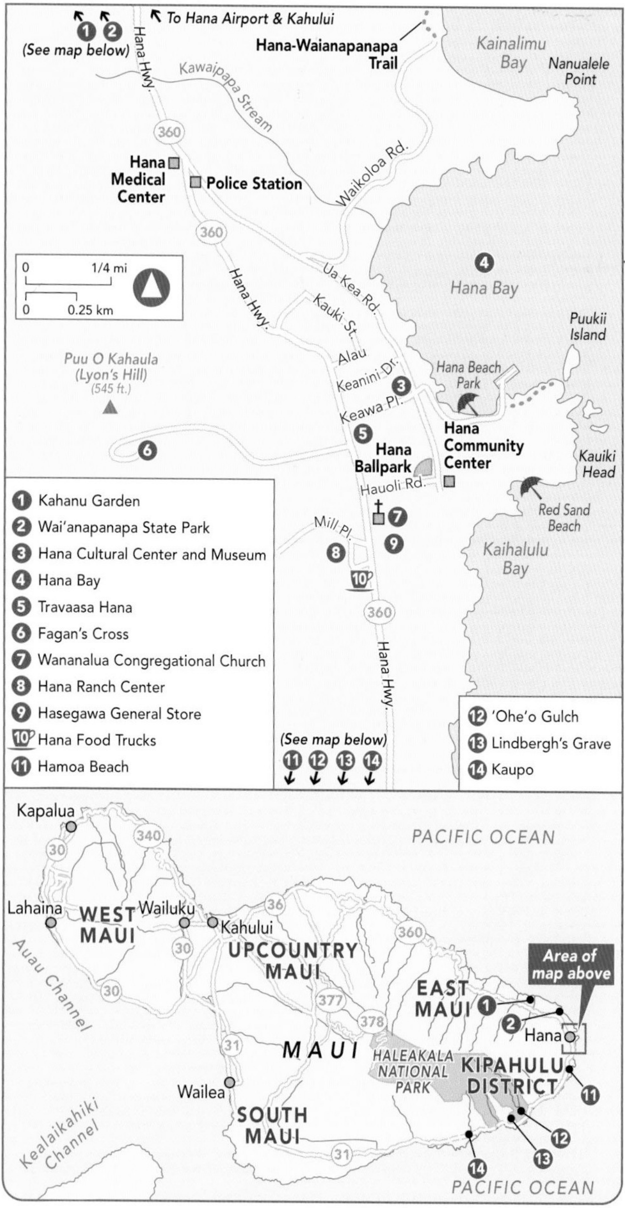
To Hana Airport & Kahului
(See map below)
Hana-Waianapanapa Trail
Kainalimu Bay
Nanualele Point
Hana Hwy.
Kawaipapa Stream
360
Waikoloa Rd.
Hana Medical Center
Police Station
1/4 mi
0.25 km
Ua Kea Rd.
Hana Bay
Kauki St.
Puukii Island
Puu O Kahaula (Lyon's Hill) (545 ft.)
Alau
Keanini Dr.
Hana Beach Park
Keawa Pl.
Hana Community Center
Hana Ballpark
Kauiki Head
Hauoli Rd.
Red Sand Beach
Mill Pl.
Kaihalulu Bay
1 Kahanu Garden
2 Wai'anapanapa State Park
3 Hana Cultural Center and Museum
4 Hana Bay
5 Travaasa Hana
6 Fagan's Cross
7 Wananalua Congregational Church
8 Hana Ranch Center
9 Hasegawa General Store
10 Hana Food Trucks
11 Hamoa Beach
12 'Ohe'o Gulch
13 Lindbergh's Grave
14 Kaupo
Kapalua
340
30
PACIFIC OCEAN
Lahaina
WEST MAUI
Wailuku
Kahului
36
UPCOUNTRY MAUI
Auau Channel
EAST MAUI
Area of map above
377
378
Hana
31
MAUI
HALEAKALA NATIONAL PARK
KIPAHULU DISTRICT
Wailea
SOUTH MAUI
Kealaikahiki Channel
PACIFIC OCEAN

Hana is where islanders come for vacation. After the long journey to get here, take a deep breath. Inhale the scent of sea salt, white ginger, and ripe guava. Ahhhh . . . *this* is probably what you came to Maui in search of. Hana enjoys more than 90 inches of rain a year, more than enough to keep the scenery lush. Banyans, bamboo, breadfruit trees—everything seems larger than life in this rainforested coastal town. Explore the magical landscape: red and black sand beaches, valleys threaded with silver waterfalls, and sparkling blue pools. Be extra kind to the locals; remember, you're only one of hundreds of visitors who breeze through their humble community every day. START: **Hana.**

Travel Tip

Wake early to see the sun rise out of the sea. In the morning hours you'll have Hana's waterfalls and beaches all to yourself. Day-trippers arrive in town around 11am and stay until about 4pm; during that window, the area is overrun with hundreds of people, all in a hurry. By staying here overnight, you can avoid them and soak up the extra solitude.

From Hwy. 360 turn toward the ocean on Ula'ino Road, just past MM 31.

1 ★★ Kahanu Garden. Allow yourself plenty of time to explore this 472-acre (191ha) garden and cultural site, including a thatched canoe house and the world's largest collection of breadfruit trees. Across the wide lawn, you'll see the imposing **Pi'ilanihale Heiau,** a massive temple built by a lineage of powerful Maui chiefs. The structure's mammoth proportions are humbling: 3 acres (1.2 ha) with stacked rock walls 50 feet (15m) tall and 8-to-10 feet (2.4m–3m) thick. Historians believe it was built in several stages, beginning as early as the 13th century, with basalt rocks hand-carried from Hana Bay, some 5 miles (8km) away. The breadfruit trees at the base of the back wall are likely descendants of those planted in ancient times.

1 hr. 650 Ula'ino Rd. www.ntbg.org. ☎ 808/248-8912. Guided tours $25; self-guided tours $10; children 12 and under free. Mon–Fri 9am–4pm, Sat 9am–2pm.

Continuing east on Hwy. 360, just past MM 32, turn left and take Honokolani Rd. to the ocean.

2 ★★★ kids Wai'anapanapa State Park. Get up early to see shiny black-sand Wai'anapanapa Beach and hike the coastal trail. Plan to spend at least a couple of hours at this 120-acre (49ha) park

Take plenty of time to roam Kahanu Garden's 472 acres.

that appears like a vivid dream, with bright-green jungle foliage on three sides and cobalt-blue water lapping at its shore. Swimming in the ocean is not recommended here (rough seas, strong currents), but you can plunge into a fresh-water cave pool just above the beach. Warm up by walking the coastal trail past blowholes, sea arches, and *hala* groves. *End of Honokalani Rd., off Hana Hwy. (Hwy. 360), Hana. ☎ 808/248-4843. Open daily 24 hours.*

Continue on Hwy. 360. As you enter Hana, the road splits about ½ mile (.8km) past MM 33, at the police station. Both roads will take you to Hana, but Uakea Road is more scenic.

3 ★★ kids Hana Cultural Center and Museum. With the sun starting to reach its zenith, take a cooling break while touring this small museum's excellent collection of Hawaiian quilts, artifacts, books, and photos. Kids will love the tiny jail cell and thatched *hale* (huts) for cooking and canoe storage. *30 min. 4974 Uakea Rd. www.hanaculturalcenter.org. ☎ 808/248-8622. Mon–Fri 10am–4pm; $3 donation.*

The black sands of Wai'anapanapa Beach.

From Uakea Rd., turn left on Keawa Place to the bay.

4 ★ kids Hana Bay. Come here to watch the activities in the bay—fishermen throwing nets, paddlers pulling their canoes into the water, and local kids belly-flopping off the pier. You'll find restrooms, showers, picnic tables, barbecues, and a snack bar here. The red cinder cone looming over the southeast side of the bay is **Kau'iki Hill,** the birthplace in 1768 of Queen Ka'ahumanu, who played a huge role in Hawai'i's history by breaking traditional *kapu* (taboos) after Kamehameha the Great's death and encouraging her people to convert to Christianity.

Return to Hana Hwy. 360. Park across the street from the hotel.

5 Travaasa Hana. If you can afford it, this is *the* place to stay in Hana (and one of the state's top resorts). If they aren't too busy, the staff generally is amenable to taking you on a tour in their speedy golf carts. Ask to see the sausage tree, and the dogtooth anklet in the lobby. They have an excellent spa here, too. Plan on a half-hour to see this elegant resort, longer if you want to get a meal or a drink at one of the restaurants here. See p 150.

6 kids Fagan's Cross. Across the street from Travaasa Hana, find the trailhead for an uphill hike to the 30-foot-high (9m) white cross (made of lava rock), erected in memory of Paul Fagan, who founded Hana Ranch as well as Hotel Hana-Maui, now Travaasa

Fagan's Cross.

Hana. The 3-mile (4.8km) round-trip hike provides a gorgeous coastal view, especially at sunset. The uphill trail starts across Hana Highway from Travaasa Hana. (Enter the pastures at your own risk; they're often occupied by glaring bulls and cows with new calves.) Watch your step as you ascend this steep hill. The hike can take 1 to 2 hours, depending on how fast you hike and how long you linger at the top admiring the breathtaking view.

South on Hwy. 360, just past Hauoli Rd., the next four sites are in close proximity.

7 Wananalua Congregation Church. Stop for photos of this historic church, built from coral stones from 1838 to 1842 during the missionary rush to convert the natives. *15 min. 10 Hauoli Rd., just off Hana Hwy. 360. 808/248-8040.*

8 Hana Ranch Center. This small cluster of buildings composes Hana's entire commercial center, with a post office, bank, general store, and **Hana Ranch Restaurant.** *1 Mill Place, off Hana Hwy. 360.*

9 ★ Hasegawa General Store. This legendary general store, established in 1910 and immortalized in song since 1961, is a good place to find picnic items (chips, fruit, cookies, soda, bread, lunch fixings) and Hana-specific souvenirs. There's also an ATM if you're low on cash for fruit stands and food trucks. *5165 Hana Hwy. 360. 808/248-8231. Daily 7am–7pm.*

10 Hana Food Trucks. A caravan of food trucks has rushed to fill the void of culinary options in this remote outpost. A minute down the road from Hasegawa's, Ono Organic Farms has a stand open daily 10am to 6pm selling gorgeous, ripe tropical fruit, coffee, and cacao beans grown in nearby Kipahulu. The trucks behind the stand have a decent selection of plate lunches and fish tacos.

Head south on Hwy. 360 and turn left on Haneo'o Rd.

11 ★★ Hamoa Beach. See p 79. En route to Hamoa, look also for the dark red sand of **Koki Beach,** which is visible from Haneo'o Road.

Haneo'o Rd. rejoins Hana Hwy. 360. Continue south another 7 miles (11km).

12 ★★★ kids 'Ohe'o Gulch. If conditions permit, it's time to hit the water again, in the Kipahulu section of **Haleakala National Park** (see p 84). For years people called this series of stair-step waterfalls "Seven Sacred Pools." It's a misnomer; there are more than seven pools—and all water in Hawai'i is considered sacred. Park rangers

Waimoku Falls.

offer safety information, exhibits, books, and a variety of walks and hikes year-round; check at the station for current activities. Don't miss the magnificent 400-foot (122m) **Waimoku Falls,** reachable via an often-muddy, but rewarding, hour-long uphill hike through a magical bamboo forest. Expect showers on the Kipahulu coast. *www.nps.gov/hale. ☎ 808/248-7375. Admission $25 per car.*

Continue 1 mile (1.6km) past 'Ohe'o Gulch on the ocean side of Hwy. 360.

⓭ **Lindbergh's Grave.** Aviation fans make the trek to honor renowned pilot Charles A. Lindbergh (1902–1974), who was the first to fly solo across the Atlantic. He settled in Kipahulu, where he died of cancer in 1974, and was buried under river stones in a seaside graveyard behind the 1857 **Palapala Ho'omau Congregational Church.** You'll have no trouble finding his tombstone, which is engraved with his favorite words from the 139th Psalm: "If I take the wings of the morning and dwell in the uttermost parts of the sea."

Drive about 6 miles (9.6km) farther on Hwy. 360, which becomes Pi'ilani Hwy. 31.

⓮ **Kaupo.** If you still have daylight, continue on (or wait until the next day) to remote, rural Kaupo. The road turns to gravel at times, but isn't too bad—despite what your rental car agent might claim. Kaupo highlights include the lovingly restored 1859 **Huialoha Church** (www.huialohachurchkaupo.org) with its old schoolhouse ruins and lovely pebble beach; and farther down the road, the **Kaupo Store,** an eclectic old country store that carries a range of bizarre goods and doesn't always keep its posted hours, but is a fun place to "talk story" with the staff about this area, which at one time supported a substantial population. Donations are requested for restroom use. *Store: 217 Kaupo Rd. ☎ 808/248-8054. Mon–Sat 10am–5pm.* ●

'Ohe'o Gulch.

5 The Best **Beaches**

Beaches Best Bets

Best **Black Sand**
★★★ Wai'anapanapa State Park, *MM 32, Hana Highway (Hwy. 360), Hana (p 82)*

Best for **Body Surfing**
★ Kama'ole III Beach Park, *South Kihei Road, Kihei (p 80)* and ★★ Hamoa Beach, *Haneo'o Road, Hana (p 79)*

Best for **Families**
★ Kama'ole III Beach Park, *S. Kihei Road, Kihei (p 80)*

Longest **White-Sand Beach**
★★★ Big Beach (Makena Beach), Makena State Park *South Makena Road, Makena (p 78)*

Best for **Kayaking**
★★ Makena Landing, *Makena Road, Makena (p 98)*

Best for **Picnicking**
★ Wahikuli County Wayside, *MM 23, Honoapi'ilani Highway (Hwy. 30), Lahaina (p 81)*

Most **Romantic**
★★ Wailea Beach, *Wailea Alanui Road, Wailea (p 82)*

Best for **People-Watching**
★★ Ka'anapali Beach, *Ka'anapali (p 80)*

Safest for **Kids**
★★ H. A. Baldwin Park ("Baby Beach" at far west end), *MM 6, Hana Highway (Hwy. 360), btw. Spreckelsville and Pa'ia (p 79)*; and ★★ Launiupoko Beach Park, *MM 18, Honoapi'ilani Highway (Hwy. 30), Lahaina (p 81)*

Safest for **Swimming**
★ Kama'ole III Beach Park, *South Kihei Road, Kihei (p 80)*

Best for **Snorkeling**
★★★ Kahekili Beach Park, *Pu'ukoli'i Road, Ka'anapali (p 80)*

Best **View**
★★★ Maluaka Beach, *Makena Road, Makena (p 81)* and Koki Beach, *Haneo'o Road, Hana (p 81)*

Best for **Learning to Surf**
★ Cove Park, *'Ili'ili Road at South Kihei Road, Kihei (p 78)*

Best for **Windsurfing**
★★★ Ho'okipa Beach Park, *just before MM 9, Hana Highway (Hwy. 36), Paia (p 79)*

Best for **Sunbathing**
★★ Hamoa Beach, *Haneo'o Road, Hana (p 79)*

Below: The gray sands of Hamoa Beach are a mix of coral and lava. Previous page: The view along a beach in South Maui.

Maui Beaches A to Z

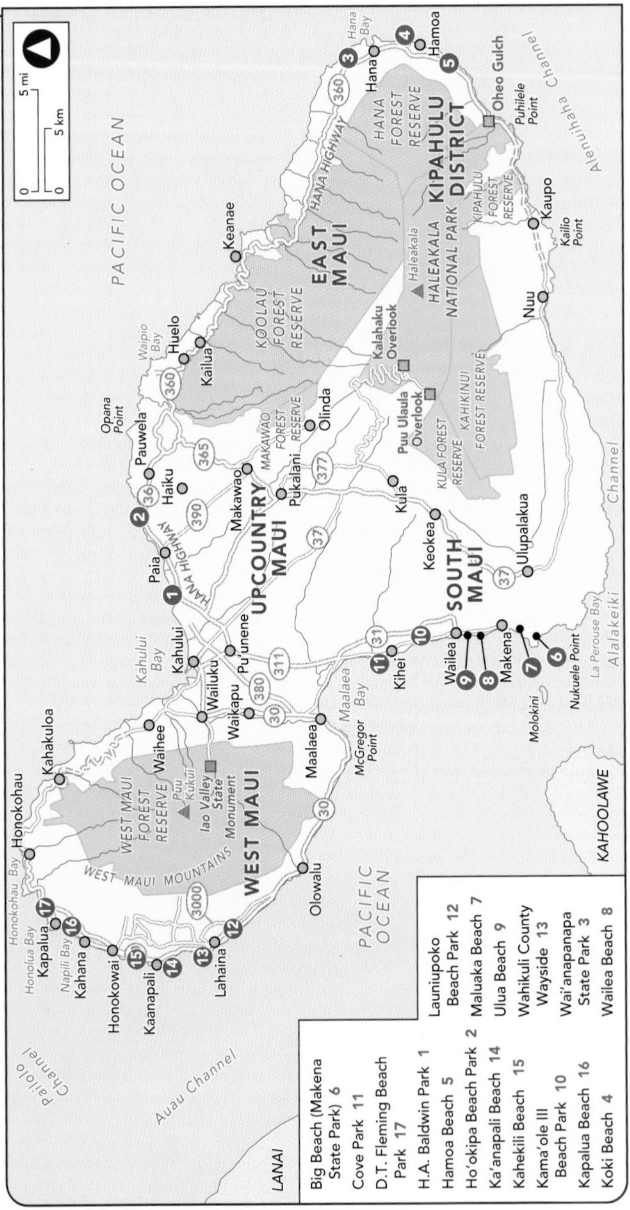
Big Beach (Makena State Park) 6
Cove Park 11
D.T. Fleming Beach Park 17
H.A. Baldwin Park 1
Hamoa Beach 5
Ho'okipa Beach Park 2
Ka'anapali Beach 14
Kahekili Beach 15
Kama'ole III Beach Park 10
Kapalua Beach 16
Koki Beach 4
Launiupoko Beach Park 12
Maluaka Beach 7
Ulua Beach 9
Wahikuli County Wayside 13
Wai'anapanapa State Park 3
Wailea Beach 8
PACIFIC OCEAN
WEST MAUI
EAST MAUI
UPCOUNTRY MAUI
SOUTH MAUI
KIPAHULU DISTRICT
HALEAKALA NATIONAL PARK
LANAI
KAHOOLAWE

Maui's Beaches—Open to All

Maui has more than 80 accessible beaches of every conceivable description, from rocky black-sand beauties to powdery golden ones. The ones I list in this chapter represent my personal favorites, carefully chosen to suit a variety of needs, tastes, and interests. All beaches, even those in front of exclusive resorts, are public property; Hawai'i state law requires resorts and hotels to offer public right-of-way access to the beach, as well as public parking. So don't be shy—just because a beach fronts a hotel doesn't mean you can't enjoy it.

★★★ **Big Beach (Makena), Makena State Park.** One of the most popular beaches on Maui, Big Beach (*Oneloa* in Hawaiian) is so vast it never feels crowded. Also known as Makena Beach, it's more than 100 feet wide, it stretches out 3,300 feet from Pu'u 'Olai, the tall cinder cone on its north end, to its southern rocky point. The golden sand is luxuriant, deep, and soft, but the shorebreak is steep and powerful—many a visitor has broken an arm in the surf here. If you're an inexperienced swimmer, better to watch the pros shred waves on skimboards. Facilities are limited to portable toilets, but there's plenty of parking and lifeguards at the first two entrances. Dolphins often frequent these waters, and nearly every afternoon a heavy cloud rolls in, providing welcome relief from the sun. Clamber up Pu'u 'Olai to find **Little Beach** on the other side, a small crescent of sand where assorted nudists defy the law to work on their all-over tans. *Three entrances off of South Makena Rd., Makena.*

★ **Cove Park.** Just south of the 36-acre (14.6ha) skate park and athletic complex of Kalama Park, this small sandy cove provides perfect waves for learning to surf, or practicing your skills before trying more expert waves elsewhere on Maui. The compact facilities include parking and restrooms. *2120 'Ili'ili Road, Kihei.*

Makena State Park's Big Beach.

Lovely Baldwin Beach Park.

★ D. T. Fleming Beach Park. This wide, quiet, out-of-the-way beach cove is good for families. Immediately north of the Ritz-Carlton, Kapalua, it's bordered by ironwood trees, which provide plenty of shade, and the water is generally good for swimming and snorkeling. Facilities include restrooms, showers, picnic tables, barbecue grills, lifeguards, and a paved parking lot. *Past MM 30, Honoapi'ilani Hwy. (Hwy. 30), Kapalua.*

★★ H. A. Baldwin Park. This beach park draws lots of locals: dog walkers, yoga enthusiasts, boogie boarders, fishermen, and young families. The far ends of the beach are safest for swimming: the cove in the lee of the rocks at the north end, and "Baby Beach" at the south end, where an exposed reef creates a natural sandy swimming pool. Facilities include a pavilion with picnic tables, barbecue grills, restrooms, showers, a semi-paved parking area, a soccer field, and lifeguards. The park is busy on weekends and late afternoons; weekday mornings are much quieter. *At MM 6, Hana Hwy. (Hwy. 36), btw. Spreckelsville and Pa'ia, turn left on Alawai Rd., follow to the ocean.*

★★ Hamoa Beach. Viewed from above, this half-moon-shaped, gray-sand beach is a vision of paradise. The wide stretch of sand (a mix of coral and lava) is three football fields long and sits below 30-foot black-lava sea cliffs. Swells on this unprotected beach break offshore and roll in, making it a popular surfing and bodysurfing area. Hamoa is often swept by powerful rip currents, so take care. The calm left side is best for snorkeling in summer. Travaasa Hana resort has numerous facilities for guests, plus outdoor showers and restrooms for nonguests. Parking is limited. Look for the Hamoa Beach turnoff from Hana Highway. *Haneo'o Rd., off Hana Hwy. (Hwy. 360), Hana.*

★★★ Ho'okipa Beach Park. Ho'okipa means "hospitality," and this sandy beach on Maui's North Shore certainly rolls out the red carpet for wave-riders–it's among the world's top spots for windsurfing and kiting. Daring watermen and women paddle out to carve waves up to 25 feet tall on the reef's multiple surf breaks. Spectators are welcome as well; head to the clifftop parking lot for a bird's-eye view of the action. On flat days, you can snorkel over the reef's trove of marine life. Check out the sea turtles napping on the sand below the

cliff (but give the resting reptiles at least 15 ft. leeway). Facilities include restrooms, showers, pavilions, picnic tables, barbecue grills, and parking. *2 miles past Pa'ia on the Hana Hwy. (Hwy. 36).*

★★ Ka'anapali Beach. Four-mile-long (6.4km) Ka'anapali is one of Maui's best beaches, with grainy gold sand as far as the eye can see. Because Ka'anapali is so long, and because most hotels have adjacent swimming pools, the beach is crowded only in pockets—you'll find plenty of spots to be alone. Summertime swimming is excellent. There's decent snorkeling around **Black Rock (Pu'u Keka'a)**, in front of the Sheraton. The water is clear, calm, and populated with clouds of tropical fish. You might even spot a turtle or two. Facilities consist of outdoor showers. Parking is a problem, though. *Look for* PUBLIC BEACH ACCESS *signs off Ka'anapali Pkwy., off Honoapi'ilani Hwy. (Hwy. 30), at the Ka'anapali Resort.*

★★★ Kahekili Beach Park. This beach gets top marks for everything: a grassy park with pavilion and palm trees, plenty of soft golden sand, and a vibrant coral reef only a few fin-kicks from shore. Herbivorous fish (such as surgeonfish and rainbow-colored parrotfish) are off-limits to fishermen here, so the snorkeling is truly excellent. Facilities include picnic tables, barbecues, showers, restrooms, and paved parking—a real bonus on a stretch of coast where parking is often a problem. *From Honoapi'ilani Hwy. (Hwy. 30) just north of Ka'anapali Resort, follow Pu'ukoli'i Rd. to its end.*

★ Kama'ole III Beach Park. On weekends this beach is jampacked with picnickers, swimmers, and snorkelers, but during the week, "Kam-3" (as locals call it), is often empty. There's a playground for children and a grassy lawn that meets the sand; swimming is safe, although scattered lava rocks are toe stubbers at the water line, and parents should watch to make sure kids don't venture too far out—the bottom slopes off quickly. Both the north and south shores are rocky fingers with a surge big enough to attract fish (and snorkelers that watch them), while winter waves attract bodysurfers. Facilities include restrooms, showers, picnic tables, barbecue grills, swing set, and lifeguards. *S. Kihei Rd., across from Keonekai Rd., Kihei.*

★★★ Kapalua Beach. This is a postcard-perfect beach: a golden crescent bordered by two palm-studded points. Protected from strong winds and currents by lava-rock promontories, Kapalua's calm waters are great for snorkelers and swimmers of all ages and abilities, and the bay is big enough to paddle a kayak around without getting into the more challenging channel that separates Maui from Moloka'i. Facilities include outdoor showers, restrooms, lifeguards, a rental

Kama'ole III Beach Park.

Kapalua Beach.

shack, and plenty of shade. Parking is limited to about 30 spaces in a small lot. *Past MM 30, by Napili Kai Beach Resort, Honoapi'ilani Rd., Kapalua.*

★★ **Koki Beach.** While unwary visitors trespass and routinely get injured on an unstable trail to reach a different red-sand beach in Hana, this one—only a short drive south—has safe, easy access along with stunning views. Although swimming is not recommended, due to rip tides and strong currents, it's a lovely place to picnic while admiring the red cinder cone known as **Ka Iwi O Pele** ("The Bones of Pele") or tiny **'Alau Island,** a bird sanctuary. The huli huli (barbecue) chicken stand often onsite is also worth a visit. *From Travaasa Hana, 5031 Hana Hwy., Hana, head 1.7 miles (2.7km) south on Hana Hwy. 360 to a left turn onto Haneo'o Rd.*

★★ kids **Launiupoko Beach Park.** Families with children will love this small, shady park with a large wading pool for kids and a small sandy beach with good swimming when conditions are right. The view from the park is one of the best, with the islands of Kaho'olawe, Lana'i, and Moloka'i in the distance. Facilities include a paved parking lot, restrooms, showers, picnic tables, and barbecue grills. It's crowded on weekends. *MM 18, Honoapi'ilani Hwy. (Hwy. 30), Lahaina.*

★★★ **Maluaka Beach.** Talk about views: With Molokini Crater and Kaho'olawe both visible in the distance, this short, wide, palm-fringed crescent of golden sand is set between two black-lava points and bounded by big dunes topped by a grassy knoll. Swimming and kayaking in the mostly calm bay are first-rate. Facilities include restrooms, showers, grass park, and paved parking. *From Makena Alanui, turn left on Makena Keonoio.*

★ **Ulua Beach.** One of the most popular beaches in Wailea, Ulua is a long, wide crescent of gold sand between two rocky points. When the ocean is calm, Ulua offers Wailea's best snorkeling; when it's rough, the waves are excellent for bodysurfers. Crowded conditions make it perfect for meeting people. Facilities include showers and restrooms. *Look for the blue shoreline access sign, on Wailea Alanui Dr., Wailea.*

★ **Wahikuli County Wayside.** One of Lahaina's most popular beach parks, Wahikuli is packed on weekends, but during the week it's a prime spot for swimming, snorkeling, sunbathing, and picnicking.

Wailea Beach.

Facilities include paved parking, restrooms, showers, and small pavilions with picnic tables and barbecue grills. *MM 23, Honoapi'ilani Hwy. (Hwy. 30), btw. Lahaina and Ka'anapali.*

★★★ **Wai'anapanapa State Park.** This 120-acre (49ha) beach park is wonderful for shoreline hikes and picnicking, although swimming is generally unsafe (powerful rip currents, strong waves breaking offshore). The black-sand beach gets crowded on weekends; weekdays are generally a better bet. Facilities include 12 cabins, a beach park, picnic tables, barbecue grills, restrooms, showers, and a parking lot. *MM 32, Hana Hwy. (Hwy. 360), Hana.* *See p 91.*

★ **Wailea Beach.** From this beach, the view out to sea is magnificent, framed by neighboring Kaho'olawe and Lana'i and the tiny crescent of Molokini. Grab your sweetie at sunset and watch the clear waters tumble to shore; this is as romantic as it gets. Facilities include restrooms, outdoor showers, and limited free parking. *Look for blue shoreline access sign, on Wailea Alanui Dr., Wailea.* ●

The Legend of Wai'anapanapa

Wai'anapanapa State Park gets its name from the legend of the Wai'anapanapa Cave. Chief Ka'akea, a jealous and cruel man, suspected his wife, Popo'alaea, of having an affair. Popo'alaea left her husband and hid herself in a chamber of the Wai'anapanapa Cave. A few days later, when Ka'akea was passing by the cave, the shadow of a servant gave away Popo'alaea's hiding place, and Ka'akea killed her. During certain times of the year, the water in the tide pool turns red as a tribute to Popo'alaea, commemorating her death. (Killjoy scientists claim, however, that the change in color is due to the presence of small red shrimp.)

6 The Great Outdoors

Haleakala National Park

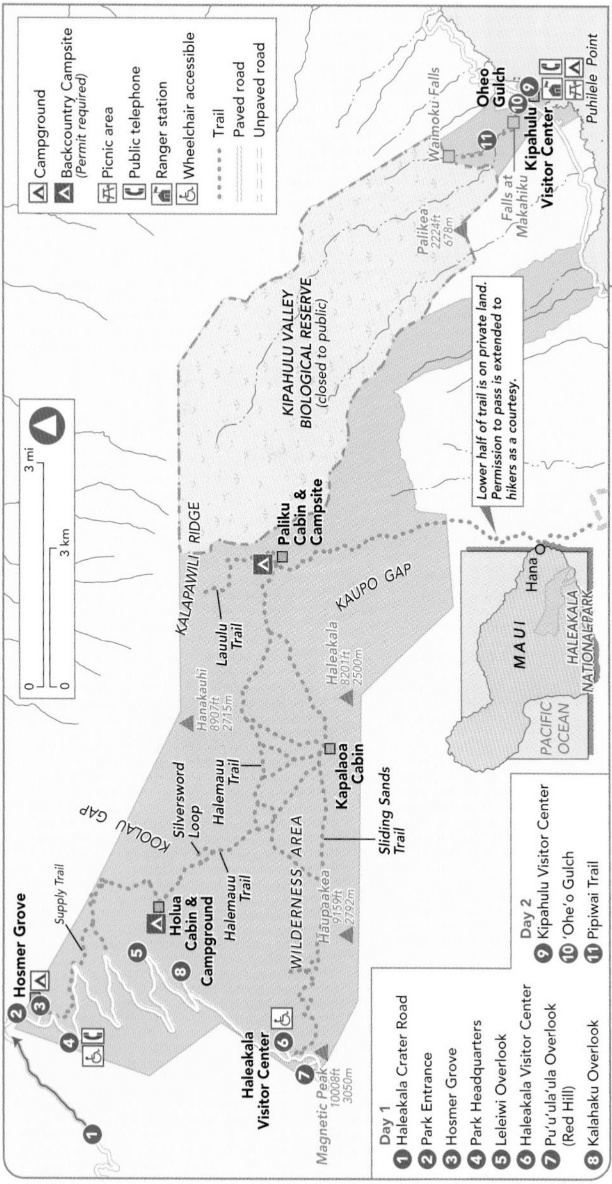
Campground
Backcountry Campsite (Permit required)
Picnic area
Public telephone
Ranger station
Wheelchair accessible
Trail
Paved road
Unpaved road
0
3 mi
0
3 km
KIPAHULU VALLEY BIOLOGICAL RESERVE (closed to public)
KALAPAWILI RIDGE
Paliku Cabin & Campsite
Lauulu Trail
KAUPO GAP
Haleakala 8201ft 2500m
Hanakauhi 8907ft 2715m
Kapalaoa Cabin
Halemauu Trail
Silversword Loop
KOOLAU GAP
Sliding Sands Trail
WILDERNESS AREA
Haupaakea 9159ft 2792m
Holua Cabin & Campground
Supply Trail
Hosmer Grove
Haleakala Visitor Center
Magnetic Peak 10008ft 3050m
Palikea 2224ft 678m
Waimoku Falls
Oheo Gulch
Falls at Makahiku
Kipahulu Visitor Center
Puhilele Point
Lower half of trail is on private land. Permission to pass is extended to hikers as a courtesy.
Hana
MAUI
HALEAKALA NATIONAL PARK
PACIFIC OCEAN
Day 1
1 Haleakala Crater Road
2 Park Entrance
3 Hosmer Grove
4 Park Headquarters
5 Leleiwi Overlook
6 Haleakala Visitor Center
7 Pu'u'ula'ula Overlook (Red Hill)
8 Kalahaku Overlook
Day 2
9 Kipahulu Visitor Center
10 'Ohe'o Gulch
11 Pipiwai Trail

Previous page: Those in the know say Maui is the best Hawaiian isle for wind surfing.

The summit of Haleakala, the House of the Sun, is a spectacular natural phenomenon. More than 1.3 million people a year ascend the 10,023-foot-high mountain to peer into the world's largest dormant volcano. (Haleakala has not erupted for at least 4 centuries, but it's still officially considered active.) Haleakala National Park's lunar-like landscape is home to numerous rare and endangered plants, birds, and insects. There are actually two parts: **Haleakala Summit** and **Kipahulu** (p 87), in the dense rainforest on Maui's east coast. No roads link the two sections; you'll visit them separately, taking at least a day to explore each place. Whichever you visit first, save your park receipt to get free entry at the other section. START: **Kahului.**

Travel Tips

The town of Pukalani is the last stop for food and gas (there are no facilities within the national park). On the way back down the mountain, put your car in low gear so you won't destroy your brakes on the descent.

Day One

From Kahului, take Hwy. 37 to Hwy. 377 to Hwy. 378.

1 ★★★ Haleakala Crater Road. Just driving up the mountain is an experience. On Haleakala Crater Road (Hwy. 378), 33 switchbacks travel through numerous climate zones, passing in and out of clouds, fog, and rain, to finally deliver a view that extends for more than 100 miles (161km). Be on the lookout for downhill bicyclists, stray cattle, and native nene, the native Hawaiian geese.

2 Park Entrance. A ranger will collect an entrance fee of $25 per car (or $20 per motorcycle), good for 3 days of unlimited entry at both the summit and Kipahulu districts.

3 ★★★ Hosmer Grove. Birders should make a beeline to this small campground and forest. In Hawai'i's territorial days, forester Ralph Hosmer tried to launch a timber industry. It failed, but a few of his sweet-smelling cedars and pines remain. A half-mile loop trail snakes from the parking lot through the evergreens to a picturesque gulch, where rare **Hawaiian honeycreepers** flit above native *'ohi'a* and sandalwood trees.

4 ★★ Park Headquarters Visitor Center. Stop here to pick up park information and camping permits, use the restroom, fill your water bottle, and purchase park swag. Keep an eye out for the native Hawaiian goose, the gray-brown **nene** with its black face, buff cheeks, and partially webbed feet. Nene once flourished throughout Hawai'i, but habitat destruction and

A view from atop Haleakala.

Hawaii's endangered nene, or Hawaiian goose.

non-native predators (rats, cats dogs, mongooses) nearly caused their extinction. By 1951 there were only 30 left. Boy Scouts helped to reintroduce them into Haleakala. The species remains endangered, but is now protected as Hawai'i's state bird. *www.nps.gov/hale.* ☎ *808/572-4459. Daily 8am–4pm.*

❺ ★★ **Leleiwi Overlook.** Just beyond MM 17, pull into the parking area. From here a short trail leads you to a stellar view of the crater. When the clouds are low and the sun is in the right place—usually around sunset—you might experience a phenomenon known as the "Specter of the Brocken": You can see a reflection of your shadow, ringed by a rainbow, in the clouds below. This optical illusion occurs only three places on the planet: Haleakala, Scotland, and Germany.

❻ ★★★ **Haleakala Visitor Center.** Just before the summit, this small building offers a panoramic view of the volcanic

Going to the Summit

You need reservations to view sunrise from the summit. The National Park Service now limits how many cars can access the summit between 3am and 7am. Book your spot up to 60 days in advance at www.recreation.gov. A fee of $1 (on top of park entrance fees) applies. You'll need to show your reservation receipt and photo I.D. to enter the park. Watching the sun's first golden rays break through the clouds is indeed spectacular, although I recommend sunset instead: It's equally beautiful—and warmer! Full-moon nights can be ethereal, too.

Whenever you go, know that weather at the summit is extreme, ranging from blazing sun to sudden snow flurries. Glorious views aren't guaranteed; the summit may be misty or overcast at any time of day. As you ascend the slopes, the temperature drops about 3 degrees every 1,000 feet (305m), so the top can be 30 degrees cooler than sea level—and the alpine wind can really sting. Come prepared with warm layers and rain gear. Before you head up the mountain, get current weather conditions from the park (☎ 808/572-4400) or the **National Weather Service** (☎ 866/944-5025, option 4).

landscape, with photos identifying the various features and exhibits that explain its history, ecology, geology, and volcanology. (Restrooms and water are available here, too.) Rangers offer excellent free **naturalist talks** daily in the summit building and lead guided hikes from here (check website for times). *www.nps.gov/hale.* ☎ *808/572-4459. Daily sunrise–noon.*

❼ ★★★ **Pu'u'ula'ula Overlook (Red Hill).** Here, at the volcano's highest point, a glass-enclosed windbreak makes a prime viewing spot, crowded with shivering folks at sunrise. (You'll also notice a mysterious cluster of buildings: Haleakala Observatories, unofficially dubbed **Science City.**) This is also the best place to see a rare **silversword,** a botanical wonder that's like a spacy artichoke with attitude. Silverswords grow only in Hawai'i, take from 4 to 90 years to bloom, and then, usually between May and October, send up a 1- to 6-foot stalk covered in dark purple, sunflower-like blooms. Don't walk too close to silversword plants—footfalls can damage their roots.

❽ ★★ **Kalahaku Overlook.** On your way back down the summit, stop here to gaze into the distance. On a clear day you can see all the way across Alenuihaha Channel to the often-snowcapped summit of Mauna Kea on the Big Island.

Day Two

❾ **Kipahulu Visitor Center.** Eleven wiggly miles (18km) past Hana on Hwy. 360, the Kipahulu center offers information, books, exhibits, and ranger-led walks year-round. The entry fee is $25 per car or $20 per motorcycle (also good for entry at Haleakala summit district). Restrooms and drinking water are available. *www.nps.gov/hale.* ☎ *808/248-7375. Daily 9:30am–5pm.*

❿ ★★★ **'Ohe'o Gulch.** A one-lane stone bridge passes over this charismatic stream, which breaks into multiple waterfalls cascading down to the tumultuous ocean. Often called the Seven Sacred Pools (a misnomer—there are more than seven pools, and in Hawai'i *all* water is sacred), the famous pools are gorgeous, though often packed with visitors. (Don't be tempted to enter when the park service closes them for safety reasons—flash floods have swept some to their death here.) The surrounding forest includes native species such as *hala* (screwpine) and *hau* (tree hibiscus).

⓫ ★★★ **Pipiwai Trail.** A short hike above 'Ohe'o Gulch will take you to two spectacular **waterfalls.** The trail begins across the street from the ranger station's central parking area. Follow the trail .5 miles to the overlook for **Makahiku Falls,** a 200-foot-tall beauty. Continue another 1.5 miles, across two bridges and through a bamboo forest, to the dazzling 400-foot-tall **Waimoku Falls.** It's a hard uphill hike, but worth every step. Beware of falling rocks; never stand beneath the falls.

A waterfall of 'Ohe'o Gulch.

Go with a Guide

Maui's oldest hiking company is **Hike Maui ★★** (www.hikemaui.com; ☎ 866/324-6284 or 808/879-5270), which offers numerous treks island-wide, ranging from an easy 1-mile, 3-hour hike to a waterfall ($95) to a strenuous full-day hike in Haleakala Crater ($190). On Hike Maui's popular East Maui waterfall trips ($133), you can swim and jump from the rocks into rainforest pools. Guides share cultural and botanical knowledge along the trail. All prices include equipment and transportation. Hotel pickup costs an extra $30 per person.

The Maui chapter of the **Sierra Club ★★** offers the best deal by far: guided hikes for a $5 donation. Volunteer naturalists lead small groups along historic coastlines and up into forests with waterfalls. Go to www.mauisierraclub.org or call ☎ 808/419-5143.

so that each is a day's walk from the previous one: **Holua** is just off Halemau'u Trail at 6,920 feet (2,109m), **Kapala'oa** is on the Sliding Sands Trail in the center of the crater, and **Paliku** is on the eastern end by Kaupo Gap. Each offers a cozy cabin with 12 padded bunks (bring your own bedding), cooking utensils, a propane stove, and a wood-burning stove with firewood. Cabins can be reserved up to 180 days in advance at www.recreation.gov or call ☎ 877/444-6777; a flat rate of $75 is charged for the entire cabin. You will need a valid credit card to reserve by phone. The person who made the reservation must pick up the permit at the Haleakala Visitor Center. **Holua** and **Paliku** also offer tent camping, with pit toilets and nonpotable catchment water. Free permits are issued daily at park headquarters (first-come, first-served); campers are limited to 2 nights in one cabin and 3 nights total in the wilderness per month.

Ke'anae Arboretum

Hiking. An easy, family-friendly 2-mile (3.2km) walk through the Ke'anae Arboretum explores a forest with both native and introduced plants. Allow 45 minutes, longer if you want to swim. Bring rain gear and mosquito repellent. *47 miles (76km) from Kahului, along the Hana Hwy. 360.*

Olowalu

★ Camping. Halfway to Lahaina, **Camp Olowalu** abuts one of the island's best coral reefs. It's perfect for snorkeling and (during winter) whale watching; kayak rentals are available. Tent sites and car camping are $24 per adult ($7 ages 9–17) with access to bathrooms and outdoor showers. Closer to the highway are "tentalows" with two or four twin beds with linens, as well as private outdoor showers; they're $140–$195 per night. For $1,500 a night, large groups can rent a set of six A-frame cabins (each sleeps 6) with bathrooms, showers, and a kitchen. *800 Olowalu Village Rd., off of Honoapi'ilani Hwy. www.campolowalu.com. ☎ 808/661-4303.*

Polipoli Spring State Recreation Area

★ Hiking. Halfway up the slope of Haleakala, this state park doesn't feel like typical Hawai'i (it's downright cold at 6,200 ft./1,890m). But

Wai'anapanapa State Park.

there's great hiking on the Polipoli Loop, an easy 3.5-mile (5.6km) hike that takes about a couple hours and branches out to a variety of longer trails. Dress warmly to meander through groves of eucalyptus, swamp mahogany, and hybrid cypress. *Take Hwy. 37 to Keokea and turn right on Hwy. 337; after less than ½ mile (.8km) turn on Waipoli Rd. and continue for 10 miles (16km) to the park.*

Wai'anapanapa State Park ★★★ Hiking & Camping. Tucked in a tropical rainforest on the outskirts of Hana, dreamy Wai'anapanapa State Park features a black-sand beach set in an emerald forest, with camping and hiking. The coastal trail is an easy, 3-mile (4.8km) round-trip hike that parallels the sea, traveling past lava cliffs and a forest of *hala* trees. The park has 12 cabins and a tent campground. (Go for the cabins; it rains torrentially here.) Tent sites are $18 per night for up to six people. Cabins ($90 per night, 2-night minimum) sleep six and have minimally stocked kitchens and covered lanai; reserve online at camping.ehawaii.gov/camping or call ☎ 808/984-8109. *Just after MM 32 on the Hana Hwy. (Hwy.360), turn off at* WAI'ANAPANAPA STATE PARK *sign at Honokolani Rd. and head toward the ocean.*

Safe Hiking & Camping

Most of the dangers to avoid while out adventuring involve water. **Flash floods** in Hawai'i happen suddenly, as downpours up the mountain cause streams to rise 4 feet in less than 10 minutes. People have been swept away, trapped, or forced to spend the night wet and shivering on the mountain. Don't let this happen to you. Watch the weather while hiking and never cross a flooding stream (even in a car). **Don't drink** stream water and don't swim if you have open wounds—feral pigs and deer spread *leptospirosis,* a bacterium that produces flulike symptoms and can be fatal. Don't jump into a fresh or saltwater pool without checking for **submerged rocks,** and don't ever approach **blowholes**—they can suck you in. At the shoreline, be aware that **rogue waves** can knock you over. Don't turn your back to the ocean.

Other do's and don'ts: Do carry your trash out and head back before sundown. Twilight near the equator is short-lived; it gets dark quickly! Finally, Maui is not crime free: Don't leave valuables unprotected. Carry a day pack if you're camping, and avoid camping alone.

Maui's Best Golf Courses

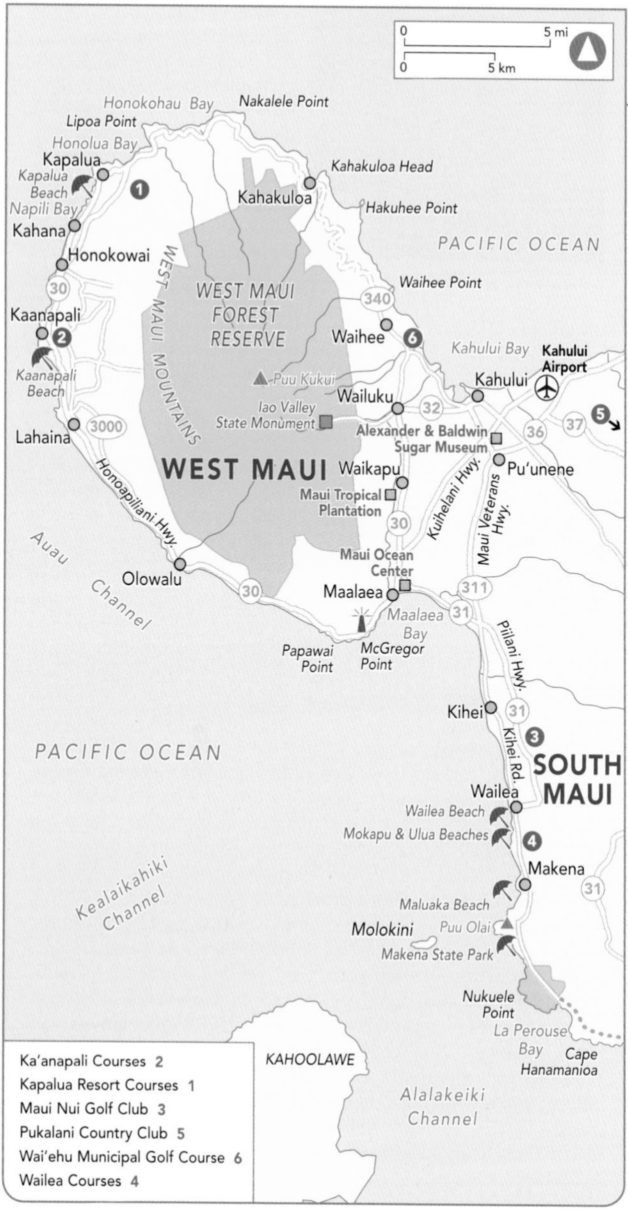

- Ka'anapali Courses 2
- Kapalua Resort Courses 1
- Maui Nui Golf Club 3
- Pukalani Country Club 5
- Wai'ehu Municipal Golf Course 6
- Wailea Courses 4

In some circles, Maui is synonymous with golf. Golfers have many outstanding layouts to choose from, from world championship courses to municipal parks with oceanfront views. Greens fees are pricey, but twilight tee times can be a giant deal. Be forewarned: The trade winds in the afternoon can seriously alter your game.

Renting Golf Gear

Standby Golf (www.hawaiistandbygolf.com; ☎ 888/645-2665) rents clubs ($25–$30) and offers savings on greens fees at Ka'anapali, Wailea Gold and Emerald, and Pukalani golf courses.

Golf Club Rentals (www.mauiclubrentals.com; ☎ 808/665-0800) has custom-built clubs for men, women, and juniors (right- and left-handed), which can be delivered islandwide; rates start at $25 a day.

Maui Nui Golf Club (formerly Elleair). Unspooling across the foothills of Haleakala, this playground is just high enough to afford spectacular ocean vistas from every hole. It's beautiful and forgiving. *Just one caveat:* Go in the morning. Not only is it cooler, but more important, it's less windy. In the afternoon the winds bluster down Haleakala with great gusto. Facilities include a clubhouse, driving range, putting green, pro shop, and lessons. *470 Lipoa Pkwy., Kihei. www.mauinuigolfclub.com.* ☎ *808/874-0777. Greens fees $99; twilight rate $49–$89.*

★ **Ka'anapali Courses.** The courses at Kaanapali offer a challenge to all golfers, from high handicappers to near pros. The par-72, 6,305-yard **Royal Ka'anapali Course** is a true Robert Trent Jones, Sr., design, with lots of wide bunkers, long stretched-out tees, and the largest, most-contoured greens on Maui. The par-72, 6,250-yard **Ka'anapali Kai,** an Arthur Jack Snyder design, is shorter than the Royal course, but its narrow, hilly fairways require more accuracy. Facilities include a driving range, putting course, and clubhouse with dining. Weekdays are your best bet for tee times. *Off Hwy. 30, Ka'anapali. www.kaanapaligolfcourses.com.* ☎ *808/661-3691. Greens fees Royal Ka'anapali Course*

Golf Tips

If you're trying to get a tee time at a public course, weekdays are always better than weekends. You'll have better luck teeing off after 9am, and afternoons are generally wide open. And, of course, book in advance, as soon as you have your travel dates. Bring extra balls: The rough is thick, water hazards are everywhere, and the wind will mess with your game. Trade winds of 10 to 30 mph (16–48kph) are not unusual between 10am and 2pm; you may have to play two to three clubs up or down to compensate. On the greens, your putt will *always* break toward the ocean. Hit deeper and more aggressively in the sand—the sand used on most Hawai'i courses is firmer and more compact than on mainland courses. Plan on taking lots of photos of the spectacular views, too.

Kapalua Resort is home to two top golf courses.

$255 ($179 resort guests), twilight rate $149, super twilight (starting at 3pm) $109; Ka'anapali Kai Course $205 ($139 resort guests), twilight rate $99, super twilight $79. At southernmost stoplight in Ka'anapali, turn onto Ka'anapali Pkwy. Clubhouse is the first building on your right.

★★★ Kapalua Resort Courses. The views from these two championship courses are worth the greens fees alone. The par-72, 6,761-yard **Bay Course,** designed by Arnold Palmer and Ed Seay, is relatively forgiving, with wide fairways, but the greens are tricky to read. The par-73, 6,547-yard **Plantation Course,** site of the Hyundai Tournament of Champions, is a Ben Crenshaw and Bill Coore design set on a rolling hillside, which rewards low shots and precise chipping. Facilities include locker rooms, a driving range, and a good restaurant. Weekdays are your best bet for tee times. *Off Hwy. 30, Kapalua. www.golfatkapalua.com. ☎ 877/527-2582. Greens fees: Bay Course $229 ($209 resort guests), twilight rates (1pm on) $169, super twilight (3:30pm on) $149; Plantation Course $329 ($299 resort guests), twilight rates $249, super twilight $199.*

Pukalani Country Club. This cool par-72, 6,962-yard course offers a break from the resorts' steep greens fees, and it's really fun to play. High handicappers will love this course; more experienced players can increase the challenge by playing from the back tees. Facilities include club and shoe rentals, practice areas, lockers, a pro shop, and a restaurant. *360 Pukalani St., Pukalani. www.pukalanigolf.com. ☎ 808/572-1314. Greens fees (including cart) $89, $69 11am–1pm, $39 1–2:30pm, $29 after 2:30pm. Take Hana Hwy. 36 to Haleakala Hwy. 37 to the Pukalani exit; turn right onto Pukalani St. and go 2 blocks.*

Wai'ehu Municipal Golf Course This par-72 links course is like two courses in one: The first 9 holes, built in 1930, are set along the dramatic coastline, while the back 9 holes, added in 1966, head toward the mountains. It's a fun course that probably won't challenge your handicap. The only hazard is the wind, which can rip off the ocean and play havoc with your ball. Facilities include a snack bar, driving range, practice greens, golf-club rental, and clubhouse. It's a public course, so greens fees are low—but getting a tee time is tough. *2199 Kaho'okele*

Golfing on a Budget

If your heart is set on playing on a resort course, book at least a week in advance. Ardent golfers on a budget should play in the afternoon, when discounted twilight rates are in effect. There's no guarantee you'll get 18 holes in, especially in winter when it's dark by 6pm, but you'll have an opportunity to experience these world-famous courses at half the usual fee.

For discount tee times, call **Standby Golf** (www.hawaiistandbygolf.com; ☎ 888/645-BOOK [2665] or 808/665-0800) between 7am and 10pm. Stand-by offers discounted (up to 50% off) greens fees and guaranteed tee times for same-day or future golfing.

St., Wailuku. www.mauicounty.gov/facilities/Facility/Details/157. ☎ 808/240-7400. Greens fees $58–$63; cart $21. From Kahului Airport, turn right on the Hana Hwy. 36, which becomes Ka'ahumanu Ave. (Hwy. 32). Turn right at stoplight onto Wai'ehu Beach Rd. (Hwy. 340). Go another 1½ miles (2.4km) to entrance on your right.

★★ **Wailea Courses.** You can choose among three courses at Wailea. The **Blue Course,** a par-72, 6,758-yard course designed by Arthur Jack Snyder and dotted with bunkers and water hazards, is for duffers and pros alike. A little more difficult is the par-72, 7,078-yard championship **Gold Course,** designed by Robert Trent Jones, Jr., with narrow fairways, several tricky dogleg holes, and natural hazards like lava-rock walls. Wailea's youngest is the **Emerald Course,** also by Jones, Jr., with tropical landscaping and a player-friendly design. With 3 courses, getting a weekend tee time is slightly easier here than at other resorts, but weekdays are still best (the Emerald Course is usually toughest to book). Facilities include two pro shops, restaurants, locker rooms, and a golf training facility. *Wailea Alanui Dr. (off Wailea Iki Dr.), Wailea. www.waileagolf.com. ☎ 888/328-MAUI [6284] or 808/875-7450. Greens fees $209–$250 ($179–$225 for Wailea or Maui resort guests), twilight rates $115–$175.*

The Emerald Course in Wailea.

Maui's Best Snorkeling

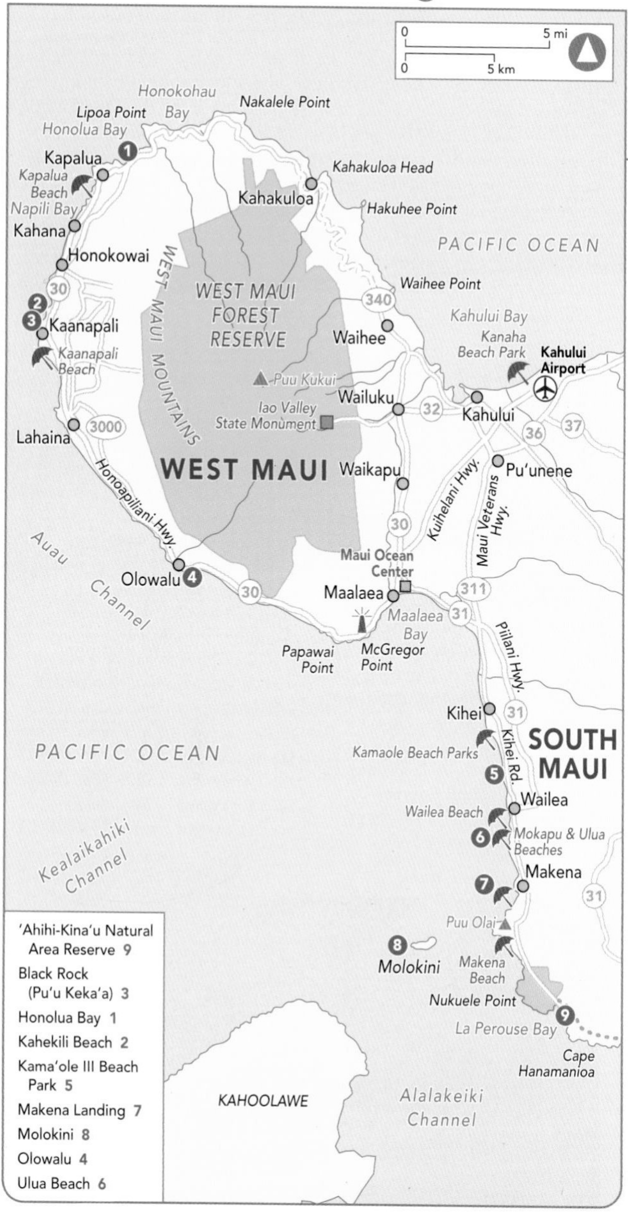
0
5 mi
0
5 km
Honokohau Bay
Nakalele Point
Lipoa Point
Honolua Bay
Kapalua
Kapalua Beach
Napili Bay
Kahana
Honokowai
Kahakuloa Head
Kahakuloa
Hakuhee Point
PACIFIC OCEAN
WEST MAUI MOUNTAINS
WEST MAUI FOREST RESERVE
Waihee Point
Kahului Bay
Kanaha Beach Park
Kahului Airport
Kaanapali
Kaanapali Beach
Waihee
Puu Kukui
Wailuku
Kahului
Iao Valley State Monument
Lahaina
WEST MAUI
Waikapu
Pu'unene
Honoapiilani Hwy.
Kuihelani Hwy.
Maui Veterans Hwy.
Auau Channel
Olowalu
Maui Ocean Center
Maalaea
Maalaea Bay
Papawai Point
McGregor Point
Piilani Hwy.
Kihei
PACIFIC OCEAN
Kamaole Beach Parks
Kihei Rd.
SOUTH MAUI
Wailea
Wailea Beach
Mokapu & Ulua Beaches
Kealaikahiki Channel
Makena
Puu Olai
Molokini
Makena Beach
Nukuele Point
La Perouse Bay
Cape Hanamanioa
KAHOOLAWE
Alalakeiki Channel
'Ahihi-Kina'u Natural Area Reserve 9
Black Rock (Pu'u Keka'a) 3
Honolua Bay 1
Kahekili Beach 2
Kama'ole III Beach Park 5
Makena Landing 7
Molokini 8
Olowalu 4
Ulua Beach 6

Snorkeling is the main attraction in Maui. All you need are a mask, a snorkel, fins, and some basic swimming skills. If you've never snorkeled before, most resorts and excursion boats offer instruction, but it's easy to figure it out for yourself: In many places all you have to do is wade into the water and look down. Just be sure to go with a buddy, keep breathing steadily, and don't overexert yourself. Below are my favorite snorkeling spots in Maui.

★★ 'Ahihi-Kina'u Natural Area Reserve. 'Ahihi Bay is a 2,000-acre (809ha) state natural area reserve in the lee of Cape Kina'u, on Maui's rugged south coast, where Haleakala's red-hot lava last ran to the sea some 4 centuries ago. Fishing is strictly *kapu* (forbidden) here, and the fish know it; they're everywhere in this series of rocky coves and black-lava tide pools. After you snorkel, check out La Pérouse Bay on the south side of Cape Kina'u, where French admiral La Pérouse became the first European to set foot on Maui. ***Note:*** The state has indefinitely restricted access to portions of the reserve; go to hawaii.gov/dlnr/dofaw/nars/ reserves/maui/ahihikinau for updated information or call ☎ 808/984-8800. *Drive south on Makena on Makena Alanui Rd.*

★ Black Rock. At the north edge of Ka'anapali Beach, in front of the Sheraton, Black Rock (Pu'u Keka'a) has an easy entry and clouds of tropical fish. You might even spot an eagle ray or turtle or two. *Look for* PUBLIC BEACH ACCESS *signs off Ka'anapali Pkwy. (off Honoapi'ilani Hwy./Hwy.30), in the Ka'anapali Resort.*

★★★ Honolua Bay. Spectacular coral formations glitter beneath the surface of this gemlike bay, a Marine Life Conservation District, at the upper northwest tip of the island. You'll have to swim a fair distance to reach the coral, though. Walk through a thick grove (take care with the boat ramp entry; it's slippery); once you're in the water, head to the right. Turtles, rays, and a variety

One of the creatures you may encounter while snorkeling in Maui.

of snappers and goatfish will cruise along beside you. In the crevices are eels, lobster, and an array of rainbow-hued fish. Dolphins sometimes come here to rest. No facilities. *MM 32 on Honoapi'ilani Hwy.*

★★★ Kahekili Beach. The north side of Ka'anapali Beach happens to be A+ for snorkeling, thanks to active marine management. Herbivorous species (surgeon fish and colorful parrotfish) are off-limits to fishermen here. A vibrant, healthy reef beckons just a few fin-kicks from shore. Count the different types of coral you see and look for eels poking out of holes. *End of Pu'ukoli'i Rd., off of Honoapi'ilani Hwy. in Ka'anapali.*

kids Kama'ole III Beach Park. Locals love this beach: Not only does it have wide pockets of golden sand, but it's also the only one with a playground for children and a grassy lawn. For snorkeling, look toward the rocky fingers extending out in the north and south shores; they are fish magnets. *S. Kihei Rd., across from Keonekai Rd., Kihei.*

Where to Get Snorkel Gear

You'll find rental gear and ocean toys all over the island. Most seaside resorts are stocked with watersports equipment (complimentary or rentals). **Snorkel Bob's** (www.snorkelbob.com) rents snorkel gear, boogie boards, wetsuits, and more at numerous locations: At Napili Village, 5425 C Lower Honoapi'ilani Hwy., Lahaina (☎ 808/669-9603); Kahana Gateway Center, 4405 Honoapiilani Hwy., Lahaina (☎ 808/334-0245); 1217 Front St., Lahaina (☎ 808/661-4421); 3350 Lower Honoapi'ilani Hwy. #201, Honokowai (☎ 808/667-9999); in Azeka II Shopping Center, 1279 S. Kihei Rd., Kihei (☎ 808/875-6188); 2411 S. Kihei Rd., Kihei (☎ 808/879-7449); and 100 Wailea Ike Dr., Wailea (☎ 808/874-0011). All are open daily 8am–5pm.

Boss Frog's Dive, Surf, and Bike Shops (www.bossfrog.com) is a convenient multi-sport outlet, offering snorkel, boogie board, longboard, and stand-up paddleboard rentals and other gear; locations include: 150 Lahainaluna Rd., in Lahaina (☎ 808/661-3333); 3636 Lower Honoapi'ilani Rd. in Ka'anapali (☎ 808/665-1200); Napili Plaza, 5095 Napilihau St. in Napili (☎ 808/669-4949); and 1215 S. Kihei Rd. (☎ 808/891-0077), 1770 S. Kihei Rd. (☎ 808/874-5225), and Dolphin Plaza, 2395 S. Kihei Rd. (☎ 808/875-4477) in Kihei.

A school of raccoon butterflyfish.

★★ Makena Landing. If you're a confident swimmer, head to Makena Landing, hug the north end of the bay, and round the point. You'll be treated to diverse corals and fish, turtles and caves. Look closely and you might spy a shy white-tip reef shark hiding in a cavern. A great place to dive or launch kayaks. *On Makena Rd., just north of juncture with Honoiki St.*

★★★ Molokini. Like a crescent moon fallen from the sky, the crater of Molokini sits almost midway between Maui and the uninhabited island of Kaho'olawe. The 100-foot-deep bowl serves as a natural sanctuary for tropical fish and snorkelers, who arrive daily in a fleet of dive boats to this marine-life preserve. Note that in high season, Molokini can be crowded. See "Sail-Snorkel Trips," facing page, for information on getting to Molokini.

★★ Olowalu. Great snorkeling around MM 14, where, about 150 to 225 feet (46–69m) from shore, turtles line up to have cleaner wrasses pick off small parasites. Manta rays congregate here as well. *MM 14, Honoapi'ilani Hwy. 5 miles (8km) south of Lahaina.*

Ulua Beach. Come here in the morning when the waters are calm,

Sail-Snorkel Trips

Trilogy ★★★ (www.sailtrilogy.com; ☎ 888/MAUI-800 [628-4800] or 808/TRILOGY [874-5649]) offers my favorite snorkel-sail trips, on a fleet of custom-built catamarans. Their full-day **Maui-to-Lana'i sail** from Lahaina Harbor to Hulopo'e Marine Preserve is the only cruise that includes a ground tour of the island and Hulopo'e Beach. The trip costs $220 for adults, $189 for ages 13–18, $120 for children 3–12. Trilogy's half-day **snorkel-sail trips to Molokini,** leaving from Ma'alaea Harbor; cost $135 for adults, $101 for teens, $68 for kids 3 to 12. All trips include breakfast (Mom's homemade cinnamon buns) and a barbecue lunch. In winter, 2-hour **whale watches** depart Ka'anapali Beach ($59 adults, $44 teens, $30 children).

Maui Classic Charters ★★ (Ma 'alaea Harbor, slip 55 and slip 80; www.mauicharters.com; ☎ 800/736-5740 or 808/879-8188) offers morning and afternoon **snorkel cruises to Molokini** on *Four Winds II*, a 55-foot glass-bottom catamaran. Rates for the morning sail are $105 for adults and $75 for children 3 to 12, with continental breakfast and barbecue lunch. The afternoon sail is a steal at $52, though the captain usually only visits Coral Gardens, which is accessible from shore. Hoping to catch sight of dolphins? Try the 5-hour **snorkel journey to Molokini and Makena** on the catamaran *Maui Magic* (cost $120 adults, $90 children 5–12). All Maui Classic trips include beer, wine, and soda, plus snorkeling gear and instruction; the 5-hour *Maui Magic* trip also includes continental breakfast and barbecue lunch. In whale season (Dec 22–Apr 22), the *Four Winds II* runs a 3½-hour **whale-watching trip** for $52 adults, $38 ages 3 to 12.

The **Pacific Whale Foundation ★★** (101 N. Kihei Rd., Kihei; www.pacificwhale.org; ☎ 800/249-5311 or 808/249-8811) supports its whale research and conservation programs by offering **whale-watch cruises, dolphin encounters,** and **snorkel tours** out of both Lahaina and Ma'alaea harbors. Options include a fun **Island Rhythms Sunset Cruise** ($85 adults, $45 ages 3–12) with Marty Dread, a local entertainer who woos whales with rollicking tunes, and **Sunset and Celestial Cruises** ($69 adults, $45 children) with astronomer-storyteller Harriet Witt. Snorkel trips start at $69, whale watches at $38.

Owned by a Native Hawaiian family, the luxury catamaran ***Kai Kanani*** (34 Wailea Gateway Center, Kihei; www.kaikanani.com; ☎ 808/879-7218) launches its **sunset, whale-watching and snorkel cruises** from Makena. Leaving at 6:15am, the 3-hour sunrise cruise ($198 adults, $161 children ages 2–12) provides the most privacy at busy Molokini, with a gourmet breakfast afterward. Add a Mercedes shuttle from select Wailea resorts for $15 per person.

before trade winds kick up, to look for camouflaged frogfish. *Look for blue shoreline access sign on Wailea Alanui Dr., Wailea.*

Adventures on Land

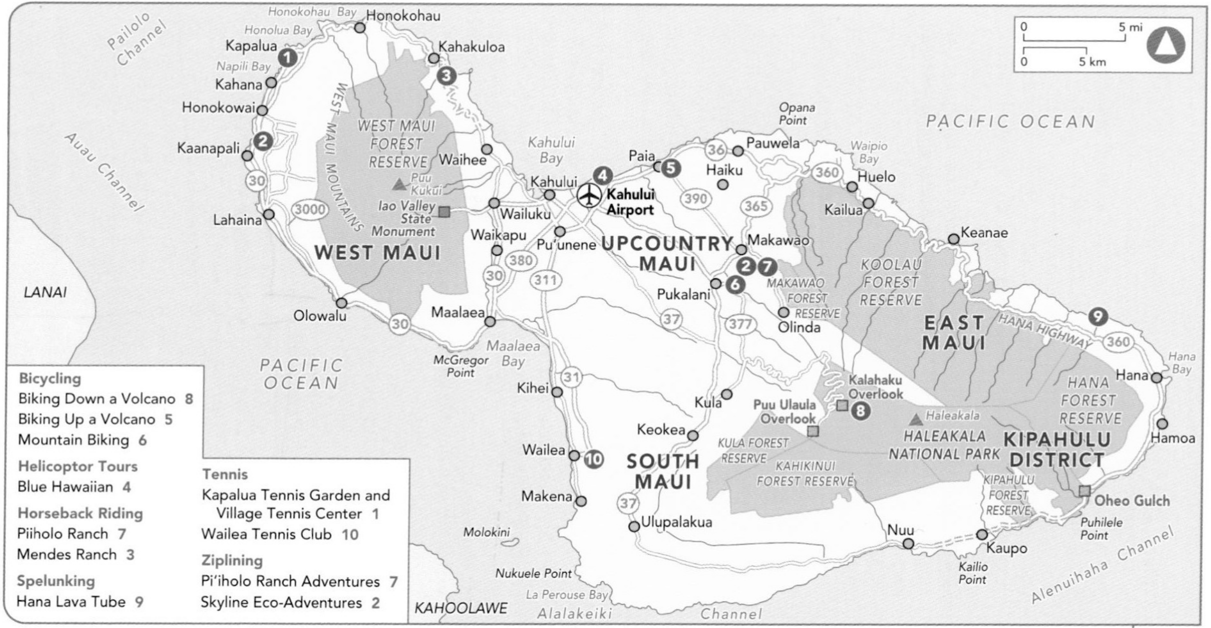
PACIFIC OCEAN
PACIFIC OCEAN
0 5 mi
0 5 km
Pailolo Channel
Auau Channel
LANAI
KAHOOLAWE
Alalakeiki Channel
Alenuihaha Channel
Honokohau Bay
Honokohau
Honolua Bay
Kapalua
Napili Bay
Kahana
Honokowai
Kaanapali
Lahaina
Olowalu
Kahakuloa
Waihee
WEST MAUI FOREST RESERVE
WEST MAUI MOUNTAINS
Puu Kukui
Iao Valley State Monument
WEST MAUI
Wailuku
Waikapu
Maalaea
Maalaea Bay
McGregor Point
Kahului Bay
Kahului
Kahului Airport
Pu'unene
Paia
Haiku
Pauwela
Opana Point
Waipio Bay
Huelo
Kailua
Keanae
UPCOUNTRY MAUI
Makawao
Pukalani
MAKAWAO FOREST RESERVE
Olinda
KOOLAU FOREST RESERVE
EAST MAUI
HANA HIGHWAY
Hana
Hana Bay
Hamoa
HANA FOREST RESERVE
KIPAHULU DISTRICT
Oheo Gulch
Puhilele Point
KIPAHULU FOREST RESERVE
Kaupo
Kailio Point
Nuu
Haleakala
HALEAKALA NATIONAL PARK
Kalahaku Overlook
Puu Ulaula Overlook
KULA FOREST RESERVE
KAHIKINUI FOREST RESERVE
Kula
Keokea
SOUTH MAUI
Ulupalakua
Kihei
Wailea
Makena
Molokini
Nukuele Point
La Perouse Bay
Bicycling
Biking Down a Volcano 8
Biking Up a Volcano 5
Mountain Biking 6
Helicoptor Tours
Blue Hawaiian 4
Horseback Riding
Piiholo Ranch 7
Mendes Ranch 3
Spelunking
Hana Lava Tube 9
Tennis
Kapalua Tennis Garden and Village Tennis Center 1
Wailea Tennis Club 10
Ziplining
Pi'iholo Ranch Adventures 7
Skyline Eco-Adventures 2

Maui is known for its inviting waters, but you'll also discover plenty of land-based adventures to enjoy. Haleakala is perfect for scenic horseback rides; the warm, sunny days are terrific for tennis, and real daredevils can try ziplining.

Bicycling

Biking Down a Volcano. Several companies offer the opportunity to coast down Haleakala, from near the summit to the shore, on basic cruiser bikes. It can be a thrilling experience—but be careful if you aren't a seasoned cyclist; serious accidents are not uncommon. Bike tours aren't allowed in Haleakala National Park, so your van will take you to the summit first, then drop you off just outside of the park. You'll descend through multiple climates and ecosystems, past eucalyptus groves and flower-filled gulches. Bear in mind: The roads are steep and curvy, with no designated bike lanes and little-to-no shoulder. In winter and the rainy season, conditions can be harsh; temperatures at the summit can drop below freezing and 40mph winds howl. Wear warm layers whatever the season. **Mountain Riders Bike Tours** offers several good options, including a guided **sunrise tour** ($197) that includes seeing dawn at the summit and an unguided express tour ($75). All rates include hotel pickup (starting at 2am for sunrise tours!), bicycle, and safety gear; some include snacks. *www.mountainriders.com. ☎ 800/706-7700. From $175 (check website for discounts).*

Biking Up a Volcano. If you've got the chops to pedal *up* Haleakala, the pros at **Maui Cyclery ★★★** can outfit you and provide a support vehicle. Tour de France athletes launch their Maui training sessions from this full-service Pa'ia bike shop, which rents top-of-the-line equipment and offers a range of guided tours and cycling camps. *99 Hana Hwy., Pa'ia; www.gocyclingmaui.com. ☎ 808/579-9009.*

Mountain Biking. If muddy trails are more your style, hit up Moose at **Krank Cycles ★★★** for a tricked-out bike and directions to the Makawao Forest trails. *1120 Makawao Ave., Makawao; www.krankmaui.com. ☎ 808/572-2299.*

Helicopter Flights

Maui from the Air. Only a helicopter can bring you face-to-face with remote sites like Maui's little-known Wall of Tears, near the

Coasting down Haleakala.

summit of Pu'u Kukui in the West Maui Mountains. You'll glide through canyons etched with 1,000-foot (305m) waterfalls and over dense rainforests; you'll climb high enough to glimpse the summit of Haleakala, and fly by the dramatic sea cliffs of Moloka'i. **Blue Hawaiian's ★★★** pilots are part Hawaiian historian, part DJ, part tour guide, and part amusement-ride operator. As you soar through the clouds, you'll learn about the island's flora, fauna, history, and culture. Blue Hawaiian is the only helicopter company in the state using high-tech, environmentally friendly (and quiet) Eco-Star helicopters. *Kahului Airport. www.bluehawaiian.com. ☎ 800/745-2583 or 808/871-8844. Flights vary 50–90 min. for $259–$429 per person.*

Horseback Riding

Makawao. Maui has spectacular adventure rides through rugged ranch lands, into tropical forests, and to remote swimming holes. My favorite is **Pi'iholo Ranch ★★**, in Makawao, a working cattle ranch owned by the *kama'aina* (long-time resident) Baldwin family, where a variety of 2- to 3-hour private rides meander across the misty slopes of Haleakala with picnic stops (starting at $229). You can play "Cowboy for a Day" and learn how to round up cattle ($349); on the "Heli Ranch Experience" ($3,340 for two people), a limo takes you to the Kahului heliport to board an Eco-Star helicopter and fly to a private ranch cabin for breakfast and a 2-hour horseback ride. *325 Waiahiwi Rd., Makawao. www.piiholo.com. ☎ 808/270-8750. Rides start at $229.*

Kahakuloa. For an "out west" type of adventure, I like **Mendes Ranch & Trail Rides ★★**. The 300-acre (121ha) spread is a real-life working cowboy ranch with a full

A Blue Hawaiian helicopter tour.

array of natural wonders: waterfalls, palm trees, coral-sand beaches, lagoons, tide pools, a rainforest, and its own volcanic peak (more than a mile high). Wrangler guides will take you from the edge of the rainforest out to the sea and even teach you to lasso. They'll field questions and point out native flora, but generally just let you soak up Maui's natural splendor. A 1½-hour morning or afternoon ride costs $135; call Sunshine Helicopters (☎ 808/871-0722) for packages with varying helicopter tours (currently $490 for 60-min. Moloka'i tour with trail ride). *3530 Kahekili Hwy., 5 miles (8km) past Wailuku. www.mendesranch.com. ☎ 808/244-7320.*

Spelunking

★ Hana Lava Tube. When you're out in Hana, you can descend into darkness to explore a million-year-old underground lava tube/cave. See for yourself how the Hawaiian Islands were made. Wander through the subterranean world, then take a spin through the red ti-leaf maze above ground. The self-guided tours take 30 to 45 minutes. *205 Ulaino Rd. just north of Hana. www.mauicave.com. ☎ 808/248-7308. Daily 10:30am–4pm. Admission $12 ages 6 and up.*

Tennis

★★★ Kapalua Tennis Garden and Village Tennis Center. Opened in 1979, the Tennis Garden

has 10 Plexi-Pave courts paired in tiered clusters, with four lit for night play and surrounded by lush tropical foliage. Each set of courts is secluded in landscaped privacy with its own viewing lanai. Also available: private lessons, stroke-of-the-day clinics, drop-in clinics, and tournaments. The staff can match you up with a partner if you need one. *Kapalua Resort. www.golfatkapalua.com/tennis. ☎ 808/662-7730. Courts $25 per person per hour. Passes available.*

★★ Wailea Tennis Club. One of Maui's best tennis facilities, this resort club features 11 Sportsmaster courts (3 nighttime courts), backboard, pro shop, lessons, and doubles clinics. *131 Wailea Iki Place, Wailea. www.waileatennis.com. ☎ 808/879-1958. Courts $25 per person per day.*

Ziplining

★ Pi'iholo Ranch Adventures. Explore this family ranch (see p 102) in the Makawao forest from above—flying through the eucalyptus canopy on one of six ziplines. Tour packages include access to the aerial bridge, tree platforms, ziplines (including side-by-side lines that you can ride with friends), and a trip to nearby waterfalls where you can take a refreshing dip. *799 Pi'iholo Rd., Makawao. www.piiholo zipline.com. ☎ 808/572-1717. Tours: $140–$165.*

★ Skyline EcoAdventures. Go on, let out a wild holler as you soar above a rainforested gulch or down the slope of a mountain. Pioneers of this internationally popular activity, the Skyline owners brought the first ziplines to the U.S. and launched them from their home, here on Maui. Eco-conscious and carbon-neutral, the company donates thousands of dollars to local environmental agencies. Skyline has two courses, one on the west side and the other halfway up Haleakala. Both are fast and fun, the guides are savvy and safety-conscious, and the scenery is breathtaking. In Ka'anapali, you can even "zip and dip": drop off your line into a mountain pool. Tours operate daily and take riders ages 12 and up, weighing between 80 and 300 pounds. *Haleakala: 2½ miles up Haleakala Hwy., Makawao. www.zipline.com. ☎ 808/878-8400. Ka'anapali: Fairway Shops, 2580 Keka'a Dr. #122, Lahaina; ☎ 808/662-1500. Tours: $170–$190.*

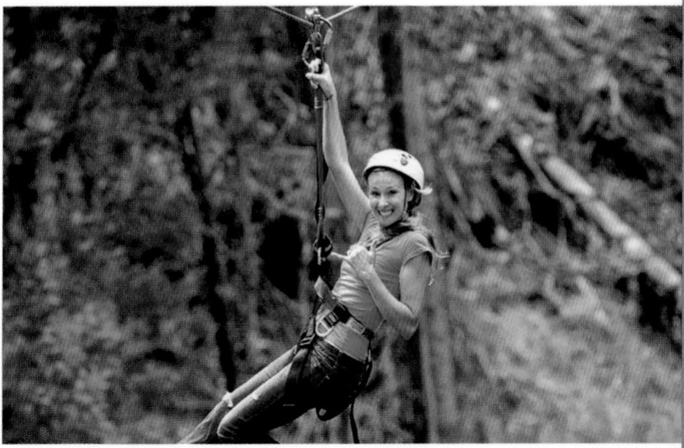

Ziplining the Haleakala course of Skyline EcoAdventures.

Adventures in the Ocean

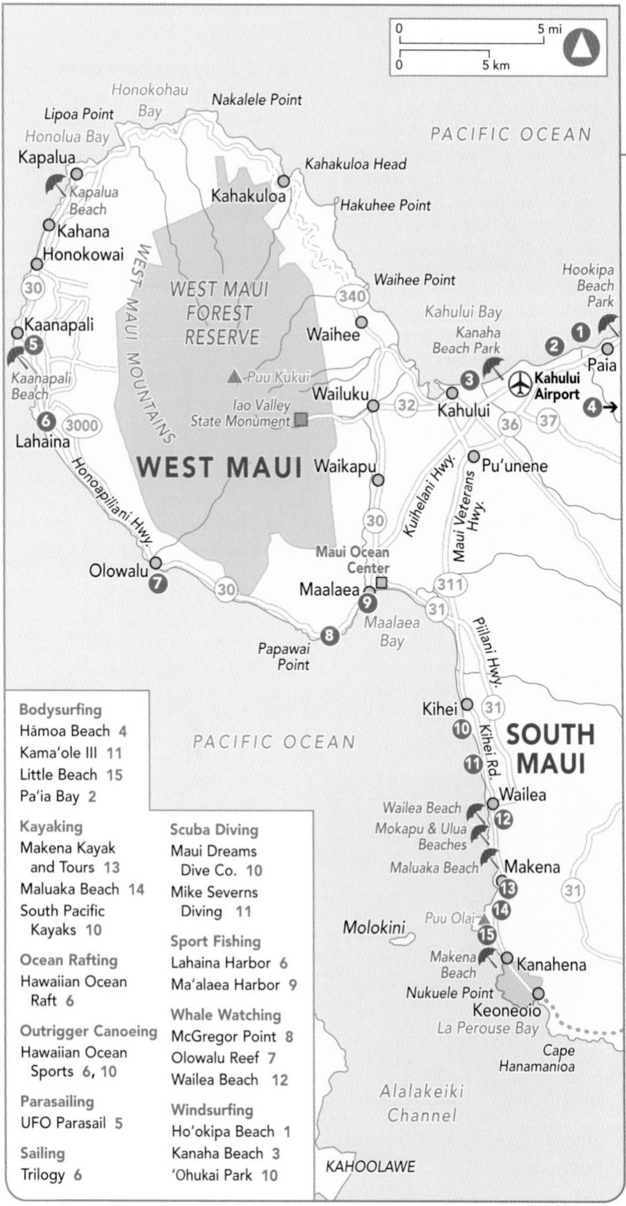
0
5 mi
0
5 km
Honokohau Bay
Nakalele Point
Lipoa Point
Honolua Bay
PACIFIC OCEAN
Kapalua
Kahakuloa Head
Kapalua Beach
Kahakuloa
Hakuhee Point
Kahana
Honokowai
WEST MAUI MOUNTAINS
Waihee Point
Hookipa Beach Park
30
340
WEST MAUI FOREST RESERVE
Kahului Bay
Kaanapali
Kanaha Beach Park
Waihee
Paia
Kaanapali Beach
Puu Kukui
Kahului Airport
Wailuku
Iao Valley State Monument
32
Kahului
3000
36
37
Lahaina
Pu'unene
WEST MAUI
Waikapu
Honoapiilani Hwy.
Kuihelani Hwy.
Maui Veterans Hwy.
Maui Ocean Center
Olowalu
311
Maalaea
31
Maalaea Bay
Piilani Hwy.
Papawai Point
Kihei
Kihei Rd.
SOUTH MAUI
PACIFIC OCEAN
Wailea
Wailea Beach
Mokapu & Ulua Beaches
Makena
Maluaka Beach
Molokini
Puu Olai
Makena Beach
Kanahena
Nukuele Point
Keoneoio
La Perouse Bay
Cape Hanamanioa
Alalakeiki Channel
KAHOOLAWE
Bodysurfing
Hāmoa Beach 4
Kama'ole III 11
Little Beach 15
Pa'ia Bay 2
Kayaking
Makena Kayak and Tours 13
Maluaka Beach 14
South Pacific Kayaks 10
Ocean Rafting
Hawaiian Ocean Raft 6
Outrigger Canoeing
Hawaiian Ocean Sports 6, 10
Parasailing
UFO Parasail 5
Sailing
Trilogy 6
Scuba Diving
Maui Dreams Dive Co. 10
Mike Severns Diving 11
Sport Fishing
Lahaina Harbor 6
Ma'alaea Harbor 9
Whale Watching
McGregor Point 8
Olowalu Reef 7
Wailea Beach 12
Windsurfing
Ho'okipa Beach 1
Kanaha Beach 3
'Ohukai Park 10

To really appreciate Maui, you need to get off the land and into the sea. Trade winds off the Lahaina coast and the strong wind that rips through Maui's isthmus make sailing around the island exciting. Or you can go head-to-head with a 1,000-pound marlin in a big game fishing battle; slowly glide over the water in a kayak; hover high above it in a parasail; or get into the water and scuba dive, bodysurf, board surf, or windsurf.

Bodysurfing

Riding the waves without a board, becoming one with the rolling water, is an exquisite art. Some bodysurfers just rely on their hands to ride the waves; others use a pair of open-heeled swim fins to help propel them through the water. The best bodysurfing beach for beginners is **Kama'ole III** in Kihei. Secluded **Hamoa Beach** in Hana offers up steady swells, and in winter **Pa'ia Bay,** just outside of Pa'ia town, has great waves. If you don't mind nudity (illegal, but still practiced here), clamber over the Pu'u 'Olai cinder cone at Makena State Park to find **Little Beach,** probably the best bodysurfing cove on the island.

Kayaking

Gliding silently over the water, propelled by a paddle, seeing Maui from the sea the way the early Hawaiians did—that's what ocean kayaking is all about. One of Maui's best kayak routes is south along the coast from **Maluaka Beach** in Makena, where there's easy access, calm water, and sensational views. Go out in the early mornings; the wind comes up around 11am, making seas choppy and paddling difficult.

Ocean Rafting

If you're semi-adventurous and looking for a more intimate experience with the sea, try ocean rafting, cruising along the coast on inflatable rafts that hold 6 to 24 passengers. One of the best (and most reasonable) outfitters is **Hawaiian Ocean Raft;** its 5-hour tour includes three stops for snorkeling and stops to search for dolphins, plus continental breakfast and midmorning snacks. *Lahaina Harbor. www.hawaiioceanrafting.com. ☎ 808/661-7238. $85 adults, $72 for children ages 5–12.*

Plan Ahead

Kayak tours, surf lessons, and other paid activities are prohibited on county beaches on Sundays and state holidays.

Outrigger Canoe

Learn how to paddle a six-person canoe in sync with family or friends, just as the ancient Polynesians did when colonizing these islands. Several hotels (including Fairmont Kea Lani and Andaz Maui) have their own boats and offer wonderful cultural trips right off the beach. Otherwise, book with **Hawaiian Ocean Sports ★★★**. The Native Hawaiian–owned company shares knowledge about Maui's culture, history, and marine life on tours departing from Wailea Beach Park; some include snorkeling. You may spot turtles, whales, manta rays, or

Ocean kayaking lets you see Maui as the early Hawaiians did.

Kayak Tours

For beginners, **Makena Kayak and Tours ★** (www.makenakayak.com; ☎ 808/879-8426) is an excellent choice. Professional guide Dino Ventura leads a 2½-hour trip from Makena Landing and loves taking first-timers over the secluded coral reefs and into remote coves. His $65 tour includes snorkel and kayak equipment; the 4-hour tour costs $95. If Dino is booked, try **South Pacific Kayaks** (www.southpacifickayaks.com; ☎ 800/776-2326 or 808/875-4848). Maui's oldest kayak-tour company leads trips that run from 3 to 5 hours, starting at $74 per person ($129 per person for private trips with minimum of 4). The company rents equipment, too, and will meet you at Makena Landing with kayaks ready to go.

monk seals, too. *www.hawaiianoutriggerexperience.com. ☎ 808/633-2800. From $89 for ages 5 and older.*

Parasailing
Soar high above the crowds (at around 800 ft./244m) for a bird's-eye view of Maui. This adventure sport, a cross between skydiving and waterskiing, involves sailing through the air, suspended under a large parachute attached by towline to a speedboat. Keep in mind that parasailing tours don't run during whale season (roughly mid-December through mid-April). My favorite time is 8am, when the light is fantastic. Book with **UFO Parasail,** which picks you up at Ka'anapali Beach. *www.ufoparasail.net. ☎ 800/FLY-4-UFO (359-4836). $89 for 800 ft.(244m) or $99 for 1200 ft. (366m), $49 for observer.*

Sailing
Trilogy ★★★ (see box p 99) offers my favorite snorkel-sail trips.

Scuba Diving
Maui offers plenty of undersea attractions worth strapping on a tank for. Most divers start with **Molokini,** which can only be reached by boat. The sunken crater offers astounding visibility (you can often peer down 100 ft.) and an abundance of marine life, from clouds of yellow butterflyfish to manta rays. Experienced divers can explore Molokini's dramatic **back wall ★★★**, which plunges 350 feet and is frequented by larger marine animals. Other top sites include **Mala Wharf,** the ***St. Anthony*** (a sunken longliner), and **Five Graves** at Makena Landing. Don't be scared off by the latter's ominous name—it's a magical spot with sea caves and arches. Most operators offer no-experience-necessary dives, ranging from $100 for one tank to $150 for two tanks. Visit the scuba gurus at **Maui Dreams Dive Company** (www.mauidreamsdiveco.com; ☎ 808/879-3584), for advice, equipment, and to book an intro beach dive ($99) or guided scooter dives ($139–$169) to WWII wrecks and frogfish hideouts. **Mike Severns Diving** (www.mikeseverns diving.com; ☎ 808/879-6596), is also great, offering two-tank dives for $159 ($139 with your own equipment).

Sport Fishing
Marlin (as big as 1,200 lb.), tuna, *ono* (wahoo) and mahimahi swim in Maui's coastal and channel waters. No license is required; just book a sport-fishing vessel out of **Lahaina** or **Ma'alaea** harbors. Most charter

You might encounter a whale shark while diving.

boats carry a maximum of 6 passengers; you can walk the docks, inspect boats, and talk to captains and crews; or book through **Sportfish Hawaii** (www.sportfishhawaii.com; ☎ 877/388-1376). A shared boat for a half-day of bottom-fishing starts at $149. A half-day exclusive (you get the entire boat) starts at $699; a full-day exclusive starts at $1,399. Many captains tag and release marlin or keep the fish for themselves (sorry, that's Hawai'i style). If you want to eat your mahimahi for dinner or have your marlin mounted, tell the captain before you go.

Surfing

If you'd like to try out the ancient Hawaiian sport of *he'e nalu* (wave

Whale-Watching

Maui is a favorite destination for Hawaiian humpback whales, who make the 3,000-mile (4,828km) swim from the chilly waters of Alaska to bask in Maui's warmth. The massive marine mammals get downright frisky from about December to April (though January and February are the peak months). Seeing whales leap out of the sea or perfect their tail slap is mesmerizing. You can hear them sing underwater, too! Just duck your head a foot below the surface and listen for creaks, groans, and otherworldly serenades. Bring binoculars to one of the following spots: **McGregor Point,** on the way to Lahaina, scenic lookout at MM 9; **Olowalu Reef,** along the straight part of Honoapi'ilani Highway, between McGregor Point and Olowalu; or **Wailea Beach Resort & Spa** (3700 Wailea Alanui Dr., Wailea), on the Wailea coastal walk, with a telescope installed for whale-watching.

For a closer look, I recommend jumping aboard a maneuverable high-speed raft. **Capt. Steve's Rafting Excursions** (www.captainsteves.com; ☎ 808/667-5565) offers 2-hour whale-watches out of Lahaina Harbor (from $55 adults, $45 children 5–12).

Maui's warm waters are prime habitat for humpback whales.

sliding), call **Tide and Kiva Rivers,** two local boys (actually twins), who have been surfing since they could walk. Lessons are 1½-hours long and include equipment and instruction. They decide where the lesson will take place, based on their client's ability and where the surf is on that day. Tide claims he has beginners standing up in their first lesson. *www.riverstothesea.com. ☎ 808/280-8795. 1½-hr. lessons $119 for group (ages 11 and older), $139 semi-private for two (ages 7 and older), $219 private (ages 7 and older).*

Windsurfing

Maui has Hawai'i's best windsurfing beaches. In winter, windsurfers from around the world flock to the town of **Pa'ia** to ride the waves. **Ho'okipa Beach,** internationally known for its brisk winds and excellent waves, is the site of several world-championship contests. **Kanaha,** west of Kahului Airport, also has dependable winds. When the winds turn northerly, the northern end of **Kihei** is the spot to be, especially **'Ohukai Park,** the first beach as you enter South Kihei Road from the northern end; it has good winds, easy access, parking, and a long strip of grass to assemble your gear. **Hawaiian Sailboarding Techniques,** 425 Koloa St., Kahului (www.hstwindsurfing.com; ☎ 800/968-5423 or 808/871-5423), offers rentals and 2½-hour lessons from $99 at Kanaha Beach early in the morning before the breeze gets too strong for beginners. **Maui Windsurf Company,** 22 Hana Hwy., Kahului (www.mauiwindsurfcompany.com; ☎ 808/877-4816), rents top quality equipment (Goya boards, sails, and roof racks) from $64, and offers 2½-hour group lessons from $99. ●

Windsurfers in Ho'okipa on Maui's North Shore.

7 The Best Shopping

Shopping Best Bets

Best **Alohawear**
★★ Moonbow Tropics, *multiple locations (p 115)*

Best **Antiques**
★★ Bird of Paradise Unique Antiques, *56 N. Market St., Wailuku (p 115)*

Best **Art**
★★★ Hui No'eau, *2841 Baldwin Ave., Makawao (p 116)* and
★★★ Village Galleries, *120 Dickenson St., Lahaina (p 117)*

Best **Bookstore**
★★★ Maui Friends of the Library, *In Queen Ka'ahumanu Center, 275 Ka'ahumanu Ave., Kahului (p 117)*

Best **Flower Lei**
★ Pukalani Superette, *15 Makawao Ave., Pukalani (p 118)* and
★★★ Native Intelligence, *1980 Market St., Wailuku (p 118)*

Best **Gifts for Kids**
★★ Maui Ocean Center, *192 Ma'alaea Rd., Ma'alaea (p 118)*

Best **Handblown Glass**
★★ Hot Island Glass, *3620 Baldwin Ave., Makawao (p 116)*

Best **Hawaiian Art & Gifts**
★★★ Hana Coast Gallery, *at Travaasa Hana (p 115)* and
★★★ Native Intelligence, *1980 Market St. #2, Wailuku (p 118)*

Best **Local Fashion**
★★ Ha Wahine, *53 N. Market St., Wailuku (p 118)*

Best **Shoes**
★★ Island Sole, *728 Front St., Lahaina (p 119)*

Best **Souvenir to Ship Home**
★★ Proteas of Hawai'i, *phone orders only, ☎ 808/878-2533 (p 118)*

Best **Swimwear**
★★★ Maui Girl, *12 Baldwin Ave., Pa'ia (p 120)*

Best **T-Shirt Selection**
★ Crazy Shirts, *multiple locations (p 120)*

Flying with Food

Maui's delicious jams, preserves, and honey make tasty souvenirs, as do locally made rum, vodka, and wine, but don't forget to pack them in checked bags before flying home. Otherwise, they'll be confiscated by security.

Previous page: Maui Girl clothing store.

Maui Shopping

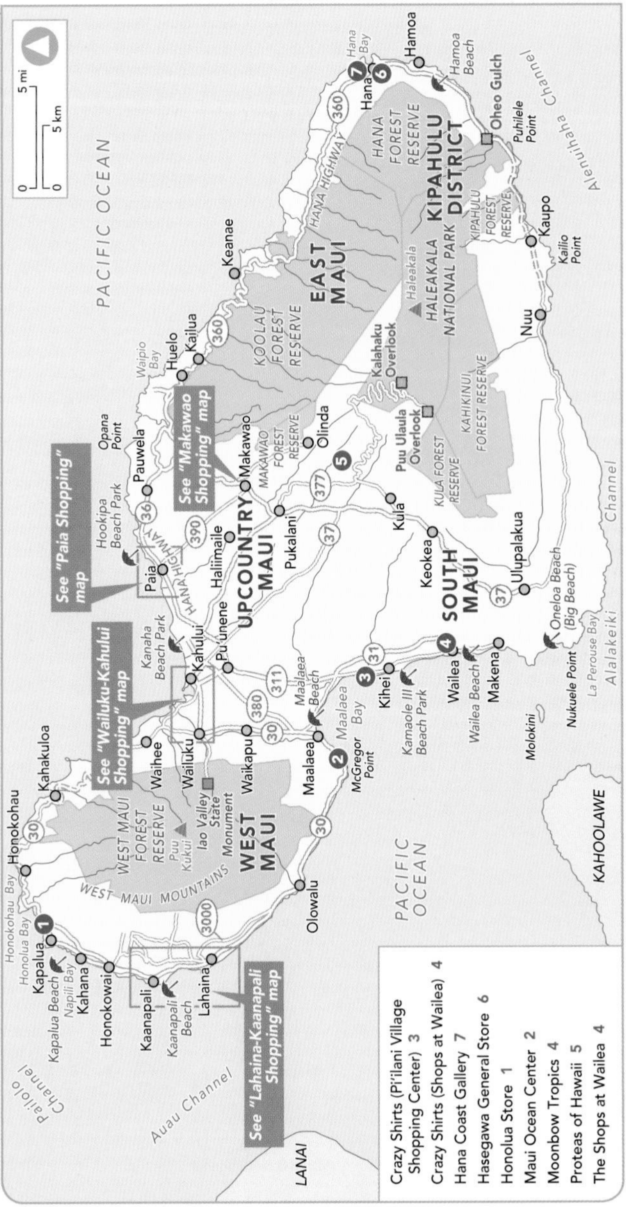

PACIFIC OCEAN
0 5 mi
0 5 km
See "Paia Shopping" map
See "Makawao Shopping" map
See "Wailuku-Kahului Shopping" map
See "Lahaina-Kaanapali Shopping" map
WEST MAUI
UPCOUNTRY MAUI
EAST MAUI
SOUTH MAUI
KIPAHULU DISTRICT
HALEAKALA NATIONAL PARK
WEST MAUI MOUNTAINS
WEST MAUI FOREST RESERVE
KOOLAU FOREST RESERVE
MAKAWAO FOREST RESERVE
HANA FOREST RESERVE
KIPAHULU FOREST RESERVE
KULA FOREST RESERVE
KAHIKINUI FOREST RESERVE
HANA HIGHWAY
Kapalua
Kahana
Honokowai
Kaanapali
Lahaina
Olowalu
Honokohau
Kahakuloa
Waihee
Wailuku
Waikapu
Maalaea
McGregor Point
Kahului
Pu'unene
Paia
Haliimaile
Pukalani
Makawao
Pauwela
Huelo
Kailua
Keanae
Olinda
Kula
Keokea
Ulupalakua
Kihei
Wailea
Makena
Hana
Hamoa
Kaupo
Nuu
Oheo Gulch
Kalahaku Overlook
Puu Ulaula Overlook
Haleakala
Iao Valley State Monument
Puu Kukui
Molokini
Nukuele Point
La Perouse Bay
Oneloa Beach (Big Beach)
Kapalua Beach
Kaanapali Beach
Kanaha Beach Park
Hookipa Beach Park
Kamaole III Beach Park
Wailea Beach
Maalaea Beach
Hamoa Beach
Opana Point
Puhilele Point
Kailio Point
Waipio Bay
Hana Bay
Maalaea Bay
Honokohau Bay
Honolua Bay
Napili Bay
Pailolo Channel
Auau Channel
Alalakeiki Channel
Alenuihaha Channel
LANAI
KAHOOLAWE
Crazy Shirts (Pi'ilani Village Shopping Center) 3
Crazy Shirts (Shops at Wailea) 4
Hana Coast Gallery 7
Hasegawa General Store 6
Honolua Store 1
Maui Ocean Center 2
Moonbow Tropics 4
Proteas of Hawaii 5
The Shops at Wailea 4

Lahaina & Ka'anapali Shopping

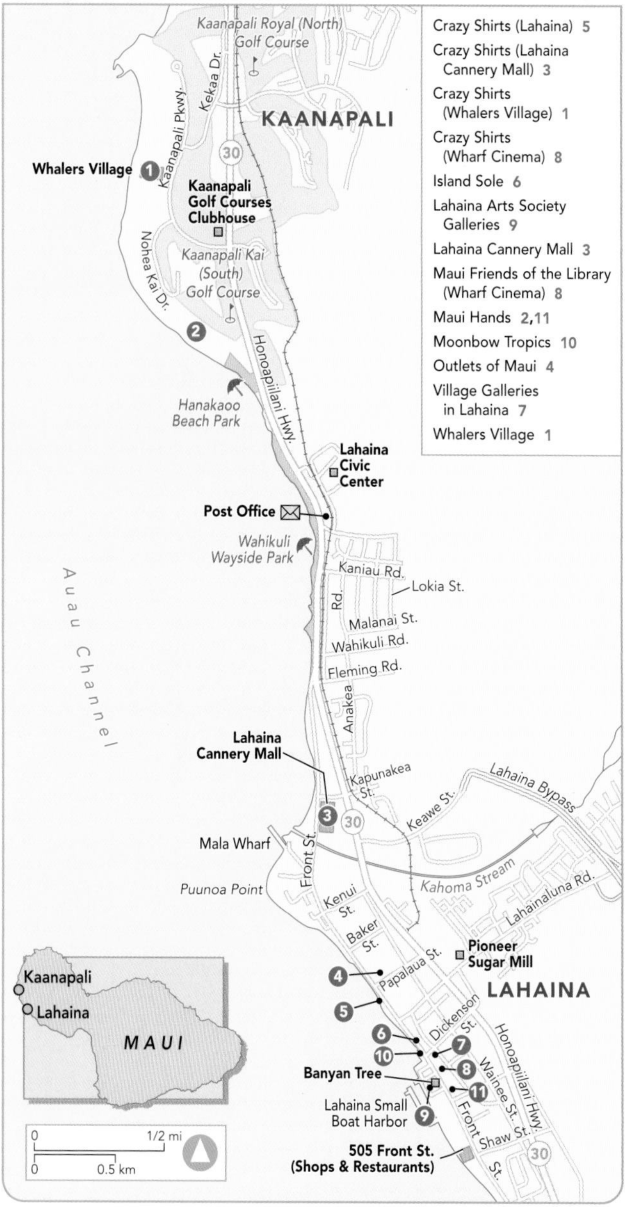
Crazy Shirts (Lahaina) 5
Crazy Shirts (Lahaina Cannery Mall) 3
Crazy Shirts (Whalers Village) 1
Crazy Shirts (Wharf Cinema) 8
Island Sole 6
Lahaina Arts Society Galleries 9
Lahaina Cannery Mall 3
Maui Friends of the Library (Wharf Cinema) 8
Maui Hands 2,11
Moonbow Tropics 10
Outlets of Maui 4
Village Galleries in Lahaina 7
Whalers Village 1
Kaanapali Royal (North) Golf Course
Kekaa Dr.
Kaanapali Pkwy.
KAANAPALI
30
Whalers Village
Kaanapali Golf Courses Clubhouse
Kaanapali Kai (South) Golf Course
Nohea Kai Dr.
Honoapiilani Hwy.
Hanakaoo Beach Park
Lahaina Civic Center
Post Office
Wahikuli Wayside Park
Kaniau Rd.
Lokia St.
Rd.
Malanai St.
Wahikuli Rd.
Fleming Rd.
Anakea
Auau Channel
Lahaina Cannery Mall
Kapunakea St.
Lahaina Bypass
Keawe St.
Mala Wharf
Front St.
Kahoma Stream
Puunoa Point
Kenui St.
Baker St.
Lahainaluna Rd.
Pioneer Sugar Mill
Papalaua St.
LAHAINA
Dickenson St.
Banyan Tree
Wainee St.
Lahaina Small Boat Harbor
Front St.
Shaw St.
505 Front St. (Shops & Restaurants)
Kaanapali
Lahaina
MAUI
0 1/2 mi
0 0.5 km

Wailuku & Kahului Shopping

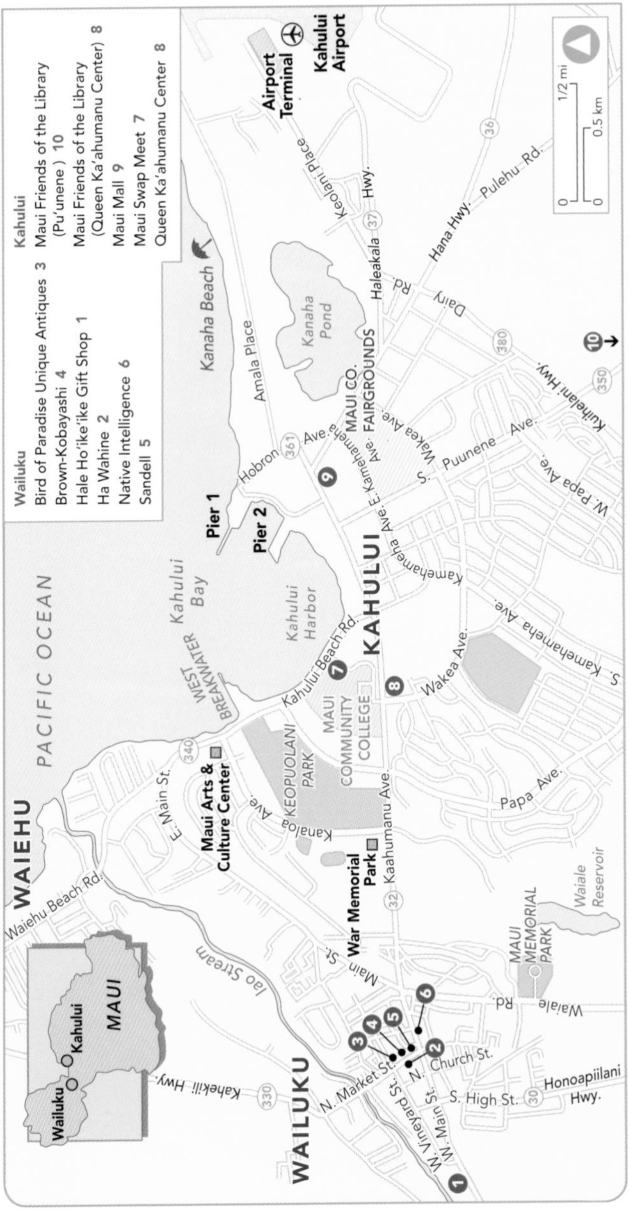

Pa'ia Shopping

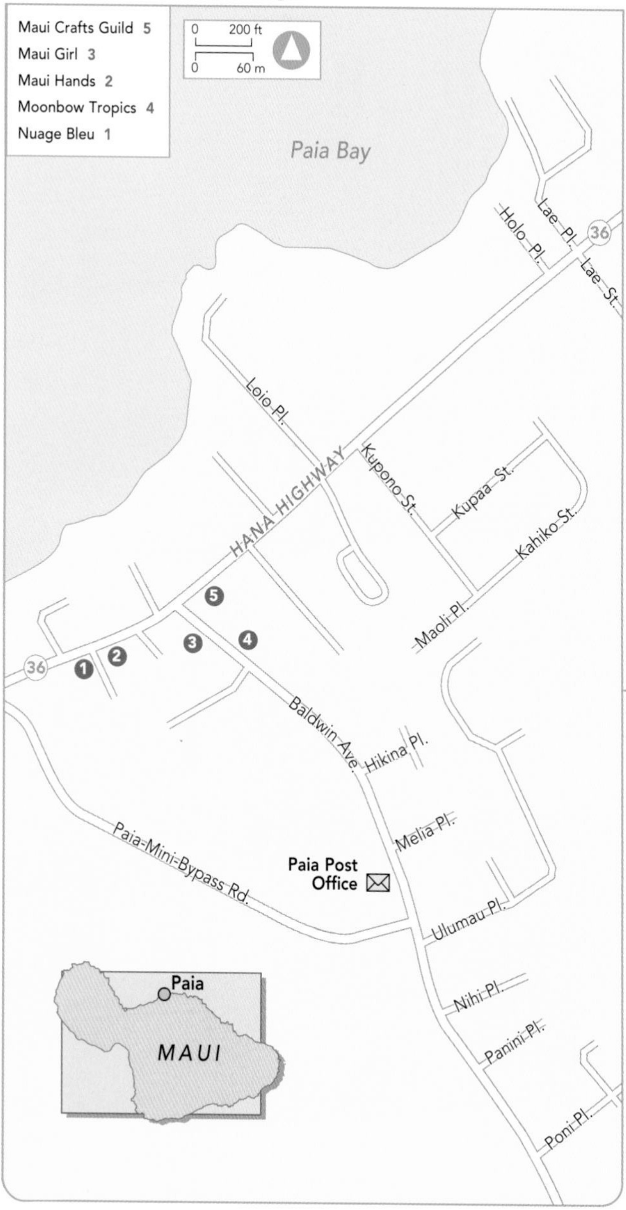
Maui Crafts Guild 5
Maui Girl 3
Maui Hands 2
Moonbow Tropics 4
Nuage Bleu 1
0 200 ft
0 60 m
Paia Bay
Lae Pl.
Holo Pl.
36
Lae St.
Loio Pl.
HANA HIGHWAY
Kupono St.
Kupaa St.
Kahiko St.
Maoli Pl.
Baldwin Ave.
Hikina Pl.
Melia Pl.
Paia-Mini-Bypass Rd.
Paia Post Office
Ulumau Pl.
Nihi Pl.
Panini Pl.
Poni Pl.
Paia
MAUI

Makawao Shopping

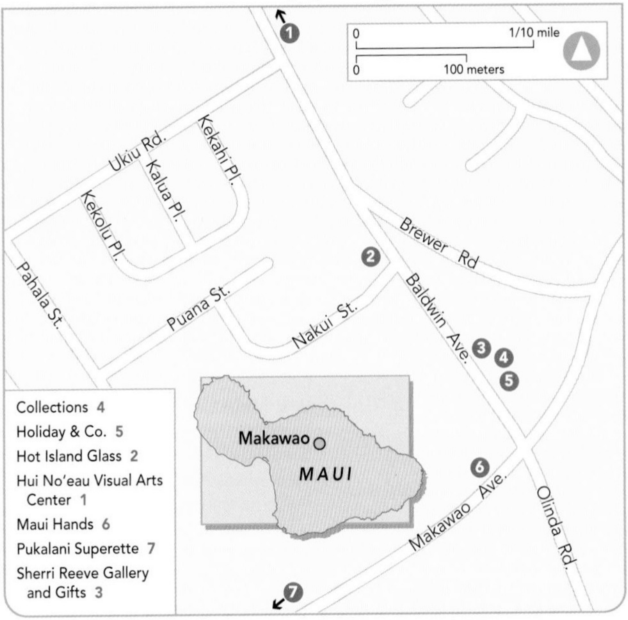

Maui Shopping A to Z

Alohawear

★★ Moonbow Tropics LAHAINA, PA'IA, WAILEA Find classy Aloha shirts, flowing skirts, and colorful Maui caps here. *707 Front St., Lahaina. www.moonbowtropics.com. ☎ 808/667-7998. Also at 27 Baldwin Ave., Pa'ia, ☎ 808/579-3131; and Shops at Wailea, 3750 Wailea Alanui Dr., Wailea, ☎ 808/874-1170. AE, DISC, MC, V. Map p 111, 112, and 114.*

Antiques & Collectibles

★★ Bird of Paradise Unique Antiques WAILUKU I love wandering through the nostalgic Hawaiiana here. Items range from 1940s rattan furniture to vintage Aloha shirts and classic Hawaiian music on cassettes. *56 N. Market St. ☎ 808/242-7699. AE, MC, V. Map p 113.*

★ Brown-Kobayashi WAILUKU The focus is gracious living with Asian antiques. You'll find Japanese kimonos and obi, exotic Chinese woods, and more. *38 N. Market St. ☎ 808/242-0804. AE, MC, V. Map p 113.*

Art

★★★ Hana Coast Gallery HANA If you only go to one gallery, make it this award-winning one devoted entirely to Hawai'i's top artists. It has Maui's best selection under one roof (sculptures, paintings, prints, feather work, stonework, and carvings). *Travaasa Hana hotel, 5031 Hana Hwy. www.hanacoast.com. ☎ 808/248-8636. AE, MC, V. Map p 111.*

You'll find classic Hawaiian music for sale at Bird of Paradise Unique Antiques.

★★ **Hot Island Glass** MAKAWAO Watch artists transform molten glass into works of art in this Makawao Courtyard studio, where an award-winning family of glass blowers built its own furnaces. The colorful works displayed range from small jellyfish paperweights to large museum-quality vessels. *3620 Baldwin Ave. www.hotislandglass.com. ☎ 808/572-4527. AE, DISC, MC, V. Map p 115.*

★★★ **Hui No'eau Visual Arts Center** MAKAWAO Visit this wonderful gallery and then browse the gift shop, which features local artists' ceramics, jewelry, and screenprints. *2841 Baldwin Ave. www.huinoeau.com. ☎ 808/572-6560. AE, DISC, MC, V. Map p 115.*

★ **Lahaina Arts Society Galleries** LAHAINA Changing monthly exhibits of the Maui artist-members range from paintings to fiber art, to ceramics, sculpture, prints, jewelry, and more. The galleries host fairs at Lahaina Cannery Mall every second and fourth weekend of the month. *648 Wharf St. www.lahainaarts.com. ☎ 808/661-0111. MC, V. Map p 112.*

★★ **Maui Crafts Guild** PA'IA The high quality and unique artwork at this artist-owned and -operated guild encompasses everything from pit-fired raku to hand-painted fabrics, jewelry, beadwork, traditional Hawaiian stonework, and even banana bark paintings. *120 Hana Hwy. www.mauicraftsguild.com. ☎ 808/579-9697. AE, MC, V. Map p 114.*

★★ **Maui Hands** KA'ANAPALI, LAHAINA, MAKAWAO, PA'IA Great Hawaiian gifts can be found here, where 90% of the items are made by Maui artists and sold at prices that aren't inflated. *1169 Makawao Ave., Makawao. www.mauihands.com. ☎ 808/572-2008. Also 612 Front St., Lahaina, ☎ 808/667-9898; in the Hyatt Regency, 210 Nohea Kai Dr., Ka'anapali ☎ 808/667-7997; and at 84 Hana Hwy., Pa'ia. ☎ 808/579-9245. AE, MC, V. Map p 112, 114, and 115.*

Intriguing paintings at the Hui No'eau Visual Arts Center.

Can you say you've actually been to Hawaii if you don't get an Aloha shirt?

★ Sherri Reeve Gallery and Gifts MAKAWAO Want to take a bit of the vibrant color and feel of the islands home with you? This open-air gallery sells everything from inexpensive cards, hand-painted tiles, and T-shirts to original works and limited editions. *3669 Baldwin Ave. www.sreeve.com. ☎ 808/572-8931. AE, DISC, MC, V. Map p 115.*

★★★ Village Galleries in Lahaina LAHAINA The oldest continuously operated gallery on Maui is known among art collectors as a showcase for regional artists. *120 Dickenson St.. Lahaina. www.villagegalleriesmaui.com. ☎ 808/661-4402 or 808/661-5559. Map. p 112. Also at the Ritz-Carlton, Kapalua, 1 Ritz-Carlton Dr. ☎ 808/669-1800. Map p 143.*

Books

★★★ kids Maui Friends of the Library KAHULUI, LAHAINA, PU'UNENE This non-profit, all-volunteer organization collects cast-off books and sells them for a song. You'll discover Hawaiian titles, kids' books, mysteries, and even board games on the well-curated shelves. Proceeds fund public libraries and the island's brand-new bookmobile. Finding the Pu'unene location is a worthwhile adventure—books there cost only 25¢! *In the Queen Ka'ahumanu Center, 275 Ka'ahumanu Ave., Kahului. www.mfol.org. ☎ 808/877-2509. Also in the Wharf Center, Lahaina, ☎ 808/667-2696; and in Pu'unene, ½ mile past HC&S sugar mill, behind Pu'unene School (follow the "BOOKS" signs), ☎ 808/871-6563. Map p 112 and 113.*

Fashion

★ Collections MAKAWAO This eclectic shop is filled with spirited clothing reflecting the ease and color of island living. *3677 Baldwin Ave. www.collectionsmauiinc.com. ☎ 808/572-0781. MC, V. Map p 115.*

Watch artists at work at the Village Art Gallery in Lahaina.

★★ **Ha Wahine** WAILUKU Local designers create the bold graphic designs based on Polynesian tattoos and other imagery for bright Aloha shirts, blouses, pareos, and dresses in flattering asymmetric cuts. *53 N. Market St. www.facebook.com/hawahine. ☎ 808/344-1642. MC, V. Map p 113.*

★★ **Holiday & Co.** MAKAWAO This chic boutique offers a luxurious collection of cashmere sweaters, leather handbags, lace lingerie, and irresistible jewelry. *3681 Baldwin Ave. www.holidayandcomaui.com. ☎ 808/572-1470. AE, DC, DISC, MC, V. Map p 115.*

★★ **Nuage Bleu** PA'IA From florals, fringes, and flounces to crisp cotton shirts and denim shorts, this "lifestyle boutique" offers a chic range of styles for women and kids, plus Tahitian pearl jewelry. *76 Hana Hwy., Pa'ia. www.nuagebleu.com. ☎ 808/579-9792. AE, MC, V. Map p 114.*

Flowers

★★ **Proteas of Hawai'i** KULA Send these other-worldly flowers back home to your friends—not only will they survive shipping anywhere in the world, but your pals will also be astounded and amazed. Phone and online orders only. *www.proteasofhawaii.com. ☎ 800/367-7768. AE, DISC, MC, V. Map p 111.*

General Stores

★★ **Hasegawa General Store** HANA I love this century-old family-run store, its aisles crammed with groceries and T-shirts and necessities of every sort. Check out the wall full of machetes above the office window. *5165 Hana Hwy. ☎ 808/248-8231. AE, MC, V. Map p 118.*

★ **Honolua Store** KAPALUA In pricey Kapalua, this is my favorite place for everyday essentials, clothing, even budget-priced deli items. *502 Office Rd. honoluastore.com. ☎ 808/665-9105. AE, DC, DISC, MC, V. Map p 111.*

★ **Pukalani Superette** PUKALANI This small, family-owned grocery has great deli items and some of the most outstanding lei on Maui at very moderate prices. Ask for the heavenly scented puakenikeni. *15 Makawao Ave. pukalanisuperette.com. ☎ 808/572-7616. MC, V. Map p 115.*

Hawaiian Art & Gifts

★★★ **Hale Ho'ike'ike at the Bailey House Gift Shop** WAILUKU For made-in-Hawaii items, this small shop is a must stop, for everything from exquisite woods, Hawaiian music, books, and traditional Hawaiian games to sarongs, *lauhala* hats, hand-sewn pheasant hatbands, jams and jellies, and an occasional Hawaiian quilt. *2375-A Main St. www.mauimuseum.org. ☎ 808/244-3326. MC, V. Map p 113.*

★★★ **Native Intelligence** WAILUKU It's like a museum, only you can take these marvelous Polynesian artifacts home. Stock up on locally made clothing, finely woven *lauhala* hats, carved shell jewelry, and fresh flower lei. *1980 Main St. #2. www.native-intel.com. ☎ 808/242-2421. AE, MC, V. Map p 113.*

Kids

★★ kids **Maui Ocean Center** MAALAEA Stop here for plush stuffed marine animals, nature books, T-shirts, and an array of fine artwork, jewelry, and Hawaiian art created by prominent island artists; aquarium admission not required. *Ma'alaea Harbor Village, 192 Ma'alaea Rd. (the triangle btw. Honoapi'ilani Hwy. and Ma'alaea Rd.). www.mauioceancenter.com.*

Native Intelligence shop.

☎ 808/270-7000. AE, DISC, MC, V. Map p 111.

Shoes

★★ Island Sole LAHAINA The best store for sandals, with a range of shoes from high-end OluKai "slippers" (flip-flops) to tropical-tinted Havaianas, plus hats, handbags, picture frames, and more. Prices are reasonable. *728 Front St. www.coconene.com. ☎ 808/856-3530. AE, MC, V. Map p 112.*

Shopping Centers

Lahaina Cannery Mall LAHAINA A former pineapple cannery is now an air-conditioned maze of shops and restaurants, including Longs Drugs and Starbucks. *1221 Honoapi'ilani Hwy. www.lahainacannerymall.com. ☎ 808/661-5304. Map p 112.*

Maui Mall KAHULUI This is a place for daily shopping with stores like Whole Foods and Longs Drugs. Don't miss **Tasaka Guri Guri,** a decades-old purveyor of icy treats. *70 E. Ka'ahumanu Ave. www.mauimall.com. ☎ 808/877-8952. Map p 113.*

★ Outlets of Maui LAHAINA This Front Street outlet mall features designer brands, two restaurants, a Tahitian show, and a movie-theater multiplex. *900 Front St. www.outletsofmaui.com. ☎ 808/661-8277. Map p 112.*

kids Queen Ka'ahumanu Center KAHULUI With more than 100 shops, restaurants, and theaters, Ka'ahumanu covers the basics, from **Victoria's Secret** to **Macy's,** plus local novelties like **Camellia Imports,** where you can sample lip-puckering "crack seed" (preserved fruits dusted in *li hing mui* powder). *275 Ka'ahumanu Ave. www.queenkaahumanucenter.com. ☎ 808/877-4325. Map p 113.*

A fish plate at the Maui Ocean Center's gift shop.

Whaler's Village.

★ The Shops at Wailea WAILEA This classy open-air mall sells high-end gifts, clothing, and accessories. My faves include **Ki'i Gallery,** one of Hawai'i's most comprehensive collections of fine art, and **Keliki,** a trendy beachwear boutique with locally made accessories. *3750 Wailea Alanui. www.theshopsatwailea.com. ☎ 808/891-6770. Map p 111.*

★ kids Whalers Village KA'ANAPALI Find upscale brands such as Tommy Bahama's and Louis Vuitton here, plus several good restaurants. It's fun to stroll around, gawk at the giant whale skeleton, and check out the free ukulele lessons. *2435 Ka'anapali Pkwy. www.whalersvillage.com. ☎ 808/661-4567. Map p 112.*

Swap Meets

★ Maui Swap Meet KAHULUI Some 300 vendors and plenty of parking, every Saturday from 7am to 1pm, make this a bargain shopper's paradise; from fresh vegetables to original artwork and funky antiques, there's something for everyone. *At Maui Community College, btw. Kahului Beach Rd. and Wahine Pio Ave. (access via Wahine Pio Ave.). www.mauiexposition.com/MAUISWAPMEET.html. ☎ 808/244-3100. Admission: 50¢. No credit cards. Map p 113.*

Swimwear

★★★ Maui Girl PA'IA This locally owned beach shack sells mix-and-match bikinis in every color, and must-have beach sheets. *12 Baldwin Ave. maui-girl.com. ☎ 808/579-9266. AE, MC, V. Map p 114.*

T-Shirts

★ Crazy Shirts VARIOUS LOCATIONS These 100% cotton T-shirts not only last for years, but they also make perfect souvenirs and gifts. *www.crazyshirts.com. Whalers Village, Ka'anapali, ☎ 808/661-0117, map p 112; 865 Front St., Lahaina, ☎ 808/661-4775, map p 112; Lahaina Wharf, ☎ 808/661-4712, map p 112; Pi'ilani Village Shopping Center, Kihei, ☎ 808/875-6440, map p 111; Lahaina Cannery Mall, ☎ 808/661-4788, map p 112; The Shops at Wailea, ☎ 808/875-6435, map p 111. AE, DISC, MC, V.*

Sandell WAILUKU For the inside scoop on Maui politics and a bit of social commentary, stop by to chat with artist-illustrator-cartoonist David Sandell, who has provided insight on Maui since the early 1970s through his artwork. Also check out his inexpensive T-shirts. *34 N. Market St. ☎ 808/249-2456. Map p 113.* ●

8 The Best Dining

Dining Best Bets

Best on the Beach
★★★ Mama's Fish House $$$$
799 Poho Place, Ku'au (p 129)

Best Breakfast
★★ Nalu's South Shore Grill $$
Azeka I Shopping Center, 1280 S. Kihei Rd., Kihei (p 131)

Best Brunch
★★ Fond $$ *5095 Napilihau St., Napili (p 126)*

Best on a Budget
★ CJ's Deli & Diner $ *Ka'anapali Fairway Shops (p 126)*

Best for Families
★★ Nalu's South Shore Grill $$
Azeka I Shopping Center, 1280 S. Kihei Rd., Kihei (p 131)

Best Fish Sandwich
★★ Pa'ia Fish Market $ *110 Hana Hwy., Pa'ia, 632 Front St., Lahaina, 1913 S. Kihei Rd., Kihei (p 131)*

Best Lu'au
★★★ Old Lahaina Lu'au $$$$
1251 Front St., Lahaina (p 127)

Best Pizza
★★ Flatbread & Company $$
89 Hana Hwy., Pa'ia (p 126)

Most Romantic
★★★ Gerard's $$$$
174 Lahainaluna Rd., Lahaina (p 127)

Best Splurge
★★★ Ka'ana Kitchen $$$$
Andaz Resort, Wailea (p 128)

Best Sushi
★★ Japengo $$$$ *Hyatt Regency Maui, Ka'anapali (p 127)* and
★★★ Morimoto Maui $$$$
Andaz Resort, Wailea (p 130)

Best Local Cuisine
★★★ Tin Roof $ *360 Papa Place, Kahului (p 132)*

Best Healthy Choice
★ Joy's Place $ *1993 S. Kihei Rd., Kihei (p 128)*

Best View
★★★ Mala Ocean Tavern $$$
1307 Front St., Lahaina (p 128) and
★★★ Mama's Fish House $$$$
799 Poho Place, Ku'au (p 129)

Above: The Old Lahaina Luau features traditional Polynesian dancing.
Previous page: Lunch with a view at Mill House Restaurant.

Maui & Pa'ia Dining

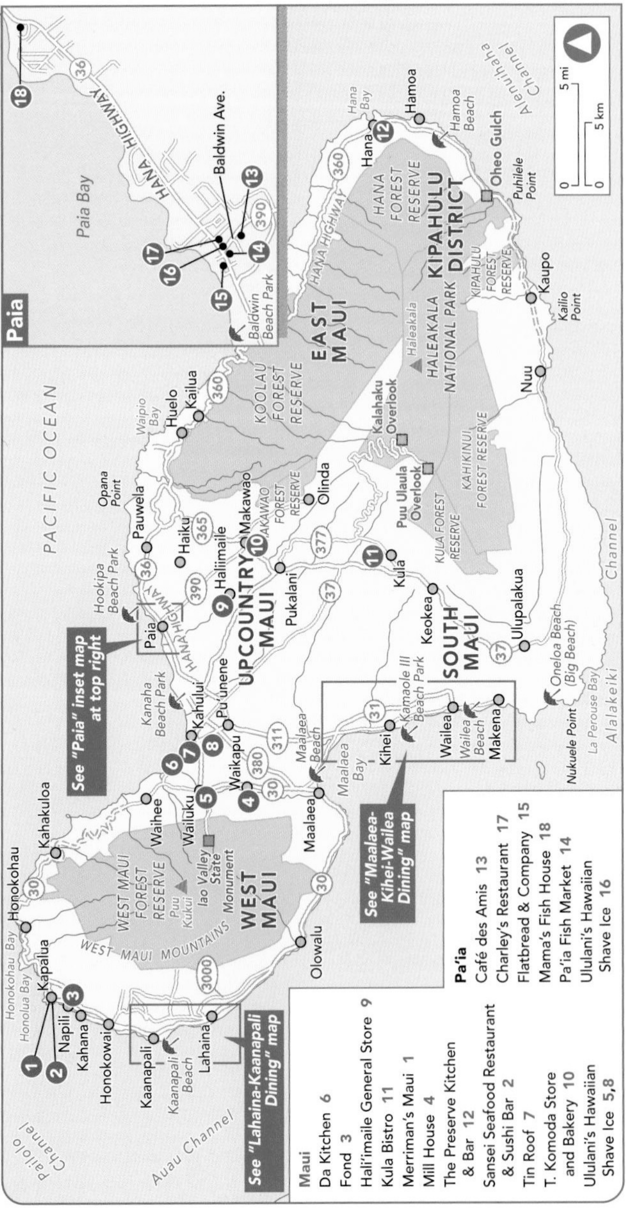
Paia
Paia Bay
HANA HIGHWAY
Baldwin Ave.
Baldwin Beach Park
PACIFIC OCEAN
See "Paia" inset map at top right
See "Maalaea-Kihei-Wailea Dining" map
See "Lahaina-Kaanapali Dining" map
WEST MAUI
WEST MAUI FOREST RESERVE
WEST MAUI MOUNTAINS
Puu Kukui
Iao Valley State Monument
UPCOUNTRY MAUI
SOUTH MAUI
EAST MAUI
KOOLAU FOREST RESERVE
MAKAWAO FOREST RESERVE
KULA FOREST RESERVE
KAHIKINUI FOREST RESERVE
HANA FOREST RESERVE
KIPAHULU FOREST RESERVE
HALEAKALA NATIONAL PARK
KIPAHULU DISTRICT
Haleakala
Kalahaku Overlook
Puu Ulaula Overlook
Oheo Gulch
Honokohau
Honokohau Bay
Honolua Bay
Kapalua
Napili
Kahana
Honokowai
Kaanapali
Kaanapali Beach
Lahaina
Olowalu
Maalaea
Maalaea Bay
Maalaea Beach
Kahakuloa
Waihee
Wailuku
Waikapu
Kahului
Kanaha Beach Park
Pu'unene
Paia
Hookipa Beach Park
Pauwela
Opana Point
Haiku
Haliimaile
Makawao
Pukalani
Olinda
Kula
Keokea
Ulupalakua
Kihei
Kamaole III Beach Park
Wailea
Wailea Beach
Makena
Oneloa Beach (Big Beach)
La Perouse Bay
Nukuele Point
Huelo
Waipio Bay
Kailua
Hana
Hana Bay
Hamoa
Hamoa Beach
Puhilele Point
Kaupo
Kailio Point
Nuu
Auau Channel
Pailolo Channel
Alalakeiki Channel
Alenuihaha Channel
0 5 mi
0 5 km
Maui
Da Kitchen 6
Fond 3
Hali'imaile General Store 9
Kula Bistro 11
Merriman's Maui 1
Mill House 4
The Preserve Kitchen & Bar 12
Sansei Seafood Restaurant & Sushi Bar 2
Tin Roof 7
T. Komoda Store and Bakery 10
Ululani's Hawaiian Shave Ice 5,8
Pa'ia
Café des Amis 13
Charley's Restaurant 17
Flatbread & Company 15
Mama's Fish House 18
Pa'ia Fish Market 14
Ululani's Hawaiian Shave Ice 16

Lahaina & Ka'anapali Dining

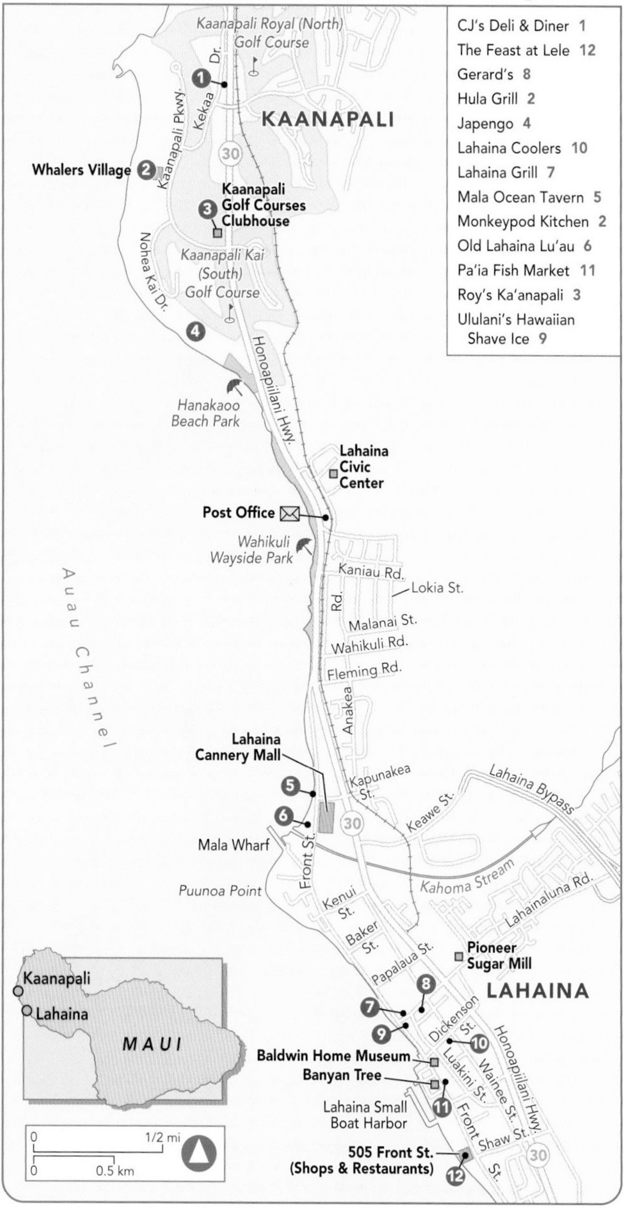
CJ's Deli & Diner 1
The Feast at Lele 12
Gerard's 8
Hula Grill 2
Japengo 4
Lahaina Coolers 10
Lahaina Grill 7
Mala Ocean Tavern 5
Monkeypod Kitchen 2
Old Lahaina Lu'au 6
Pa'ia Fish Market 11
Roy's Ka'anapali 3
Ululani's Hawaiian Shave Ice 9
Kaanapali Royal (North) Golf Course
KAANAPALI
Kekaa Dr.
Kaanapali Pkwy.
Whalers Village
Kaanapali Golf Courses Clubhouse
Nohea Kai Dr.
Kaanapali Kai (South) Golf Course
Honoapiilani Hwy.
Hanakaoo Beach Park
Lahaina Civic Center
Post Office
Wahikuli Wayside Park
Auau Channel
Kaniau Rd.
Lokia St.
Malanai St.
Wahikuli Rd.
Fleming Rd.
Anakea Rd.
Lahaina Cannery Mall
Kapunakea St.
Lahaina Bypass
Keawe St.
Mala Wharf
Front St.
Kahoma Stream
Puunoa Point
Kenui St.
Lahainaluna Rd.
Baker St.
Papalaua St.
Pioneer Sugar Mill
LAHAINA
Dickenson St.
Baldwin Home Museum
Banyan Tree
Luakini St.
Wainee St.
Lahaina Small Boat Harbor
Shaw St.
505 Front St. (Shops & Restaurants)
Kaanapali
Lahaina
MAUI
0 1/2 mi
0 0.5 km

Kihei & Wailea Dining

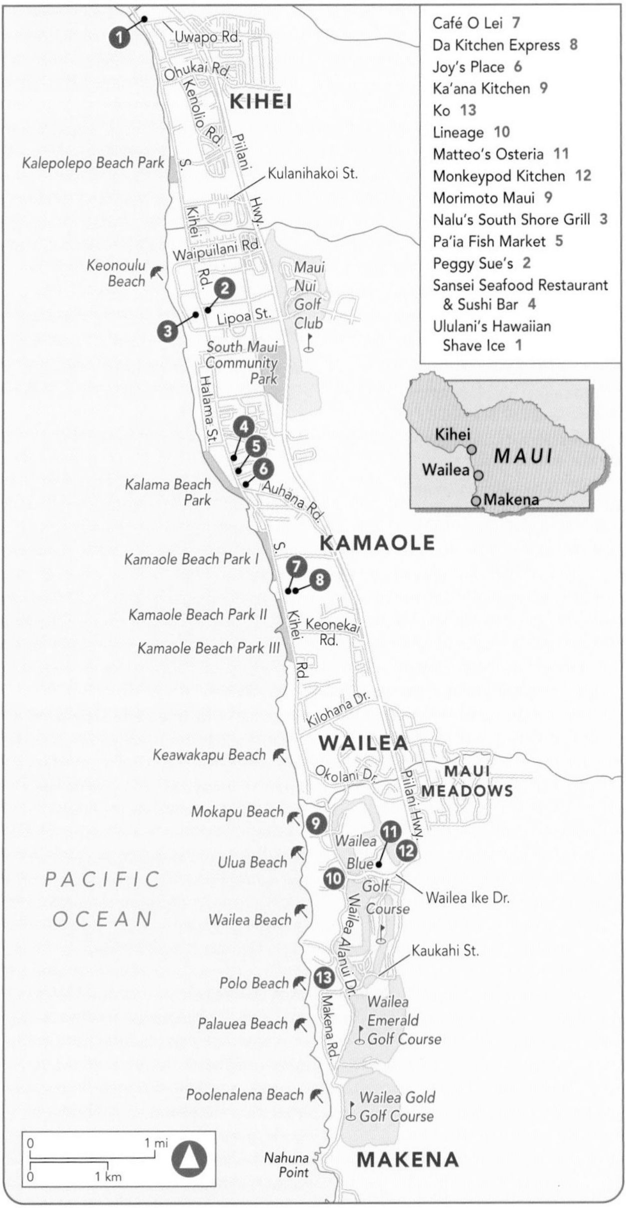

Maui Restaurants A to Z

★★ Café des Amis PA'IA *CREPES/MEDITERRANEAN/INDIAN* Savory and sweet crepes are the stars here, along with delicious Indian curries. The outdoor seating features live music in the evenings. *42 Baldwin Ave. www.cdamaui.com. ☎ 808/579-6323. Entrees $5–$18 AE, MC, V. Breakfast, lunch & dinner daily. Map p 123.*

★ kids Café o Lei KIHEI *AMERICAN/SUSHII* There's something for everyone here, from brick-oven flatbreads to sushi to juicy prime rib. The Maui onion soup is a favorite. *2439 S. Kihei Rd. www.cafeoleirestaurants.com. ☎ 808/891-1368. Entrees $9–$32. AE, MC, V. Lunch & dinner daily. Map p 125.*

★ kids Charley's Restaurant PA'IA *AMERICAN* This North Shore landmark is a mix of a 1960s hippie hangout, a windsurfers' power-breakfast spot, and a honky-tonk bar that gets going after dark. *142 Hana Hwy. www.charleysmaui.com. ☎ 808/579-9453. Entrees $10–$38. AE, DISC, MC, V. Breakfast, lunch & dinner daily. Map p 123.*

★ kids CJ's Deli & Diner KA'ANAPALI *AMERICAN/DELI* Colorful and slightly chaotic, this fun, affordable deli sports a huge billboard menu that spans the back wall and a . . . basketball hoop? Practice your free throws while ordering French toast made with Hawaiian sweet bread. *Ka'anapali Fairway Shops, 2580 Keka'a Dr. (just off the Honoapi'ilani Hwy./Hwy. 30). www.cjsmaui.com. ☎ 808/667-0968. Entrees $8–$17. AE, MC, V. Breakfast, lunch & dinner daily. Map p 124.*

★★ Da Kitchen KAHULUI, KIHEI *LOCAL/HAWAIIAN* Just off the plane? Hearty island favorites such as a plate lunch (choice of protein with two scoops rice and salad) or loco moco (beef patty, fried egg and rice smothered in gravy) will revive you quickly. **Da Kitchen Express** in Kihei's Rainbow Mall (2439 S. Kihei Rd., ☎ 808/875-7782, map p 125) is a takeout version open for lunch and dinner Tues–Sun. *Triangle Square, 425 Koloa St. #104. www.dakitchen.com. ☎ 808/871-7782. Entrees $10–$28. AE, MC, V. Lunch & dinner Mon–Sat. Map p 123.*

★★ The Feast at Lele LAHAINA *POLYNESIAN* Taking lu'au cuisine to a new level, the owners of Old Lahaina Lu'au (p 127) provide the food and dances from Hawai'i, Tahiti, New Zealand, and Samoa in an outdoor setting. Entrees from each culture are served at private, candlelit tables set on the sand. *505 Front St. www.feastatlele.com. ☎ 886/244-5353 or 808/667-5353. Set 5-course menu $130 adults, $95 children 2–12; gratuity not included. AE, MC, V. Dinner daily. Map p 124.*

★★ kids Flatbread & Company PA'IA *PIZZA* Hand-tossed organic flatbreads are sprinkled with delectable toppings: Maui goat cheese, macadamia-nut pesto, and slow-roasted pork. This fun restaurant is regularly packed; call ahead. *71 Baldwin Ave. www.flatbreadcompany.com. ☎ 808/579-9999. Entrees $14–$25. Lunch & dinner daily. AE, MC, V. Map p 123.*

★★ Fond NAPILI, *PAN-ASIAN/GLOBAL* Maui fave Jojo Vasquez prepares eclectic gourmet comfort food for brunch, from American pancakes to Mediterranean shakshuka to Filipino *silog* bowls of garlic fried rice with a fried egg and choice of protein. Dinner also criss-crosses the globe: Try the Manila

clam bucatini with locally made pasta and Chinese sausage. *Napili Plaza, 5095 Napilihau St., Napili. www.fondmaui.com. ☎ 808/856-0225. Brunch daily 8am–2pm, dinner Tues–Sat 5–9pm. Entrees $14–$18 brunch, $18–$45 dinner. AE, DC, DISC, MC, V. Map p 123.*

★★★ **Gerard's** LAHAINA *FRENCH* Chef Gerard Reversade turns out exceptional French cuisine in this elegant Victorian house. The chilled cucumber soup is transcendent, its delicacy amplified by goat cheese and fresh dill. The dessert menu has a half-dozen excellent offerings, including a marvelous millefeuille. *In the Plantation Inn, 174 Lahainaluna Rd. www.gerardsmaui.com. ☎ 808/661-8939. Entrees $39–$58. AE, DC, DISC, MC, V. Dinner daily. Map p 124.*

★★★ kids **Hali'imaile General Store** HALI'IMAILE *AMERICAN* Chef Bev Gannon, one of the 12 original Hawai'i Regional Cuisine chefs, heads up this foodie haven amid the pineapple fields with her innovative spin on good ol' American cuisine, bringing Hawaiian and Texas flavors together. *Hali'imaile Rd. www.hgsmaui.com. ☎ 808/572-2666. Entrees $14–$44. AE, DC, DISC, MC, V. Lunch Mon–Fri; dinner daily. Map p 123.*

★ kids **Hula Grill** KA'ANAPALI *HAWAI'I REGIONAL/SEAFOOD* Skip the main dining room and dig your toes in the sand at the Barefoot Bar on the beach, where you can nosh on fresh burgers, fish, pizza, and salad. *Whalers Village, 2435 Ka'anapali Pkwy. www.hulagrill.com. ☎ 808/667-6636. Entrees $10–$20 in Barefoot Bar, $20–$40 in dining room. AE, DC, DISC, MC, V. Lunch & dinner daily. Map p 124.*

★★ **Japengo** KA'ANAPALI *SUSHI/SEAFOOD* It's a rare hotel restaurant that can live up to both West Maui sunsets and locals' demanding tastes when it comes to sushi, but award-winning Japengo has done so for years. The sleek, open-air dining room includes a lounge with excellent craft cocktails, sushi bar, and wide-ranging, Japanese-inspired menu with many half-portion options; let your taste buds roam. *Hyatt Regency Maui, 200 Nohea Kai Dr., Ka'anapali. maui.hyatt.com. ☎ 808/667-4727. Sushi*

Old Lahaina Lu'au

Maui's best lu'au features terrific food and entertainment in a peerless oceanfront setting. The lu'au begins at sunset and features Tahitian and Hawaiian entertainment, including all versions of hula dancing, from ancient times to the modern era. The entertainment is riveting, even for jaded locals. The high-quality food, served from an open-air thatched structure, includes imu-roasted kalua pig, baked mahimahi in Maui-onion cream sauce, guava chicken, teriyaki sirloin steak, lomi salmon, poi, dried fish, *poke*, Hawaiian sweet potato, sautéed vegetables, seafood salad, and the ultimate treat, taro leaves with coconut milk. **Old Lahaina Lu'au** ★★★ (1251 Front St., Lahaina; www.oldlahainaluau.com; ☎ 800/248-5828 or 808/667-1998), $120 for adults, $75 for kids ages 3 to 12.

rolls $16–$24, entrees $24–$69. AE, DC, DISC, MC, V. Dinner daily. Map p 124.

★ kids **Joy's Place** KIHEI *HEALTHY DELI/SANDWICHES* If you are craving a healthy, delicious lunch, it's worth hunting for this tiny hole-in-the-wall with humongous sandwiches, fresh salads, hot soups, and smoothies. *Island Surf Bldg., 1993 S. Kihei Rd. (enter on Auhana St.). www.joysplacemauihawaii.com. ☎ 808/879-9258. All items under $12. MC, V. Mon–Fri 7:30am–4pm, Sat 7:30am–2pm. Map p 125.*

★★★ **Ka'ana Kitchen** WAILEA *HAWAI'I REGIONAL CUISINE* Foodies, don't miss dining here. Start off with a hand-mixed cocktail and the grilled octopus: fat chunks of tender meat tossed with frisée, watercress, and goat cheese. Executive chef Isaac Bancaco designed his menu like a bingo card; every choice is a winner. *At the Andaz Maui, 3550 Wailea Alanui Dr. http://maui.andaz.hyatt.com. ☎ 808/573-1234. Entrees $16–$59. AE, DC, DISC, MC, V. Breakfast & dinner daily. Map p 125.*

★★ **Ko** WAILEA *GOURMET PLANTATION CUISINE* The word *ko* means "cane," as in sugar cane, back to the old plantation days when the sugar-cane plantations had "camp" housing for each ethnic group and each had its own cuisine. There are wonderful taste treats you are only going to find here—don't miss them. *Fairmont Kea Lani, 4100 Wailea Alanui Dr., Wailea. www.korestaurant.com. ☎ 808/875-2210. Entrees $21–$50. AE, DC, DISC, MC, V. Lunch & dinner daily. Map p 125.*

★★ kids **Kula Bistro** KULA *ITALIAN/AMERICAN* Day or night, you can't go wrong at this rustic-chic spot. For breakfast, opt for frittata or eggs benedict, or peruse the tempting bakery counter. Beautifully presented pastas, paninis, and seafood are the stars at lunch and dinner; alcohol is BYOB. *4566 Lower Kula Rd. www.kulabistro.com. ☎ 808/871-2960. Breakfast entrees $10–$17, lunch & dinner $15–$35. AE, MC, V. Breakfast Tues–Sun, lunch & dinner daily. Map p 123.*

★ kids **Lahaina Coolers** LAHAINA *AMERICAN/INTERNATIONAL* This ultracasual indoor/outdoor restaurant is a hangout for hungry surfers on a tight budget. *180 Dickenson St. www.lahainacoolers.com. ☎ 808/661-7082. Entrees $8–$15 breakfast, $13–$17 lunch, $18–$33 dinner. AE, DC, DISC, MC, V. Breakfast, lunch & dinner daily. Map p 124.*

★★★ **Lahaina Grill** LAHAINA *NEW AMERICAN* This classy restaurant serves award-winning dishes: a prawn- and scallop-stuffed chile relleno, an aromatic Kona coffee-roasted rack of lamb, and triple berry pie.*127 Lahainaluna Rd. www.lahainagrill.com. ☎ 808/667-5117. Entrees $35–$62. AE, DC, DISC, MC, V. Dinner daily. Map p 124.*

★★★ **Lineage** WAILEA *MODERN ISLAND* *Top Chef* fan favorite Sheldon Simeon playfully celebrates his Hilo roots at his first high-end restaurant. Have fun choosing from a cart with small plates such as spicy boiled peanuts or *pipikaula* (beef jerky), and share rich entrees such as cold ginger chicken or silken squid lu'au. *In the Shops at Wailea, 3750 Wailea Alanui Dr. www.lineagemaui.com. ☎ 808/879-8800. Entrees $21–$62. AE, MC, V. Dinner daily 5–11pm. Map p 125.*

★★★ **Mala Ocean Tavern** LAHAINA *AMERICAN* Everything about this tiny tavern overlooking Mala Wharf is perfect: a view of surfing sea turtles, an epic brunch menu, and dinner options ranging from healthy Indonesian *gado gado*

Chef Sheldon Simeon speaks to diners at Lineage.

to hedonistic mac and cheese. *1307 Front St. www.malaoceantavern.com. ☎ 808/667-9394. Reservations recommended. Entrees $15–$49. AE, DC, DISC, MC, V. Lunch & dinner daily, weekend brunch. Map p 124*

★★★ Mama's Fish House

KU'AU *SEAFOOD* This beachfront institution is the realization of a South Pacific fantasy. Though pricey, a meal at Mama's is a complete experience from the moment you arrive. The menu lists the names of the anglers who reeled in the day's catch, and the Tahitian Pearl dessert is almost too stunning to eat. Reserve well in advance. *799 Poho Place, just off the Hana Hwy. www.mamasfishhouse.com. ☎ 808/579-8488. Entrees $44–$95. DC, DISC, MC, V. Lunch & dinner daily. Map p 123.*

★★ Matteo's Osteria WAILEA *ITALIAN/SEAFOOD* Chef-owner

Avocado toast is one of the breakfast treats at Mala Ocean Tavern.

Seafront dining at Merriman's Maui.

Matteo Mistura offers an impressive list of wines by the glass, but non-oenophiles will also appreciate his deft blend of local ingredients and classic Italian fare, such as homemade lasagne with Maui beef or poke Italiano ('ahi tuna with squid ink). *161 Wailea Ike Pl. www.matteosmaui.com. ☎ 808/891-8466. Pizzas $18–$22, entrees $26–$42. AE, MC, V. Dinner daily. Map p 125.*

★★★ Merriman's Maui KAPALUA *HAWAI'I REGIONAL* Peter Merriman, a cofounder of the Hawai'i Regional Cuisine movement, showcases classic dishes such as wok-charred 'ahi and chocolate-filled won ton purses in an elegant dining room with magnificent views of Lana'i and Moloka'i. *1 Bay Club Pl. www.merrimanshawaii.com. ☎ 808/669-6400. Entrees $31–$68. AE, MC, V. Dinner daily, Sunday brunch. Map p 123.*

★★ Mill House WAIKAPU *NEW AMERICAN* Chef Jeff Scheer's inventive menu includes beautiful hand-cut pasta, coffee-roasted beet salad, and Cornish hen with parsnip puree. Lunch is best; it's less pricey and you can see into stunning Waikapu Valley. *At Maui Tropical Plantation, 1607 Honoapi'ilani Hwy. www.millhousemaui.com. ☎ 808/270-0333. Lunch entrees $12–$28. Dinner entrees $18–$55. AE, MC, V. Lunch and dinner daily. Map p 123.*

★★ kids Monkeypod Kitchen WAILEA, KAANAPALI *HAWAII REGIONAL* Peter Merriman's lively younger siblings to his eponymous Kapalua dining room feature local ingredients in fresh, casual dishes like corn chowder, pizza, and fish tacos. The Mai Tais are a must. *10 Wailea Gateway Place, Kihei. www.monkeypodkitchen.com. ☎ 808/891-2322. Map p 125. Also in Whalers Village, 2434 Ka'anapali Pkwy., Ka'anapali. ☎ 808/878-6763. Map p 124. Lunch items $16–$30; dinner entrees $16–$50. AE, DC, DISC, M, V. Lunch & dinner daily.*

★★★ Morimoto Maui WAILEA *JAPANESE/PERUVIAN* The immaculate kitchen houses a space-age freezer full of fish bought at auction, and a rice polisher that ensures that every grain is perfect. The tasting menu starts with Morimoto-san's signature

Preparing desserts at the Mill House Restaurant.

Shave Ice: Sweet Hawaiian Snow

David and Ululani Yamashiro are near-religious about shave ice. At multiple shops around Maui under the name **Ululani's Hawaiian Shave Ice,** these wizards take the uniquely Hawaiian dessert to new heights. Ice is shaved to feather lightness and doused with your choice of syrup—any three flavors from calamansi lime to lychee to red velvet cake. David makes his own gourmet syrups with local fruit purees and a dash of cane sugar. Add a "snowcap" of sweetened condensed milk, and the resulting confection tastes like the fluffiest, most flavorful ice cream ever. Locals order theirs with chewy mochi morsels, sweet adzuki beans at the bottom, or tart *li hing mui* powder sprinkled on top. All locations are open daily. (Lahaina: 790 Front St., 10:30am–9pm; Ka'anapali: 200 Nohea Kai Dr. [in Hyatt Regency], 10am–5:30pm; Wailuku: 50 Maui Lani Pkwy, Unit E1 [in Safeway center], 10:30am–6pm; Kahului: 333 Dairy Rd., 10:30am–6pm; Kihei: 61 S. Kihei Rd., 10:30am–6:30pm, Pa'ia: 115 Hana Hwy. at Baldwin Ave. (10:30am–8pm; www.ululanisshave ice.com; ☎ 360/606-2745)

appetizer, the toro tartare. Balanced on ice, it's edible artwork. *Andaz Maui, 3550 Wailea Alanui Dr. maui.andaz.hyatt.com. ☎ 808/573-1234. Entrees $16–$150. AE, DC, DISC, MC, V. Lunch, dinner daily. Map p 125.*

★★ kids Nalu's South Shore Grill KIHEI *AMERICAN* Açai bowls for breakfast, Cubano sandwiches for lunch, burgers on brioche buns for dinner, and malasadas for dessert—this cheerful indoor/outdoor eatery has something delicious for everyone. *Azeka Shopping Center, 1280 S. Kihei Rd. nalusmaui.com. ☎ 808/891-8650. Entrees $10–$13 breakfast, $9–$18 lunch & dinner. Breakfast, lunch & dinner daily. AE, DISC, MC, V. Map p 125.*

★★ kids Pa'ia Fish Market KIHEI, LAHAINA, PA'IA *SEAFOOD* A fish sandwich with a giant slab of perfectly grilled 'ahi, opah, or 'opakapaka laid out on a bun with coleslaw and grated cheese is extra satisfying after a briny day at the beach. Also yummy: fish tacos. *www.paiafishmarket.com; 1913 S. Kihei Rd., Kihei. ☎ 808/874-8888, map p 125; 632 Front St., Lahaina, ☎ 808/662-3456, map p 124; 110 Hana Hwy., Pa'ia, ☎ 808/579-3111, map p 123. Entrees $9–$22. AE, DISC, MC, V. Lunch & dinner daily.*

kids Peggy Sue's KIHEI *AMERICAN* This 1950s-style diner has oodles of charm, with old-fashioned soda-shop stools and jukeboxes on every Formica table. You'll find shakes and floats, along with burgers, fries, and kids' meals for just $6.50. *Azeka Place II, 1279 S. Kihei Rd. ☎ 808/875-8944. Entrees $12–$16. AE, DISC, MC, V. Lunch & dinner daily. Map p 125.*

★ The Preserve Kitchen & Bar HANA *HAWAI'I REGIONAL/ AMERICAN* This ingredient-driven menu (fresh fish caught by local fishermen, produce grown by nearby farmers, and fruits in season) is served in a large dining

Sushi rolls at Sansei.

room with a view of Kau'iki Hill. *5031 Hana Hwy. ☎ 808/248-8212. Entrees $15–$45. AE, DISC, MC, V. Breakfast, lunch & dinner daily. Map p 123.*

★★ **Roy's Ka'anapali** LAHAINA *HAWAI'I REGIONAL* There's no ocean view here, but the food makes up for it. The short ribs are stellar and the "canoe for two" appetizer is fun to share. For dessert, two words: chocolate soufflé. *Ka'anapali Golf Course, 2290 Ka'anapali Pkwy. www.royyamaguchi.com. ☎ 808/669-6999. Entrees $8–$24 breakfast, $17–$22 lunch, $31–$69 dinner. AE, DC, DISC, MC, V. Breakfast, lunch & dinner daily. Map p 124.*

★★ **Sansei Seafood Restaurant & Sushi Bar** KAPALUA & KIHEI *SUSHI, PACIFIC RIM* With its creative take on sushi (foie gras nigiri and "Pink Cadillac" rolls wrapped in pink rice paper), Sansei's menu scores higher with adventurous diners than with purists. The Dungeness crab ramen is outstanding, as are the early bird specials—50% off before 6pm. *600 Office Rd., Kapalua. ☎ 808/669-6286. Map p 123. Kihei Town Center, 1881 S. Kihei Rd., Kihei. ☎ 808/879-0004. Map p 125. www.sanseihawaii.com. Entrees $16–$48. AE, DISC, MC, V. Dinner daily.*

★★★ **Tin Roof** KAHULUI *HAWAI'I REGIONAL/FILIPINO* *Top Chef* star Sheldon Simeon serves top-quality, extra-flavorful local dishes at this hole-in-the-wall lunch spot. Try the addictive mochiko chicken with a side of rice, noodles, or kale salad. No seating. *360 Papa Place. www.tinroofmaui.com. ☎ 808/868-0753. Entrees $6–$14. AE, DC, DISC, MC, V. Lunch daily. Map p 123.*

★★ kids **T. Komoda Store and Bakery** MAKAWAO *BAKERY* Get here early before this century-old institution's famous stick doughnuts and cream puffs ($1–$2) sell out; also check out the delicious pies and chocolate cake ($8–$12). *3674 Baldwin Ave. ☎ 808/572-7261. No credit cards. Map p 123. Closed Wed & Sun.*

9 The Best Nightlife & Performing Arts

Nightlife & Performing Arts Best Bets

Best **Cocktails**
★★ Monkeypod Kitchen, *10 Wailea Gateway Place, Wailea, and Whalers Village, 2434 Ka'anapali Pkwy., Ka'anapali (p 138)*

Best **Concerts**
★★★ Maui Arts & Cultural Center, *1 Cameron Way, Kahului (p 138)*

Best **Dance Floor**
★★ Casanova, *1188 Makawao Ave. , Makawao (p 137)*

Best **Place to Drink with Locals**
★★ Maui Brewing Company, *605 Lipoa Pkwy., Kihei (p 138)*

Best **Karaoke**
★★ Sansei Seafood Restaurant & Sushi Bar, *1881 S. Kihei Rd., Kihei, and 600 Office Rd., Kapalua (p 140)*

Best **Hawaiian Music**
★★★ Masters of Hawaiian Music Slack Key Guitar Series, *Napili Kai Beach Resort (p 139)*

Best **Hotel Lounge**
★★ Four Seasons Lobby Lounge, *Four Seasons Resort Maui at Wailea (p 137)*

Best **Local Brews**
★★ Maui Brewing Company, *605 Lipoa Pkwy., Kihei and 4405 Honoapi'ilani Hwy., Kahana (p 138)*

Best **Lu'au**
★★★ Old Lahaina Lu'au, *1251 Front St. (p 140)*

Best **Movies Under the Stars**
★★★ Maui Film Festival, *Wailea Golf Course (p 163)*

Sunset Cocktails

For a rocking good time, climb aboard the Pacific Whale Foundation's Friday night **Island Rhythms Sunset Cocktail Cruise ★★★** (www.pacificwhale.org; ☎ 808/249-8811). Local reggae star Marty Dread gets everybody up and dancing on the deck of the boat. During whale season, even the humpbacks may swim over to show their appreciation for his serenades. Enjoy hearty appetizers and mixed cocktails while watching the sun sink into the liquid horizon. Book online for 10% discount off regular prices, $85 adults and $45 children ages 3 to 12. Board at Ma'alaea Harbor.

Landlubbers can head to the rooftop at **Fleetwood's on Front St.,** 744 Front St., Lahaina (www.fleetwoodsonfrontst.com; ☎ 808/669-6425), where you can often catch local rock stars jamming with star owner Mick Fleetwood and his friends. If you're looking for a swank cocktail with entertainment (jazz, fine hula, etc.), visit the **Four Seasons Lobby Lounge,** 3900 Wailea Alanui Dr., Wailea (www.fourseasons.com/maui; ☎ 808/874-8000) or the **Luana Lounge** at the Fairmont Kea Lani, 4100 Wailea Alanui Dr., Wailea (www.fairmont.com/kea-lani-maui/dining/luana; ☎ 808/875-4100).

Previous page: Enjoy movies under the stars at the Maui Film Festival.

Central & South Maui Nightlife

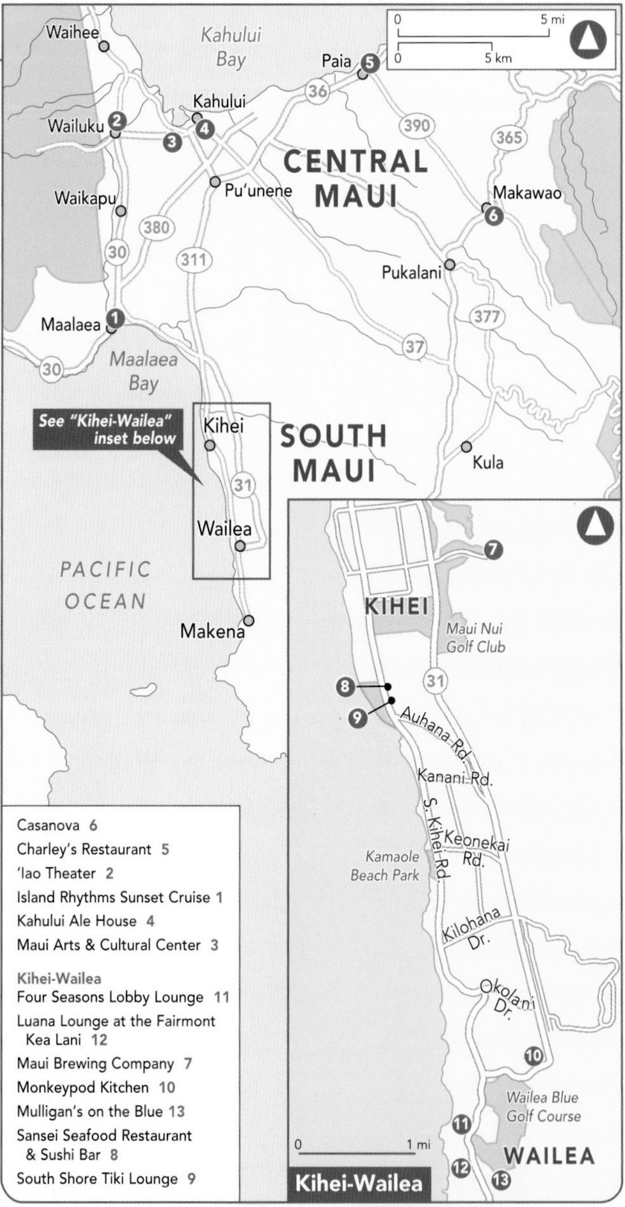

Casanova 6
Charley's Restaurant 5
'Iao Theater 2
Island Rhythms Sunset Cruise 1
Kahului Ale House 4
Maui Arts & Cultural Center 3

Kihei-Wailea
Four Seasons Lobby Lounge 11
Luana Lounge at the Fairmont Kea Lani 12
Maui Brewing Company 7
Monkeypod Kitchen 10
Mulligan's on the Blue 13
Sansei Seafood Restaurant & Sushi Bar 8
South Shore Tiki Lounge 9

Lahaina & Ka'anapali Nightlife

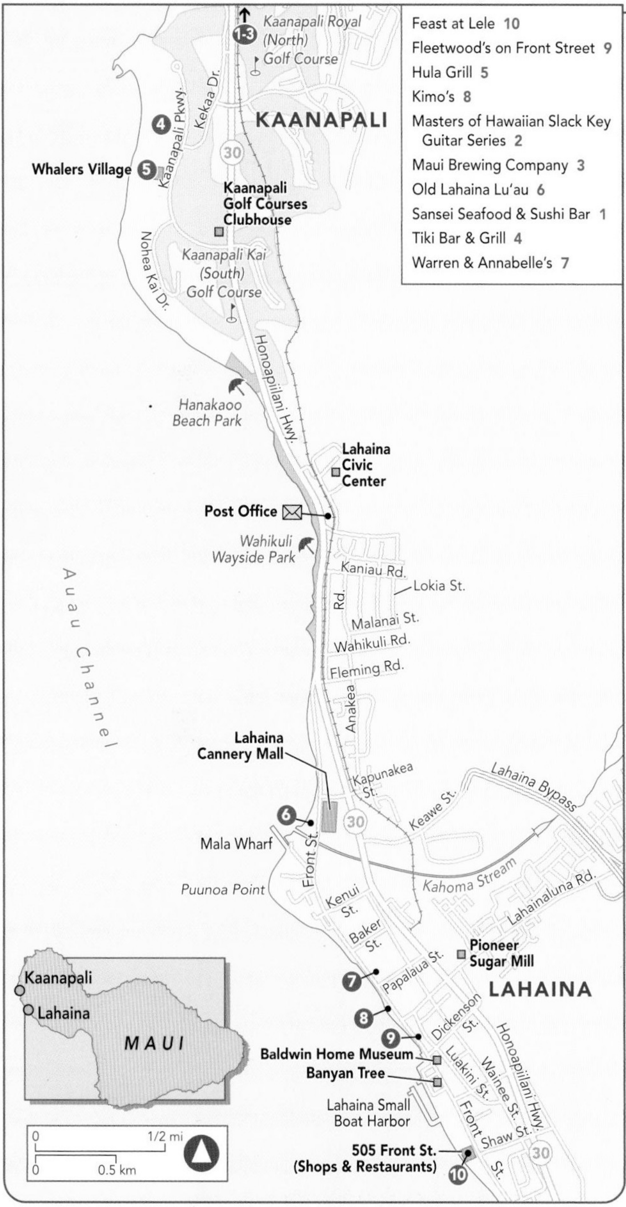

Maui Nightlife A to Z

Bars & Cocktail Lounges

★★ Casanova MAKAWAO Expect good blues, rock 'n' roll, reggae, jazz, and Hawaiian music from top local and visiting performers Friday and Saturday nights and Sunday afternoons; DJs inspire dancing on Wednesday nights. *1188 Makawao Ave. www.casanovamaui.com. ☎ 808/572-0220. Map p 135.*

★ Charley's Restaurant PA'IA This local pub features an eclectic selection of music, from country and western (Willie Nelson and son Lukas occasionally sit in) to fusion/reggae to rock 'n' roll, Tuesday through Saturday nights. *142 Hana Hwy. www.charleysmaui.com. ☎ 808/579-8085. Map p 135.*

★★ Four Seasons Lobby Lounge WAILEA For a quiet evening with gentle jazz or soft Hawaiian music, sink into the plush furniture and order an exotic drink. Nightly live music from 5:30 to 7:30pm and 8:30 to 11:30pm. *Four Seasons Resort Maui at Wailea, 3900 Wailea Alanui Dr. ☎ 808/874-8000. Map p 135.*

The oceanfront Hula Grill.

★ Hula Grill KA'ANAPALI At the oceanfront Hula Grill's Barefoot Bar, live music starts at 2pm most days (11am on Aloha Friday) and goes until 9pm, with happy hour starting at 2:30pm daily. *Whalers Village, 2435 Ka'anapali Pkwy. www.hulagrill.com. ☎ 808/667-6636. Map p 136.*

★ Kahului Ale House KAHULUI A lively sports bar with multiple taps

Sample the local beers at Maui Brewing Company.

and TVs, it also offers live music most nights. *355 E. Kamehameha Ave. ☎ 808/877-9001. Map p 135.*

★ **Kimo's** LAHAINA For the sweet sounds of Hawaiian music, check online to see who's on for the night, typically 7:30 to 9:30pm. *845 Front St. www.kimosmaui.com. ☎ 808/661-4811. Map p 136.*

★★ **Luana Lounge** WAILEA Catch the sunset from this swank lobby bar at the Fairmont Kea Lani, with live entertainment from 5 to 7pm daily and a second show 7 to 10pm Friday and Saturday. *Fairmont Kea Lani, 4100 Wailea Alanui Dr. www.fairmont.com/kea-lani-maui/dining/luana. ☎ 808/875-4100. Map p 135.*

★★ **Maui Brewing Company** KIHEI, KAHANA Sample a variety of local brews at the Kihei brewery and tasting room, which has daily live entertainment, or the Kahana brewpub. Favorites include the tasty Coconut Hiwa porter, Bikini Blonde lager, and numerous seasonal beers. *605 Lipoa Pwy., Kihei. www.mauibrewingco.com. ☎ 808/201-2337, and Kahana Gateway Center, 4405 Honoapi'ilani Hwy., Kahana. ☎ 808/669-3474. Map p 136.*

★★ **Monkeypod Kitchen** WAILEA, KA'ANAPALI The fancy signature Mai Tai with honey-lilikoi foam is a good enough reason to stop here for a beverage or two—and who can resist a libation with mezcal and honey called When Doves Cry? There's also live music daily starting at 1, 4, and 7pm. *10 Wailea Gateway Place, Wailea. www.monkeypodkitchen.com. ☎ 808/891-2322. Map p 135. Also Whalers Village, 2435 Ka'anapali Pkwy., Ka'anapali. ☎ 808/878-6763. Map p 112.*

★★ **Mulligan's On the Blue** WAILEA Toss back a pint of Guinness and catch Uncle Willie K or the Celtic Tigers at this rollicking Irish pub, with nightly live music Tuesday through Sunday (closed Monday). *100 Kaukahi St. www.mulligansontheblue.com. ☎ 808/874-1131. Map p 135.*

South Shore Tiki Lounge KIHEI This tiny, fun bar features live music daily from 4 to 6pm and dancing on the outdoor patio from 10pm to 1:30am. *1913 S. Kihei Rd. www.southshoretikilounge.com. ☎ 808/874-6444. Map p 135.*

Dance, Theater & Shows

'Iao Theater WAILUKU This beautifully restored Spanish Mission–style theater, which opened in 1928, is a great venue to catch a comedy show, Maui Chamber Orchestra concert, or live theater. *68 N. Market St. www.mauionstage.com. ☎ 808/242-6969. Map p 135.*

★★★ **Maui Arts & Cultural Center** KAHULUI Bonnie Raitt, Pearl Jam, Ziggy Marley, Tony Bennett, the American Indian Dance Theatre, the Maui Symphony Orchestra, and Jonny Lang have all performed here, in addition to the finest in local talent. The center has a visual arts gallery, an outdoor amphitheater, and two theaters. *1 Cameron Way. www.mauiarts.org. ☎ 808/242-7469. Ticket prices vary. Map p 135.*

★★ **Tiki Bar & Grill** KA'ANAPALI Nightly free Hawaiian music and hula shows, including *keiki* (children) dancers, are a great reason to order drinks or dinner at this poolside hotel bar. *Ka'anapali Beach Hotel, 2525 Ka'anapali Pkwy. www.kbhmaui.com. ☎ 808/667-0163. Map p 136.*

★★ **Warren & Annabelle's** LAHAINA This unusual magic/comedy cocktail show stars

A performance at the new Yokouchi Family pavilion at Maui Arts & Cultural Center.

illusionist Warren Gibson and "Annabelle," a ghost from the 1800s. She plays the grand piano as Warren dazzles with his sleight-of-hand magic. Guest performers also fill in throughout the year; shows (with seatings at 5 and 7:30pm) are open only to ages 21 and older. *900 Front St. www.warrenandannabelles.com. ☎ 808/667-6244. Tickets $69–$115. Map p 136.*

Hawaiian Music

★★★ Masters of Hawaiian Music Slack Key Show

NAPILI To see a side of Hawai'i that few visitors do, come to this Wednesday night production, where host George Kahumoku, Jr., presents a new slack key guitar master (see p 140) every week. George and his guests also "talk story" about old Hawai'i, music, and

Hula show at the Tiki Bar at the Ka'anapali Beach Hotel.

Hawaiian culture. *In Napili Kai Beach Resort, 5900 Lower Honoapi'ilani Rd, Napili. www.slackkeyshow.com. ☎ 808/669-3858. Tickets $38 show only, $95 with dinner. Map p 136.*

Karaoke

★★ Sansei Seafood Restaurant & Sushi Bar KIHEI, KAPALUA This super-popular Japanese restaurant hosts fun karaoke nights Thursday through Saturday 10pm to 1am. The bonus? Sushi and appetizers are half off. *1881 S. Kihei Rd., Kihei, ☎ 808/879-0004. Map p 135. Also 600 Office Rd., Kapalua. ☎ 808/669-6286. www.sanseihawaii.com. Map p 136.*

Lu'au

★★★ The Feast at Lele LAHAINA Already been to a lu'au? The nightly Feast at Lele takes it to the next level. Brought to you by the people behind Old Lahaina Lu'au (below), the Feast at Lele presents food and dances from Hawai'i, Tahiti, New Zealand, and Samoa in an outdoor seaside setting with private, candlelit tables. *505 Front St. www.feastatlele.com. ☎ 886/244-5353 or 808/667-5353. Set 5-course menu and show, $130 adults, $95 children 2–12; gratuity not included. AE, MC, V. Map p 136.*

★★★ kids Old Lahaina Lu'au LAHAINA This heartfelt, oceanfront show is the best traditional lu'au in the state. Festivities begin at sunset and feature Tahitian and Hawaiian entertainment, including ancient hula, modern hula, and an intelligent narrative on the dance's rocky survival into modern times. The food, served from an open-air thatched structure, is as much Pacific Rim as Hawaiian, and mixes in some well-known western favorites. *1251 Front St. www.oldlahainaluau.com. ☎ 808/667-1998. Tickets $120 adults, $75 children ages 3 to 12. Map p 136.* ●

Two-time Grammy-winning slack-key guitarist Keoki Kahumoku.

Slackers Welcome!

Unique to Hawai'i, slack key guitar, or *ki ho'alu* (which translates to "loosen the key") is a style achieved by loosening the guitar strings (or keys) to produce a very different sound when major chords are struck. Check it out at the **Masters of Hawaiian Music Slack Key Guitar Series** (p 139) or at the free **Ki Ho'alu Guitar Festival** held each June at the Maui Arts & Cultural Center (p 138).

10 The Best Lodging

Lodging Best Bets

Most **Romantic**
★★★ Hotel Wailea $$$ *555 Kaukahi St., Wailea (p 146)* and ★★★ Travaasa Hana $$$$$ *Hana Hwy., Hana (p 150)*

Most **Charming B&B**
★★ Old Wailuku Inn at Ulupono $$ *2199 Kaho'okele St., Wailuku (p 149)*

Most **Luxurious Condo**
★★ Ka'anapali Ali'i $$$$ *50 Nohea Kai Dr., Ka'anapali (p 147)* and ★★★ Montage Kapalua Bay $$$$$ *1 Bay Dr., Kapalua Dr. (p 148)*

Best **Family Condo**
★ Outrigger Maui Eldorado $$$ *2661 Keka'a Dr., Ka'anapali (p 149)*

Best **for Kids**
★★★ Four Seasons Resort Maui at Wailea $$$$$ *3900 Wailea Alanui Dr., Wailea (p 146)* and ★★ Wailea Beach Resort—Marriott, Maui $$$$ *3700 Wailea Alanui Dr., Wailea (p 150)*

Best **for Foodies**
★★★ Andaz Maui at Wailea $$$$$ *3550 Wailea Alanui Dr., Wailea (p 146)*

Best **View**
★★★ Napili Kai Beach Resort $$$ *5900 Honoapi'ilani Rd., Napili (p 148)*

Most **Serene Location**
★★ Hamoa Bay House & Bungalow $$ *Hana Hwy., btw. Haneo'o Loop Road, Hana (p 146)*

Best **Retreat**
★★ Lumeria Maui $$$$ *1813 Baldwin Ave., Makawao (p 148)*

Best **Club-Level Amenities**
★★★ Ritz-Carlton, Kapalua $$$$ *1 Ritz-Carlton Dr., Kapalua (p 149)* and ★★ Hyatt Regency Maui $$$$ *200 Nohea Kai Dr., Ka'anapali (p 147)*

Best **Service**
★★★ Four Seasons Resort Maui at Wailea $$$$$ *3900 Wailea Alanui Dr., Wailea (p 146)*

Best **Spa**
★★★ Montage Kapalua Bay $$$$$ *1 Bay Dr., Kapalua Dr. (p 148)*

Most **Hawaiian Resort**
★★ Ka'anapali Beach Hotel $$ *2525 Ka'anapali Pkwy., Ka'anapali (p 147)*

Best **Boutique Inn**
★★ The Inn at Mama's Fish House $$ *799 Poho Place, Ku'au (p 147)*

Most **Eco-Friendly**
★★★ The Fairmont Kea Lani Maui $$$$$ *4100 Wailea Alanui Dr., Wailea (p 146)*

Best **for Groups**
★★ Kapalua Villas $$–$$$$ *500 Office Rd., Kapalua (p 147)*

Best **Value on a Budget**
★ Nona Lani Cottages $$ *455 S. Kihei Rd., Kihei (p 148)* and ★★ Pineapple Inn Maui $$ *3170 Akala Dr., Kihei (p 149)*

Below: Aston at The Whaler on Ka'anapali Beach.
Previous page: The pool at Hotel Wailea.

Maui & Kapalua Lodging

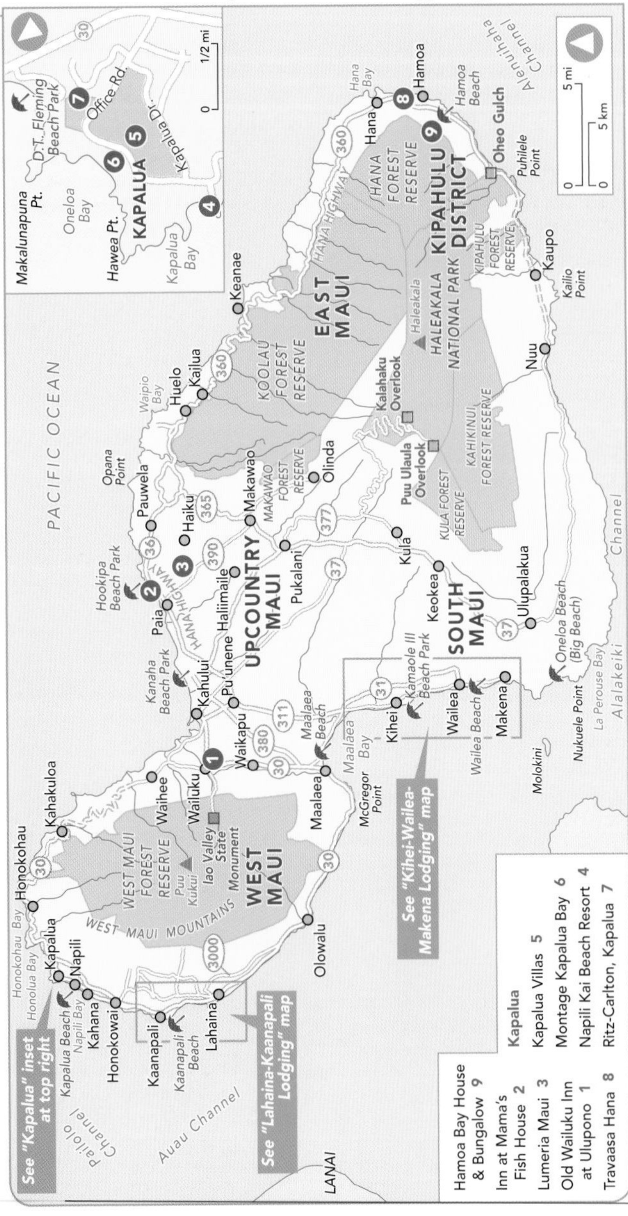
Hamoa Bay House & Bungalow 9
Inn at Mama's Fish House 2
Lumeria Maui 3
Old Wailuku Inn at Ulupono 1
Travaasa Hana 8
Kapalua
Kapalua Villas 5
Montage Kapalua Bay 6
Napili Kai Beach Resort 4
Ritz-Carlton, Kapalua 7
See "Kapalua" inset at top right
See "Lahaina-Kaanapali Lodging" map
See "Kihei-Wailea-Makena Lodging" map
PACIFIC OCEAN
WEST MAUI
UPCOUNTRY MAUI
SOUTH MAUI
EAST MAUI
KIPAHULU DISTRICT
HALEAKALA NATIONAL PARK
WEST MAUI MOUNTAINS
WEST MAUI FOREST RESERVE
KOOLAU FOREST RESERVE
MAKAWAO FOREST RESERVE
KULA FOREST RESERVE
KAHIKINUI FOREST RESERVE
HANA FOREST RESERVE
KIPAHULU FOREST RESERVE
HANA HIGHWAY
Puu Kukui
Iao Valley State Monument
Haleakala
Kalahaku Overlook
Puu Ulaula Overlook
Oheo Gulch
Honokohau
Kahakuloa
Kapalua
Napili
Kahana
Honokowai
Kaanapali
Lahaina
Olowalu
Maalaea
McGregor Point
Wailuku
Waihee
Waikapu
Kahului
Puunene
Paia
Haiku
Pauwela
Makawao
Haliimaile
Pukalani
Olinda
Kula
Keokea
Ulupalakua
Kihei
Wailea
Makena
Huelo
Kailua
Keanae
Hana
Hamoa
Kaupo
Nuu
Kaupo
Kailio Point
Puhilele Point
Hamoa Beach
Hana Bay
Alenuihaha Channel
Alalakeiki Channel
Auau Channel
Pailolo Channel
LANAI
Molokini
Nukuele Point
La Perouse Bay
Oneloa Beach (Big Beach)
Kamaole III Beach Park
Wailea Beach
Maalaea Bay
Maalaea Beach
Kanaha Beach Park
Hookipa Beach Park
Opana Point
Waipio Bay
Honokohau Bay
Honolua Bay
Napili Bay
Kapalua Beach
Kaanapali Beach
Makalunapuna Pt.
D.T. Fleming Beach Park
Oneloa Bay
Hawea Pt.
KAPALUA
Kapalua Bay
Office Rd.
Kapalua Dr.
1/2 mi
5 mi
5 km

Lahaina & Ka'anapali Lodging

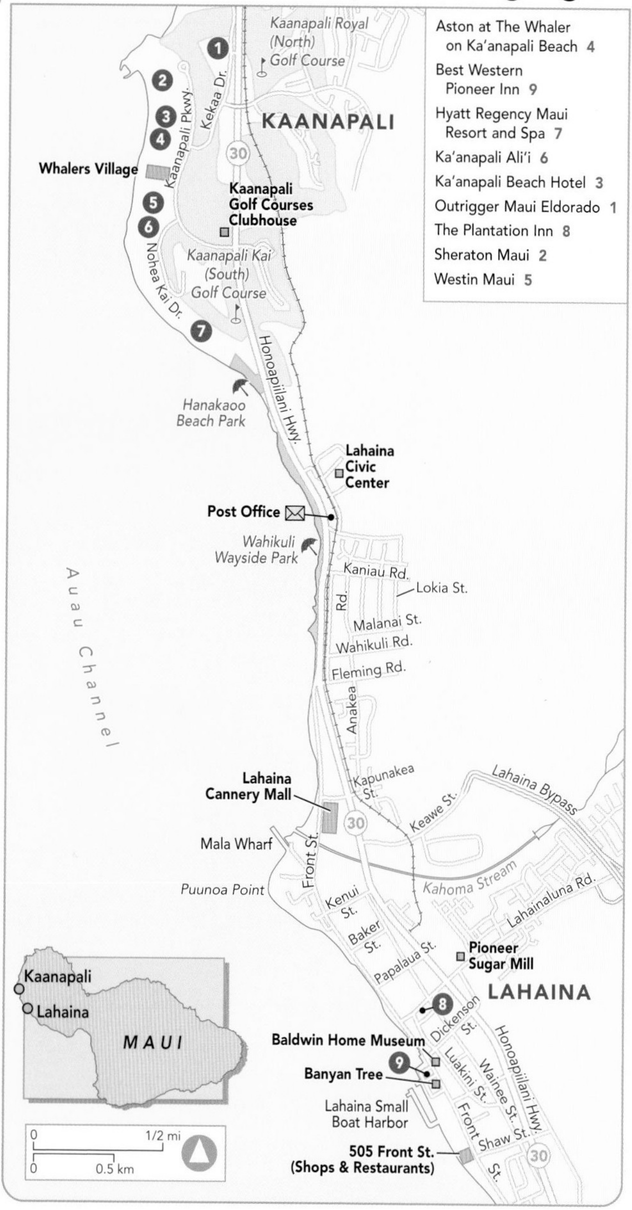
Aston at The Whaler on Ka'anapali Beach 4
Best Western Pioneer Inn 9
Hyatt Regency Maui Resort and Spa 7
Ka'anapali Ali'i 6
Ka'anapali Beach Hotel 3
Outrigger Maui Eldorado 1
The Plantation Inn 8
Sheraton Maui 2
Westin Maui 5
Kaanapali Royal (North) Golf Course
KAANAPALI
Kekaa Dr.
Kaanapali Pkwy.
Whalers Village
Kaanapali Golf Courses Clubhouse
Kaanapali Kai (South) Golf Course
Nohea Kai Dr.
Honoapiilani Hwy.
Hanakaoo Beach Park
Lahaina Civic Center
Post Office
Wahikuli Wayside Park
Kaniau Rd.
Lokia St.
Malanai St.
Wahikuli Rd.
Fleming Rd.
Anakea Rd.
Auau Channel
Kapunakea St.
Lahaina Bypass
Keawe St.
Lahaina Cannery Mall
Mala Wharf
Front St.
Puunoa Point
Kahoma Stream
Lahainaluna Rd.
Kenui St.
Baker St.
Papalaua St.
Pioneer Sugar Mill
LAHAINA
Dickenson St.
Baldwin Home Museum
Banyan Tree
Luakini St.
Wainee St.
Lahaina Small Boat Harbor
Shaw St.
505 Front St. (Shops & Restaurants)
30
Kaanapali
Lahaina
MAUI
0
1/2 mi
0
0.5 km

Kihei/Wailea/Makena Lodging

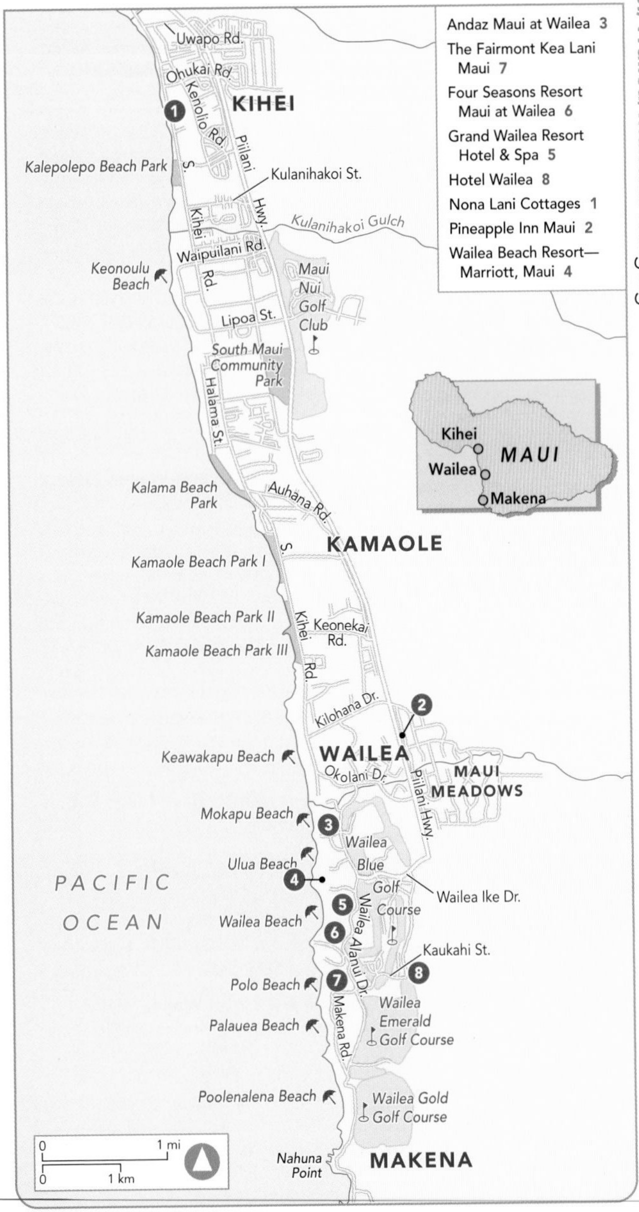

Maui Hotels A to Z

★★★ Andaz Maui at Wailea WAILEA Gourmands will love this sexy resort's two restaurants: Morimoto Maui (p 130) and Ka'ana Kitchen (p 128). The apothecary-style spa and tiered pools are also wonderful. *3550 Wailea Alanui Dr. maui.andaz.hyatt.com. ☎ 808/573-1234. 198 units. Doubles $409–$604; suites from $553; call for villa price. AE, DC, DISC, MC, V. Map p 145.*

★ Aston at The Whaler on Ka'anapali Beach KA'ANAPALI In the heart of Ka'anapali, right on the world-famous beach, lies this condo oasis of elegance, privacy, and luxury. *2481 Ka'anapali Pkwy. (next to Whalers Village). www.aquaaston.com. ☎ 888/671-5310 or 808/661-4861. 360 units. Studio $265–$359 studio; 1 bedroom (up to 4 guests) $339-$565; 2 bedroom (up to 6) $569–$1,079. Daily resort fee $20. Parking $12. AE, DC, DISC, MC, V. Map p 144.*

★ Best Western Pioneer Inn LAHAINA This turn-of-the-19th-century, two-story, plantation-style hotel overlooking Lahaina Harbor has been remodeled but kept small bathrooms. *658 Wharf St. (in front of Lahaina Pier). www.pioneerinnmaui.com. ☎ 800/457-5457 or 808/661-3636. 34 units. Doubles $197–$319. AE, DC, DISC, MC, V. Map p 144.*

★★★ kids The Fairmont Kea Lani Maui WAILEA You get your money's worth at this luxurious resort: a huge suite with kitchenette, entertainment center, bedroom, and large lanai facing Polo Beach. Villas are even more indulgent. *4100 Wailea Alanui Dr. www.fairmont.com/kealani. ☎ 800/257-7544 or 808/875-4100. 450 units. Doubles $560–$1,309. Villas from $1,218. Daily $40 resort fee. AE, DC, DISC, MC, V. Map p 145.*

★★★ kids Four Seasons Resort Maui at Wailea WAILEA Service at this stylish resort is unparalleled, and it's the most kid-friendly hotel on Maui—cookies and milk on arrival, complimentary baby gear, and a stellar kids camp. Adults get a chic infinity pool with swim-up bar and underwater music. *3900 Wailea Alanui Dr. www.fourseasons.com/maui. ☎ 800/311-0630 or 808/874-8000. 380 units. Doubles $655–$1,220; club floor doubles $1,640–$1,970; suites from $1,350. AE, DC, MC, V. Map p 145.*

★★ kids Grand Wailea Resort Hotel & Spa WAILEA This dazzling resort boasts Hawai'i's largest spa, and its most elaborate swimming pools with slides, waterfalls, rapids, a Tarzan swing, swim-up bar, even a hot tub atop an artificial volcano. *3850 Wailea Alanui Dr. www.grandwailea.com. ☎ 800/888-6100 or 808/875-1234. 780 units. Doubles $499–$969; Club floor from $939; suites from $1,339. Daily $40 resort fee AE, DC, DISC, MC, V. Map p 145.*

★★ Hamoa Bay House & Bungalow HANA Romance blooms in these gorgeous units, both with hot tubs, big lanai, and Balinese furnishings. Plus, you're close to Hamoa Beach. *Hana Hwy. www.hamoabay.com. ☎ 808/248-7884. 2 units. Doubles $285–$420. MC, V. Map p 143.*

★★★ Hotel Wailea WAILEA Secluded and serene, with a falcon's view of the Wailea coastline (and shuttle to the beach), this stylish, adults-only boutique hotel is a sexy honeymooners' paradise. *555 Kaukahi St. www.hotelwailea.com. ☎ 866/970-4167 or 808/874-0500. 72 units. Suites $529–$819; Daily $40*

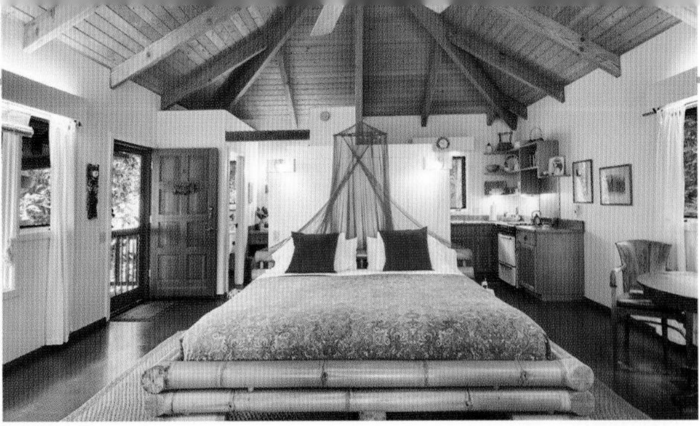

Bungalow room at Hamoa Bay.

resort fee. AE, DC, DISC, MC, V. Map p 145.

★★ kids Hyatt Regency Maui Resort and Spa KA'ANAPALI This palatial resort has a ½-acre (.2ha) outdoor pool with a lava tube slide, a cocktail bar under the falls, nine waterfalls, an Asian and Pacific art collection, and (try to top this) South African penguins in the lobby. *200 Nohea Kai Dr. maui.hyatt.com. ☎ 800/233-1234 or 808/661-1234. 806 units. Doubles $255–$551; Club level doubles $415–$641; suites from $555. Daily $32 resort fee. Parking $22. AE, DC, DISC, MC, V. Map p 144.*

★★ The Inn at Mama's Fish House KU'AU Nestled in a coconut grove on a secluded beach, these expertly decorated duplexes next to Mama's Fish House (p 129) exude the same South Pacific charm. *799 Poho Place (off the Hana Hwy., near Pa'ia). www.innatmamas.com. ☎ 800/860-4852 or 808/579-9764. 12 units. Double studio $275; 1-bedroom $300–$850; suites $425; 2-bedroom cottage $395–$850. AE, DISC, MC, V. Map p 143.*

★★ kids Ka'anapali Ali'i KA'ANAPALI These oceanfront condo units sit on 8 landscaped acres (3.2ha) right on Ka'anapali Beach, combining the amenities of a luxury hotel (yoga classes on the lawn, anyone?) with the convenience of a condominium. *50 Nohea Kai Dr. www.kaanapalialii.com. ☎ 866/664-6410 or 808/667-1400. 264 units. 1 bedroom $465–$695; 2 bedroom $680–$1,050. AE, DC, DISC, MC, V. Map p 144.*

★★ kids Ka'anapali Beach Hotel KA'ANAPALI Old Hawai'i customs reign at this modest beachfront hotel, with nightly Hawaiian hula and music and an extensive cultural program (learn to weave *lauhala*, string lei, throw a fish net). *2525 Ka'anapali Pkwy. www.kbhmaui.com. ☎ 800/262-8450 or 808/661-0011. 430 units. Doubles $205–$352; suites from $340. Parking $14. AE, DC, DISC, MC, V. Map p 144.*

★★ Kapalua Villas KAPALUA The stately townhouses dotting the

Stand up paddleboard (SUP) lessons at Ka'anapali Beach Hotel.

One of Plantation Inn's tropically themed guestrooms.

oceanfront cliffs and fairways of this idyllic coast are a (relative) bargain, especially for couples traveling together. *500 Office Rd. www.kapaluavillasmaui.com.* ☎ *800/367-2742 or 808/665-9170. 1 bedroom $225–$552; 2 bedroom $285–$425; 3-bedroom $395–$1,099. Daily $35 resort fee. Cleaning fee $250–$325. AE, DC, DISC, MC, V. Map p 143.*

★★ Lumeria Maui MAKAWAO If crystals, sacred artwork, daily yoga classes, and organic breakfasts are your jam, this is your spot, a lavishly converted women's college just above Maui's scenic North Shore. *1813 Baldwin Ave. www.lumeriamaui.com.* ☎ *808/579-8877. 25 units. Doubles $369–$539 (includes breakfast). Daily $25 resort fee. AE, MC, V. Map p 143.*

★★★ kids Montage Kapalua Bay KAPALUA The multiple pools and vast spa at this exclusive, low-density enclave of spacious luxury condos on 24 acres (9.7ha) never seem crowded. Views are dazzling and service is discreet and attentive, including at the beach. *1 Bay Dr. www.montagehotels.com.* ☎ *808/662-6200. 50 units. 1 bedroom $701–$1,495; 2 bedroom $998–$1,845; 3 bedroom $1,381–$2,425; 4 bedroom $2,401–$4,825. Daily $48 resort fee. Parking $30. AE, MC, V. Map p 143.*

★★★ kids Napili Kai Beach Resort NAPILI A secluded gold-sand beach, a weekly schedule full of entertainment and activities, units with full kitchens, and jaw-dropping views of Moloka'i and Lana'i make this vintage resort very popular. *5900 Honoapi'ilani Rd. (next to Kapalua Resort). www.napilikai.com.* ☎ *800/367-5030 or 808/669-6271. 162 units. Doubles from $335; studio double (sleeps 3–4) from $410; 1-bedroom suite from $690; 2-bedroom suite from $975; 3-bedroom suite from $1,155. AE, DISC, MC, V. Map p 143.*

★ Nona Lani Cottages KIHEI These vintage cottages, tucked among palm, fruit, and plumeria trees across the street from Sugar Beach, are a pretty sweet deal. Wi-Fi is spotty, though. *455 S. Kihei Rd. (just south of Hwy. 31). www.nonalanicottages.com.* ☎ *808/879-2497. 11 units. Double*

$183–$340. 2-night minimum. $40–$75 cleaning fee. DISC, MC, V. Map p 145.

★★ **Old Wailuku Inn at Ulupono** WAILUKU This lovingly restored 1924 former plantation manager's home offers a genuine old Hawai'i experience, plus a gourmet breakfast. *2199 Kaho'okele St. (at High St.). www.mauiinn.com. ☎ 800/305-4899 or 808/244-5897. 10 units. Doubles $185–$280. MC, V. Map p 143.*

★ kids **Outrigger Maui Eldorado** KA'ANAPALI These are great condos for families: spacious units, grassy play areas outside, safe swimming, and a beachfront with cabanas and barbecue area. *2661 Keka'a Dr. www.outrigger.com. ☎ 303/369-7777 or 808/661-0021. 204 units. Studio $145–$199; 1 bedroom $169–$389; 2 bedroom $299–$439. Daily $17 resort fee and $150–$250 cleaning fee. AE, DC, DISC, MC, V. Map p 144.*

★★ **Pineapple Inn Maui** KIHEI This charming inn offers impeccably decorated, soundproof rooms, a giant saltwater pool and Jacuzzi overlooking the ocean, and wallet-pleasing prices. *3170 Akala Dr. www.pineappleinnmaui.com. ☎ 877/212-MAUI (6284) or 808/298-4403. 5 units. Doubles $169–$219; cottage $235–$295. 3-night minimum for rooms, 6 for cottage. No credit cards. Map p 145.*

★★ **The Plantation Inn** LAHAINA This romantic, Victorian-style inn features period furniture and four-poster canopy beds. It's next door to one of Lahaina's best French restaurants, **Gerard's** (p 127), where guests get a discount. *174 Lahainaluna Rd. (1 block from Hwy. 30). www.theplantationinn.com. ☎ 800/433-6815 or 808/667-9225. 18 units. Doubles $175–$300. AE, DC, DISC, MC, V. Map p 144.*

★★★ kids **Ritz-Carlton, Kapalua** KAPALUA This elegant, art-centric enclave boasts a large, tiered pool and excellent dining options. Guests on the Club Floor also enjoy lavish food and drink in its superlative lounge. *1 Ritz-Carlton Dr. www.ritzcarlton.com. ☎ 800/262-8440 or 808/669-6200. 463 units. Doubles from $449; Club Floor from*

The Ritz-Carlton, Kapalua, has a multi-tiered swimming pool.

A bungalow at Travaasa Hana.

$1,045. Daily $35 resort fee. AE, DC, DISC, MC, V. Map p 143.

★★★ kids Sheraton Maui KA'ANAPALI The family suites are great for those traveling with kids: three beds, a sitting room with full-size couch, and two TVs (both equipped with Nintendo); plus fun activities onsite and nearby. Honeymooners enjoy the spa's couples treatments. *2605 Ka'anapali Pkwy. www.sheraton-maui.com. ☎ 866/716-8109 or 808/661-0031. 508 units. Doubles from $288; suites from $589. Daily $25 resort fee. Parking $22. AE, DC, DISC, MC, V. Map p 144.*

★★★ kids Travaasa Hana HANA This heavenly 66-acre resort wraps around Kau'iki Hill overlooking the sea. The bungalows are dreamy refuges stocked with homemade banana bread. No TVs here; instead listen to the crashing surf. *5031 Hana Hwy. www.travaasa.com/hana. ☎ 888/820-1043. 66 units. Doubles $575–$1,325. AE, DC, DISC, MC, V. Map p 143.*

★★ Wailea Beach Resort—Marriott, Maui WAILEA This meandering resort's infinity pools and fantasy kids pool are ideal spots to spend your days. Or hit neighboring Ulua Beach for A+ snorkeling. *3700 Wailea Alanui Dr. www.marriotthawaii.com. ☎ 808/879-1922. 547 units. Doubles from $451; suites from $659. Daily $35 resort fee. Parking $30. AE, DC, DISC, MC, V. Map p 145.*

★★ kids Westin Maui KA'ANAPALI Kids love the aquatic playground here, with slides, waterfalls, live flamingos, and black swans. Adults love the trademark Heavenly beds and the decked-out spa and fitness center. *2365 Ka'anapali Pkwy. www.westinmaui.com. ☎ 866/716-8112 or 808/667-2525. 759 units. Doubles $290–$689. Daily $30 resort fee. Parking $30. AE, DC, DISC, MC, V. Map p 144.*

11 The Best of Lana'i

The Best of Lana'i **in One Day**

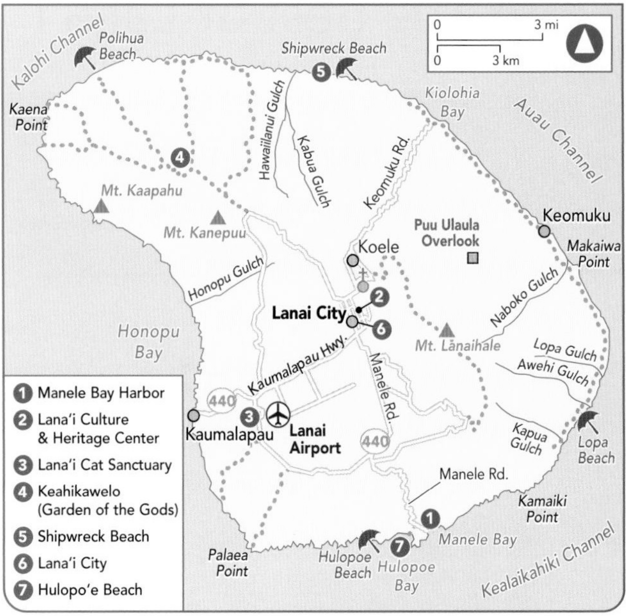

The smallest of the main Hawaiian Islands, Lana'i is now almost entirely owned by software tycoon Larry Ellison, but remains quiet and quaint with stunning beaches, ancient petroglyphs, a posh resort, and a unique cat sanctuary. It's possible to get an overview of the island in a single day if you catch the first ferry departing from Lahaina at 6:45am. You'll want to either a) book a tour with Rabaca's Limousine Service (see p 154) or b) rent a Jeep to access the island's off-road sites. The tour is the better bet, with friendly, informative drivers who know how to navigate the often washed-out roads. START: **Manele Bay Harbor. Trip length: 68 miles (109km).**

1 Manele Bay Harbor. To make the most of your day on Lana'i, take the 6:45am ferry from Lahaina Harbor. Arrive early enough in Lahaina to find all-day parking (check out side streets such as Waine'e). The ferry dock is at the north end of the harbor, next to the lighthouse. Once on board, look for dolphins, flying fish, and whales (in winter) as you travel across the channel. Rabaca's Limousine Service (p 154) will pick you up at the Manele harbor to start your tour or deliver you to pick up a rental Jeep (if available) in Lana'i City, a 20-minute trip.

2 ★★ Lana'i Culture & Heritage Center. One of your first

Previous page: Strolling on Hulopo'e Beach.

Garden of the Gods.

stops on Lana'i should be this tiny, well-curated museum in the heart of Lana'i City, where you can orient yourself to the island's cultural and natural history, and also get directions to the island's petroglyph fields. ⏱ *30 min. 730 Lana'i Ave. www.lanaichc.org.* ☎ *808/565-7177. Open weekdays 8:30am–3:30pm and Sat by appt.*

From the cultural center, it's 4.3 miles (6.9km) to Lanai Cat Sanctuary. Turn left on Lana'i Avenue, then right on Hwy. 440 (Kaumalapau Hwy.) and follow 3.6 miles (5.8km) to a left onto Kaupili Road. It's about a 10-minute drive.

3 ★★★ kids Lana'i Cat Sanctuary. This innovative, open-air shelter near the airport houses more than 600 friendly felines ready to interact with visitors, who have made it the island's most popular attraction. ⏱ *30 min. 1 Kaupili Rd. www.lanaicatsanctuary.org.* ☎ *808/565-7177. Open daily 10am–3pm.*

4 ★★★ kids Keahiakawelo (Garden of the Gods). Boulders strewn by volcanic forces have been sculpted by the elements into varying shapes and colors—brilliant reds, oranges, ochers, and yellows—in this rugged, beautiful landscape. Modern visitors nicknamed this otherworldly place "the Garden of the Gods," but its

Shipwreck Beach is named for this rusting offshore hulk.

Getting to & Around Lana'i

To fly to Lana'i, you'll have to make a connection on O'ahu or Maui, where you catch a puddle-jumper for the 25-minute flight. **'Ohana by Hawaiian** (www.hawaiianairlines.com; ☎ 800/367-5320) flies 48-seat turboprops five times daily to Lana'i from Honolulu; **Mokulele Airlines** (www.mokuleleairlines.com; ☎ 866/260-7070) flies twice daily from Maui's main airport in Kahului on nine-passenger Cessnas.

The **Expeditions Lahaina/Lana'i Passenger Ferry** (go-lanai.com; ☎ 800/695-2624) runs five times a day, 365 days a year, between Lahaina, Maui, and the Manele Small Boat Harbor on Lana'i. The 9-mile channel crossing takes 45 minutes to an hour, depending on sea conditions. One-way tickets cost $30 adults and $20 children. Reservations are strongly recommended.

The island has very little infrastructure, so plan your transportation in advance. **Rabaca's Limousine Service** (☎ 808/565-6670) will retrieve you from the airport or harbor for $10 per person and also offers 3½-hour tours ($75 per person). Guests heading to the **Four Seasons Resort Lanai** (p 159) can hire a luxury shuttle ($22 per person from the harbor, $49 from the airport) or a private SUV ($85 per vehicle, limit four passengers); all-day Jeep rentals for guests are $150–$225. If you plan to explore the island's uninhabited areas (which I highly recommend), you'll need a four-wheel-drive (4WD) vehicle for at least a day. Book a tour and let Rabaca's do the driving, or contact **Lanai Car Rental** (www.lanaicarrental.com; ☎ 800/565-3100) to rent a Jeep Wrangler Sahara. Reserve far in advance; cars are in short supply.

Hawaiian name, *Ke-ahi-a-Kawelo*, means "the fire of Kawelo," referring to a legendary sorcerers' battle.

Return to Hwy. 430 (Keomuku Hwy.) and turn left. Continue down toward the ocean. At the junction, turn left and drive to the end of the road. Allow 1 hour to drive these 20 miles (32km) on winding, unimproved roads.

5 ★★ kids Shipwreck Beach. This 8-mile-long (13km) windswept strand on Lana'i's northeastern shore is named for the rusty ship "Liberty" stuck on the coral reef. The swimming isn't great here, nor is the snorkeling (too murky), but this is the best place in Hawai'i to beachcomb. Strong currents yield all sorts of flotsam, from glass fishing floats and paper nautilus shells to lots of junk. At the end of the road, a trail leads about 200 yards inland to the **Kukui Point petroglyphs;** follow the stacked rock *ahu* (altars) to the large boulders. Respect this historic site by not altering it or touching the petroglyphs.

It takes about 45 minutes to retrace your route back up Hwy. 430 into Lana'i City.

There's an App for That

The Lana'i Culture & Heritage Center helped create the Lana'i Guide, a GPS-enabled app that directs you to historic sites, replete with old photos, aerial videos, and chants. It's free on iTunes.

6 ★★ kids Lana'i City. This quaint old-fashioned town centered on Dole Square sits at 1,645 feet (501m) above sea level, perched amid the Cook Island pines. Built in 1924, the former pineapple plantation village is a tidy grid of tin-roofed cottages in bright pastels, with tropical fruit gardens. The charming village square has two general stores, a handful of restaurants and boutiques, and a movie theater. Turn in your rental or end your Rabaca tour here, then give yourself an hour or two to check out the shops before catching a Rabaca's shuttle down to Hulopo'e Beach.

Colorful signpost in quaint Lana'i City.

Hulopo'e Beach tide pools.

Follow Eighth Avenue to Fraser Avenue and turn left. Go right at Hwy. 440 (Kaumalapau Hwy.). Turn left at Manele Road, staying on Hwy. 440 to the end at Hulupo'e Beach Park. Allow 30 minutes for the 11-mile (18km) trip.

7 ★★★ kids Hulopo'e Beach. This wide beach is one of the best in all of Hawai'i. Not only is it a terrific snorkeling spot (especially along the rocks to your left as you face the ocean), but it is a marine preserve, where fishing and collecting marine critters is forbidden. Boats cannot anchor in the bay, so you have the entire ocean to yourself, not including the frequent visits by dolphins. For a bit of glamour, walk up to the **Four Seasons Resort Lanai** (p 159) for a cocktail.

Take the 5-minute walk from Hulopo'e Beach Park to Manele Bay to catch the last ferry back to Lahaina at 6:45pm.

The Best of Lana'i in Three Days

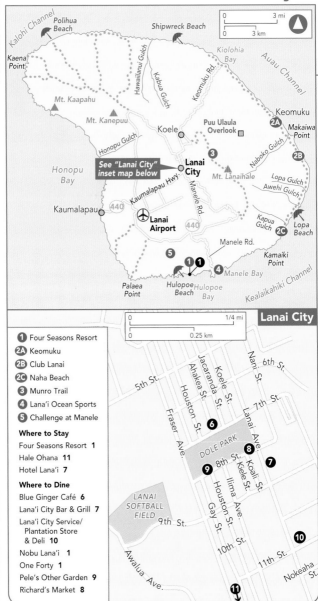

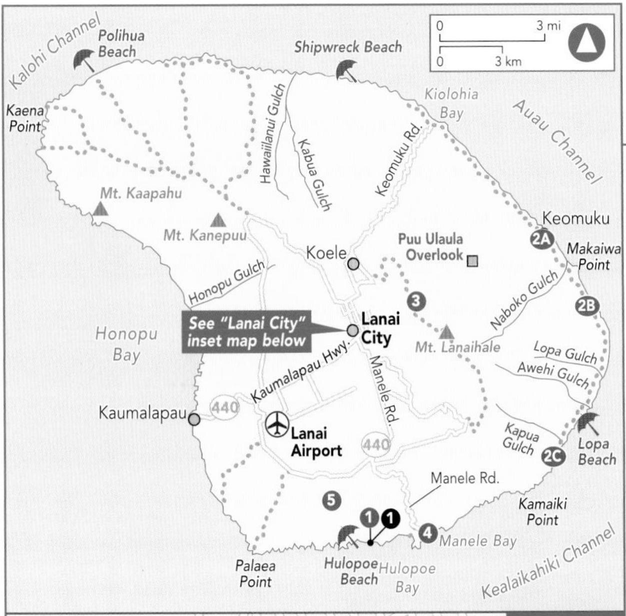

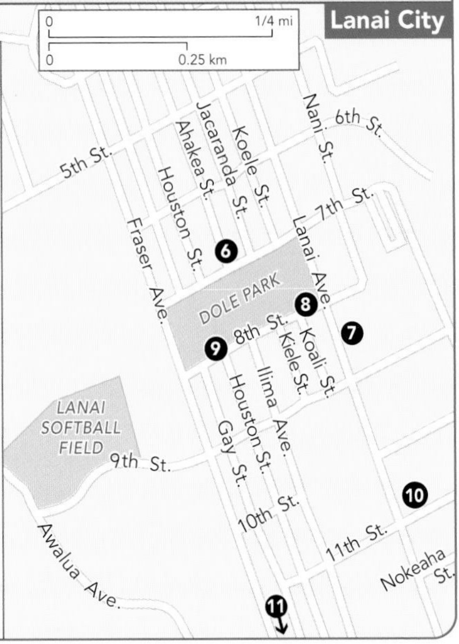

1 Four Seasons Resort
2A Keomuku
2B Club Lanai
2C Naha Beach
3 Munro Trail
4 Lana'i Ocean Sports
5 Challenge at Manele

Where to Stay

Four Seasons Resort **1**
Hale Ohana **11**
Hotel Lana'i **7**

Where to Dine

Blue Ginger Café **6**
Lana'i City Bar & Grill **7**
Lana'i City Service/ Plantation Store & Deli **10**
Nobu Lana'i **1**
One Forty **1**
Pele's Other Garden **9**
Richard's Market **8**

Three days is ideal for Lana'i, giving you enough time to explore the island, relax on the beach, and sample one of many outdoorsy activities, such as scuba diving, golfing, clay shooting, hiking, or horseback riding. Spend your first day scouting out the sights outlined in the 1-day tour on p 152. On your following days, depending on the weather, choose any of the five options described below. START: **Lana'i City or at your Lana'i lodgings.**

The beach at the Four Seasons Resort Lanai offers good snorkeling in Hulopo'e Bay.

1 ★★★ kids Four Seasons Resort Lanai and **Hulopo'e Beach.** Indulge in luxury at the Four Seasons and Hulopo'e Beach. Even if you're not a guest at the resort, you can have a resplendent brunch at **One Forty** (p 160) of made-to-order omelets, smoothies, and malasadas. Gaze out at the bay where dolphins and whales often come to rest and play. Migrate down to the beach. Watch the kids play in the surf, snorkel at the edges of the bay, and take a relaxing stroll up to **Pu'u Pehe** (Sweetheart Rock). If you're feeling energetic in the afternoon, book a horseback ride or spin around the clay-shooting course at the Four Seasons' **Island Adventure Center** (see below). For dinner, dress up and wander over to **Nobu Lana'i** (p 160) for the exquisite Japanese cuisine of Chef Nobu Matsuhisa, and a view of the sun sinking into the ocean.

Activity Central

The Island Adventure Center (1 Manele Bay Rd., Lana'i City; www.fourseasons.com/lanai; ☎ 808/565-2072) at the Four Seasons Resort Lanai offers fun activities for guests and non-guests alike. Book a horseback ride through the forest, a spin around the 14-station clay-shooting course, an archery lesson, or an ATV ride.

From Lana'i City, follow Keomoku Road (Hwy. 430) 8 miles to the coast. Here the road turns to dirt, mud, or sand; proceed with caution. Head right past beaches and old villages to the road's end. Return the way you came.

2 The East Side of the Island. If it hasn't rained recently, rent a 4×4 vehicle and explore Lana'i's untamed east side. Bring snacks and extra water; there are no facilities out here and cell service is scarce.

Explore the east side's string of empty beaches and abandoned villages, including **2A Keomoku ★★,** which is about 5¾ miles down the dirt road along the shore. This former ranching and fishing community of 2,000 was home to the first non-Hawaiian settlement on Lana'i. It's been a ghost town since the mid-1950s, after droughts killed off the Maunalei Sugar Company.

Check out **Ka Lanakila** ★, the village's sweetly restored church that dates back to 1903, and investigate the driftwood beach forts.

Continue another 2 miles south to the deserted remains of 2B **Club Lanai** ★★. A lonely pier stretches into the Pacific from a golden-sand beach populated by coconut palms, a few gazebos, and an empty bar floating in a lagoon. You can pretend you're on the set of *Gilligan's Island* here. The road ends at 2C **Naha Beach** ★ with its ancient fishponds. Return the way you came.

From Lana'i City, take Keomoku Rd. (Hwy. 430) about 2.3 miles (3.7km) to the Lana'i Cemetery, where you'll find the Munro Trail trailhead.

3 ★★ **Munro Trail.** Fit and ambitious hikers can spend the day (plan on at least 7 hours) climbing to the top of Lana'ihale on the well-marked Munro Trail. This tough, 11-mile (18km) round-trip, uphill climb through groves of Norfolk pines is a lung buster, but if you reach the top, you'll be rewarded with a breathtaking view of Kaho'olawe, Maui, Hawai'i Island, and Molokini's tiny crescent. The trail follows Lana'i's ancient caldera rim, ending up at the island's highest point, Lana'ihale. Go in the morning for the best visibility. After 4 miles (6.4km), you'll get a view of Lana'i City. If you're tired, you can retrace your steps from here, otherwise, continue the last 1.25 miles (2km) to the top. Die-hards can head down Lana'i's steep south-crater rim to join the highway to Manele Bay. Soak in a hot tub on your return.

From Lana'i City take the Kaumalapau Hwy. 440 to the end of the road at Manele Harbor. Allow 30–35 min. for the 11-mile/18km trip.

4 ★★★ **Sail-Snorkel Excursion.** To go out on (or into) the water, contact **Lana'i Ocean Sports** (www.lanaioceansports.com; ☎ 808/866-8256) about their sailing-snorkeling, whale-watching, or scuba trips from Manele Boat Harbor. Diving is particularly magical at two sites: Cathedrals I and II.

From Manele Harbor, take Hulupo'e Dr. (Hwy. 440) 1.2 miles/1.9km and turn left; golf course entrance is ahead.

5 ★★★ **Golf at the Challenge at Manele.** Golfers can test their mettle at this target-style, desert-links course designed by Jack Nicklaus, one of the toughest and most beautiful golf courses in the state. Next to the **Four Seasons Resort Lanai** (p 156), the Challenge course charges greens fees of $495 ($350 for resort guests.) To reserve a tee time, call ☎ 808/565-2222.

Hike to Lana'i's highest point on the Munro Trail.

Where to Stay & Eat

Fun in the sun at the Four Seasons.

Hotels

★★★ kids Four Seasons Resort Lanai MANELE Every inch of this opulent oasis reflects the latest in tech-savvy luxury, from the wristband room keys to the Toto toilets. Service is impeccable: The concierge texts you when dolphins or whales appear in the bay. Beach attendants set up umbrellas in the sand for you, spritz you with Evian, and deliver smoothie samples. The complimentary children's program is outstanding. *1 Manele Bay Rd. www.fourseasons.com/lanai. ☎ 800/321-4666 or 808/565-2000. 236 units. Doubles from $875, suites from $2,000. AE, DC, MC, V. Map p 156.*

★★ kids Hale 'Ohana LANA'I CITY This smartly renovated two bedroom, 1½-bath cottage on a quiet side street features bamboo floors, modern bathrooms and kitchen appliances, flatscreen TVs, and Wi-Fi, in a quiet neighborhood. *1344 Fraser Ave. www.vrbo.com/268485ha. ☎ 808/565-6961. Cottage $250 a night for up to 5 people. Cleaning fee $100. AE, DC, MC, V. Map p 156.*

★★ Hotel Lana'i LANA'I CITY This clapboard plantation-era relic overlooking Dole Park underwent a major upgrade in 2018, adding Toto toilets, air-conditioning, and flatscreen TVs while maintaining its quaint character. *828 Lana'i Ave. www.hotellanai.com. ☎ 800/795-7211 or 808/565-7211. 10 units. Doubles $250–$350 include continental breakfast. AE, MC, V. Map p 156.*

Restaurants

Blue Ginger Café LANA'I CITY *COFFEE SHOP* This cafe is a casual, inexpensive alternative to fancy hotel restaurants. Try the burgers on homemade buns. *409 7th St. (at Ilima St.). www.bluegingercafelanai.com. ☎ 808/565-6363. Breakfast and lunch items under $17;*

dinner entrees under $18. Cash only. Breakfast, lunch & dinner Thurs–Mon; breakfast & lunch Tues–Wed. Map p 156.

★ kids Lana'i City Bar & Grill LANA'I CITY *AMERICAN* Local venison is the star at this smart yet cozy restaurant in the heart of town. Bring a jacket if you want to sit outside by the fire pits and soak up the friendly ambience and fantastic live music. *In Hotel Lana'i, 828 Lana'i Ave. www.lanaicitybarandgrille.com. ☎ 808/565-7211. Entrees $18–$38. MC, V. Dinner Wed–Sun. Map p 156.*

★ Lana'i City Service/Plantation Store & Deli LANA'I CITY *DELI* The island's sole gas station includes a deli with tasty sandwiches and a few hot items. It's more gourmet than you might expect: Grilled cheese features Boursin, Swiss, provolone, and avocado, while the crab cake hoagie comes with wasabi black pepper mayo. Check the Lanai City Service Facebook page for daily specials. *1036 Lana'i Ave. www.facebook.com/lanaicityservice. ☎ 808/565-7227. Lunch items $5–$11. Deli open daily 6am–4pm (gas station and store 'til 10pm). Map p 156.*

★★★ Nobu Lanai MANELE *JAPANESE* At this classy dining room in the Four Seasons Resort Lana'i, every dish is as delicious as it is artful: the smoked Wagyu gyoza with jalapeño miso, the immaculate plates of nigiri sushi, and the ahi avocado salad with greens grown just up the road. Vegetarian? Nobu has a sophisticated menu just for you, featuring fusion tacos and tofu *tobanyaki anticucho*—a melting pot of Japanese and Peruvian flavors. *1 Manele Bay Rd. www.fourseasons.com/lanai. ☎ 808/565-2832. Entrees $19–$58. Tasting menu $195 per person. AE, DC, MC, V. Dinner daily. Map p 156.*

★ One Forty MANELE *STEAK & SEAFOOD* This casual, open-air, Hawaii-style bistro in the Four Seasons Resort Lanai serves an elaborate breakfast buffet with Asian and Western delicacies and dinner focused on Wagyu steak, Hawaiian seafood, and local venison. Book a table for dinner and watch the sun set and the stars come out. *1 Manele Bay Rd. www.fourseasons.com/lanai. ☎ 808/565-2290. Breakfast entree $16–$33; buffet $55; dinner $32–$95. AE, DC, MC, V. Breakfast and dinner daily. Map p 156.*

★ Pele's Other Garden LANA'I CITY *DELI/BISTRO* The checkered floor and vanity license plates decorating the walls set an upbeat tone at this casual bistro. For lunch, dig into an avocado and feta wrap or an Italian hoagie. Cheese lovers will swoon over the thin-crusted four-cheese pizza. *811 Houston St., Lana'i City. pelesothergarden.com/peles. ☎ 808/565-9628. Entrees $11–$17 lunch, $17–$20 dinner; pizza from $11. AE, DISC, MC, V. Lunch Mon–Fri; dinner Mon–Sat. Map p 156.*

★★ Richards Market LANA'I CITY *GROCERY* This 1946 grocery got a gourmet makeover when Larry Ellison came to town. Now find fancy wine and chocolates alongside fresh poke (raw seasoned fish), local produce, and on Tuesdays, delicious barbecue plates. *434 Eighth St., Lana'i City. ☎ 808/565-3780. AE, DISC, MC, V. Open 6am–10pm. Map p 156.* ●

The Savvy Traveler

Before You Go

Government Tourist Offices

Maui Visitors and Convention Bureau (includes Lana'i and Moloka'i), 427 Ala Makani St., Suite 101, Kahului (Maui), HI 96732; www.gohawaii.com/maui, www.gohawaii.com/lanai, www.gohawaii.com/molokai, and @mauivisit, @visitlanai and @seemolokai on Twitter; ☎ 800/525-MAUI [6284]).

The Best Times to Go

Most visitors come to Hawai'i when the weather is lousy elsewhere. Thus, the **high season**—when prices are up and resorts are often booked to capacity—is generally from mid-December to March or mid-April. In particular, the last 2 weeks of December and the first week of January are prime time for travel to Hawai'i. Spring break is also jam-packed with families taking advantage of the school holiday.

If you're planning a trip during peak season, make hotel and rental car reservations as early as possible, expect crowds, and prepare to pay top dollar. The winter months tend to be a little rainier and cooler. But there's a perk to travelling during this time: Hawaiian humpback whales are here, too.

The **off season,** when the best rates are available and the islands are less crowded, is late spring (May through the first 2 weeks of June) and fall (September to mid-December).

If you plan to travel in **summer** (mid-June–August), don't expect to see the fantastic bargains of spring and fall—this is prime time for family travel. But you'll still find much better deals on packages, airfare, and accommodations than in the winter months.

Previous page: A waterfall near Hana.

Festivals & Special Events

WINTER. **Banyan Tree Lighting Celebration** is when Lahaina's historic Banyan Tree is lit up with thousands of Christmas lights in early December (www.visitlahaina.com; ☎ 808/667-9175). The end of December and early January brings the Academy of Motion Pictures' major screenings of top films with the **First Light,** at the Maui Arts and Cultural Center (www.mauifilmfestival.com; ☎ 808/579-9244). To celebrate **Chinese New Year** (Jan–Feb), the historic Wo Hing Temple in Lahaina town holds a traditional lion dance plus fireworks, food booths, and a host of activities (www.visitlahaina.com; ☎ 808/667-9175). **Maui Whale Festival,** in February, is a month-long celebration on Maui with a variety of activities including a parade, craft fairs, games, and food (www.mauiwhalefestival.org; ☎ 808/249-8811).

SPRING. In mid-March, the entire town of Lahaina celebrates the **Whale and Ocean Arts Festival** in Banyan Tree Park, with Hawaiian musicians and hula troupes, marine-related activities, games, and a "creature feature" touch-pool exhibit for children (www.visitlahaina.com; ☎ 808/667-9175). At the end of March or beginning of April, Hana holds the **East Maui Taro Festival,** serving taro in many different forms, from fresh poi to chips. Stroll around the ballpark and check out the Hawaiian exhibits, hula demonstrations, and food booths (www.tarofestival.org; ☎ 808/264-1553). Easter weekend brings the **Annual Ritz-Carlton, Kapalua, Celebration of the Arts** to the West Maui resort. Contemporary and traditional Hawaiian

artists give free hands-on lessons during this 3-day festival, which also features song contests and rousing debates on what it means to be Hawaiian (www.celebrationofthe arts.org; ☎ 808/669-6200). On the first Saturday in April, the **Maui County Ag Fest** celebrates farmers and their bounty. Kids enjoy barn-yard games while parents sample top chefs' collaborations with local farmers. (mauiagfest.org; ☎ 808/243-2290).

May 1 is **Lei Day** in Hawai'i. Across the state, schoolchildren and public officials will be decked out in flowers. Join the fun at the **Lei Day Heritage Festival** in Wailuku at Hale Ho'ike'ike (www.mauimuseum.org; ☎ 808/244-3326) and look for special concerts at Maui Arts & Cultural Center in Kahului (www.mauiarts.org; ☎ 808/242-2787).

SUMMER. A state holiday on June 11, **King Kamehameha Day** jump-starts the summer with a massive floral parade and *ho'olaule'a* (party) (www.visitlahaina.com; ☎ 808/667-9175). Just before Father's Day weekend in June, the **Maui Film Festival** at the Wailea Resort features 5 days and nights of celebrity-splashed premieres and special films, along with fancy soireés, feasts, and stargazing. (www.maui filmfestival.com; ☎ 808/579-9244). On the last Saturday in July, on Lana'i, the **Pineapple Festival** celebrates Lana'i's history of pineapple plantation and ranching and includes eating and cooking contests, entertainment, arts and crafts, food, and fireworks (www.lanai pineapplefestival.com; ☎ 808/565-7600). The **Fourth of July** is celebrated on Maui with various activities, including fireworks in Lahaina (www.visitlahaina.com; ☎ 808/667-9175). Every weekend in June and July, a different Buddhist church on Maui hosts an **Obon Dance and Ceremony** to honor the souls of departed ancestors. The Lahaina Jodo Mission's ceremony is the prettiest, with glowing lanterns released into the sea after sunset. (☎ 808/661-4304). In early July, famous wine and food experts and oenophiles gather at the **Kapalua Wine & Food Festival** (www.kapaluawineandfoodfestival.com; ☎ 800/KAPALUA [527-2582]), for tastings, panel discussions, and samplings of new releases.

FALL. The statewide **Aloha Festivals** (www.alohafestivals.com; ☎ 808/923-2030), a series of celebrations, parades, and other events honoring the Hawaiian culture, take place in September and October. Late September brings the **Maui Ukulele Festival,** which includes a morning workshop, food booths, giveaways, and a free afternoon concert by top performers at the Maui Arts & Cultural Center in Kahului (www.ukulele festivalhawaii.org).

The Weather

Because Maui lies at the edge of the tropical zone, it technically has only two seasons, both of them warm. The dry season corresponds to summer, and the rainy season generally runs from November to March. The rainy season can cause overcast days that spoil your sunning opportunities. Fortunately, it seldom rains for more than 3 days straight, and rainy days often just consist of a mix of clouds and sun, with very brief showers.

The **year-round temperature** typically varies no more than 15 degrees, but it depends on where you are. Maui's **leeward** sides (the west and south) are usually hot and dry, whereas the **windward** sides (east and north) are generally cooler and moist. If you want arid, desertlike weather, go leeward. If you want lush, often wet, junglelike weather, go windward. Your best bets for total year-round sun are

LAHAINA-KA'ANAPALI'S AVERAGE TEMPERATURE & RAINFALL

	JAN	FEB	MAR	APR	MAY	JUNE
Daily High (°F/°C)	82/28	80/27	83/28	84/29	85/29	87/31
Daily Low (°F/°C)	64/18	6317	64/18	65/18	67/19	68/20
Water Temp	75/24	74/23	74/23	75/24	76/24	77/25
Rain in Inches	3.5	2.4	1.8	1.1	1.1	0.1

	JULY	AUG	SEPT	OCT	NOV	DEC
Daily High (°F/°C)	88/31	88/31	89/32	88/31	86/30	83/28
Daily Low (°F/°C)	69/21	69/21	70/21	69/21	67/19	65/18
Water Temp	78/26	79/26	80/27	79/26	77/25	76/24
Rain in Inches	0.2	0.2	0.3	1.1	2.2	3.2

KIHEI-WAILEA'S AVERAGE TEMPERATURE & RAINFALL

	JAN	FEB	MAR	APR	MAY	JUNE
Daily High (°F/°C)	81/27	81/27	83/28	84/29	85/29	87/31
Daily Low (°F/°C)	63/17	63/17	64/18	64/18	65/18	67/19
Water Temp	75/24	74/23	74/23	75/24	76/24	77/25
Rain in inches	4.1	2.9	2.7	1.8	0.8	0.3

	JULY	AUG	SEPT	OCT	NOV	DEC
Daily High (°F/°C)	8831	89/32	88/31	87/31	85/29	82/28
Daily Low (°F/°C)	69/21	69/21	69/21	68/20	67/19	65/18
Water Temp	78/26	79/26	80/27	79/26	77/25	76/24
Rain in inches/cm	0.4	0.5	0.4	1.3	2.6	3.3

the Kihei-Wailea and Lahaina-Kapalua coasts.

Maui is also full of **microclimates,** thanks to its interior valleys, coastal plains, and mountain peaks. If you travel into the mountains, it can change from summer to winter—from brilliantly sunny to chilly and misty—in a matter of hours, because it's cooler the higher up you go.

Useful Websites

- **www.gohawaii.com**: The Hawai'i Tourism Authority's all-around guide to islands, with pages devoted to Maui, Lana'i, and Moloka'i.
- **www.hawaiiradiotv.com**: Hawaii's radio and television guide.
- **www.calendarmaui.com**: A comprehensive look at events on Maui, with some advertise-ments for accommodations.
- **www.mauinow.com**: Maui's online news source.
- **www.omaui.com**: Daily surf report for Maui.
- **www.weather.com**: Up-to-the-minute worldwide weather reports.

Restaurant & Activity Reservations

If you've got your heart set on a particular restaurant or activity (like dinner at the Old Lahaina Lu'au or the Trilogy trip to Lana'i), book well in advance. For popular restaurants, try asking for early or late hours—often tables are available before 6:30pm and after 8pm.

Cellphones

In general it's a good bet that your cellphone will work in Maui, although coverage may not be as

good as in your hometown. Remote areas, including much of the Kahekili Highway between Kapalua and Kahului and some stretches of the road to Hana, may have no signal at all. Cell coverage on Lana'i may also be spotty (few towers). On the plus side, more locations have Wi-Fi, so you may have digital access even where voice calls are impossible. If you're in doubt about your provider's coverage (or roaming charges, if traveling from abroad), be sure to contact the company in advance for the full scoop.

Getting There

By Plane

If possible, fly directly to Maui. Doing so can save you a 2-hour layover in Honolulu and another plane ride.

If you think of the island of Maui as the shape of a person's head and shoulders, you'll probably arrive near its neck, at **Kahului Airport** (OGG). Many airlines offer direct flights to Maui from the mainland U.S., including **Hawaiian Airlines** (www.hawaiianair.com; ☎ 800/367-5320), **Alaska Airlines** (www.alaskaair.com; ☎ 800/252/7522), **United Airlines** (www.united.com; ☎ 800/241-6522), **Delta Air Lines** (www.delta.com; ☎ 800/221-1212), **American Airlines** (www.aa.com; ☎ 800/882-8880), and **Southwest Airlines** (www.southwest.com; ☎ 800/435-9792). The only international flights to Maui originate in Canada, via **Air Canada** (www.aircanada.com; ☎ 888/247-2262) and **WestJet** (www.westjet.com; ☎ 888/937-8538), which both fly year-round from Vancouver and seasonally from other cities.

Other major carriers stop in Honolulu, where you'll catch an interisland flight to Maui on **Hawaiian Airlines** (including its **'Ohana by Hawaiian** subsidiary) or **Southwest Airlines.**

If you're staying in Lahaina or Ka'anapali, you might consider flying in or out of **Kapalua–West Maui Airport** (JHM). From this tiny airfield, it's only a 10- to 15-minute drive to most hotels in West Maui, as opposed to an hour or more from Kahului. Same story with **Hana Airport** (HNM): Flying directly here will save you a 3-hour drive.

A small commuter service, **Mokulele Airlines** (www.mokuleleairlines.com; ☎ 866/260-7070) flies between Honolulu, Kahului, Kapalua, Hana, Kona, Kamuela/Waimea (Hawaii Island), Ho'olehua (Moloka'i), and Lana'i City. Check-in is a breeze: no security lines (unless leaving from Honolulu). You'll be weighed, ushered onto the tarmac, and welcomed aboard a nine-seat Cessna. The plane flies low, and the views between the islands are outstanding.

Getting Around

By Car

The best way to get around Maui is to rent a car and you'll find the best rates online. Rental cars run from $40 to $75 a day (including all state taxes and fees). Cars are usually plentiful, except on holiday weekends, which in Hawai'i also means

King Kamehameha Day (June 11), Prince Kuhio Day (March 26), and Admission Day (3rd Friday in August). Rental cars on Lana'i are expensive ($95 a day and up) and in short supply, so book well ahead.

All the major car-rental agencies have offices on Maui: **Alamo** (www.goalamo.com; ☎ 877/222-9075), **Avis** (www.avis.com; ☎ 800/331-1212), **Budget** (www.budget.com; ☎ 800/214-6094), **Dollar** (www.dollar.com; ☎ 800/800-4000), **Hertz** (www.hertz.com; ☎ 800/654-3131), and **National** (www.nationalcar.com; ☎ 800/227-7368).

There are also a few frugal car-rental agencies offering older cars at discount prices. **Aloha Rent a Car** (www.aloharentacar.com; ☎ 877/452-5642 or 808/877-4477) has used, older vehicles and requires a 4-day minimum rental. Rates start at $31 a day, with free airport pickup and drop-off included. **Maui Cruisers,** in Wailuku (www.mauicruisers.net; ☎ 877/749-7889 or 808/249-2319), also offers free airport pickup and return; rentals start at $28 a day (4-day minimum) or $122 a week (including tax and insurance).

To rent a car in Hawai'i, you must be at least 25 years old and have a valid driver's license and a credit card.

One more thing on car rentals: Hawai'i is a no-fault state, which means that if you don't have collision-damage insurance, you are required to pay for all damages before you leave the state, whether or not the accident was your fault. Your personal car insurance back home may provide rental-car coverage; read your policy or call your insurer before you leave home. Bring your insurance card if you decline the optional insurance, which usually costs from $12 to $20 a day. Obtain the name of your company's local claim representative before you go. Some credit card companies also provide collision-damage insurance for their customers; check with yours before you rent.

By Bus

The **Maui Bus** (www.mauicounty.gov/bus; ☎ 808/871-4838) provides limited public transit across the island. Expect hour-long waits between rides. Air-conditioned buses serve 13 routes, including several that stop at the airport. Simply cross the street at baggage claim and wait under the awning. Unfortunately, bus stops are few and far between, so you may end up lugging your suitcase a long way to your destination. All routes operate daily, including holidays. Suitcases (one per passenger) and bikes are allowed; surfboards are not. The fare is $2.

By Airport Shuttle

If there's just one or two of you traveling, book a shuttle van from the airport to your destination from **Roberts Hawai'i Airport Express Shuttle** (www.airportshuttlehawaii.com/shuttles/maui; ☎ 866/898-2523 or 808/439-8800), which offers curb-to-curb service in a shared van or small bus. Booking is a breeze online. Plan to pay $24 (one-way) to Wailea and $34 to Ka'anapali. Another option is **SpeediShuttle Maui** (www.speedishuttle.com; ☎ 877/242-5777); prices (one-way, from the airport, for a shared van) range from $45 to Wailea to $62 to Ka'anapali. You need to book in 24 hours in advance. Bonus: You can request a fresh flower-lei greeting for an added fee.

By Taxi & Ride-Share

Taxi service on Maui is quite expensive—expect to spend around $80 for a ride from Kahului to Ka'anapali and $60 from the

airport to Wailea. For islandwide 24-hour service, call **Alii Cab Co.** (☎ 808/661-3688 or 808/667-2605). You can also try **Kihei Taxi** (☎ 808/879-3000), **Wailea Taxi** (☎ 808/874-5000), or **Maui Central Cab** (☎ 808/244-7278). **Lyft** and **Uber** are typically cheaper, although prices vary widely, with best availability and prices in busy resort and urban areas."

Fast **Facts**

ATMS You'll find **ATMs** at most banks, in supermarkets, and in most resorts and shopping centers.

BABYSITTING The first place to check is with your hotel. Many hotels have babysitting services or will provide you with lists of reliable sitters. The **Nanny Connection** (www.thenannyconnection.com; ☎ 808/875-4777) on Maui is a reputable business that sends Mary Poppins–esque nannies to resorts and beaches to watch children ($17 per hour and up, with a 3-hour minimum and $25 booking fee). You can also call **People Attentive to Children** (www.patchhawaii.org; ☎ 808/242-9232 [Maui] or 800/498-4145 [Lana'i]), which will refer you to individuals who have taken their childcare training courses.

BANKING HOURS Banks are open Monday through Thursday from 8:30am to 5pm and Friday from 8:30am to 6pm. Many banks are open until noon on Saturday.

BUSINESS HOURS Most offices are open from 8am to 5pm. Shopping centers are open Monday through Friday from 10am to 9pm, Saturday from 10am to 5:30pm, and Sunday from 10am to 5 or 6pm.

CONDOMINIUM & VACATION HOME RENTALS **Airbnb, VRBO, HomeAway** and other multinational rental agencies all have a presence on Maui. But for better service, and regularly inspected properties, we recommend the following companies: **Condominium Rentals Hawai'i** (www.crhmaui.com; ☎ 800/367-5242) offers affordable, quality properties primarily in Kihei, with a few in Wailea and Lahaina. **Bello Realty** (www.bellomaui.com; ☎ 800/541-3060) also offers a variety of condos. For vacation rentals, contact **Hawaiian Beach Rentals** (www.hawaiianbeachrentals.com; ☎ 844/261-0464).

CUSTOMS Visitors from other countries arriving by air, no matter what the port of entry, should cultivate patience and resignation before setting foot on U.S. soil. Getting through customs and immigration control can take as long as 2 hours on some days.

DENTISTS If you have dental problems, a nationwide referral service known as **1-800-DENTIST** (☎ 800/336-8478) will provide the name of a nearby dentist or clinic. Emergency dental care is available at **Hawaii Family Dental** (1847 S. Kihei Rd., Kihei; ☎ 808/856-4625 and 95 Lono Av., Ste. 210, Kahului ☎ 808/856-4626), or in Lahaina at the **Aloha Lahaina Dentists** (134 Luakini St., in the Maui Medical Group Bldg.; ☎ 808/661-4005).

DOCTORS **Urgent Care West Maui,** located in the Fairway Shops, 2580 Keka'a Dr., Suite 111, Ka'anapali (www.westmauidoctors.com; ☎ 808/667-9721), is open 365 days a year; no appointment necessary. In Kihei, visit **Urgent Care Maui** (www.minitmed.com; ☎ 808/879-7781), open weekdays

8am to 7pm ('til 6pm Sat, 'til 4pm Sun) at 1325 S. Kihei Rd., Suite 103, across from Times Market.

ELECTRICITY The United States uses 110 to 120 volts AC (60 cycles), compared to 220 to 240 volts AC (50 cycles) in most of Europe, Australia, and New Zealand. Downward converters that change 220–240 volts to 110–120 volts are difficult to find in the United States, so bring one with you.

EMERGENCIES Dial ☎ 911 for the police, an ambulance, and the fire department. District stations are located in Lahaina (☎ 808/661-4441) and in Hana (☎ 808/248-8311). For the **Poison Control Center,** call ☎ 800/222-1222.

EVENT LISTINGS The best source for listings is the Friday edition of the local daily newspaper, **Maui News** (www.mauinews.com). There are also several tourist publications with listings, including **This Week on Maui** (www.thisweek.com) and **Maui Visitor Magazine** (www.alohavisitorguides.com). You can also check small, local community newspapers, such as **Maui Time Weekly** (www.mauitime.com) and **Lahaina News** (www.lahainanews.com).

FAMILY TRAVEL Look for the kids icon throughout this book for tips on the best activities, hotels, and restaurants for families with kids. For up-to-date family-friendly events, check out **Maui Mama** (www.mauimama.com), also available in print at many island locations. **Baby's Away** (www.babysaway.com; ☎ 800/942-9030) rents cribs, strollers, highchairs, playpens, and infant seats. The staff will deliver whatever you need to wherever you're staying and pick it up when you're done.

GAY & LESBIAN TRAVELERS **Pride Guide Hawai'i** (www.gogayhawaii.com) features gay and lesbian news, blogs, business recommendations, and other information for the entire state. Also check out the website for **Aloha Maui Pride** (www.alohamauipride.org), which maintains a year-round calendar of LGBT events as well as details on its annual, weeklong Pride festivities in October.

HOLIDAYS Federal, state, and county government offices are closed on all federal holidays: January 1 (New Year's Day), third Monday in January (Martin Luther King Day), third Monday in February (Presidents' Day), last Monday in May (Memorial Day), July 4th (Independence Day), first Monday in September (Labor Day), second Monday in October (Columbus Day), November 11 (Veterans Day), fourth Thursday in November (Thanksgiving Day), and December 25 (Christmas). State and county offices also are closed on local holidays, including Prince Kuhio Day (March 26), King Kamehameha Day (June 11), and Admission Day (third Friday in August). Other special days are celebrated by many people in Hawai'i, but do not involve the closing of federal, state, or county offices: They include Chinese (Lunar) New Year (in January or February), Girls' Day (March 3), Buddha's Birthday (April 8), Father Damien's Day (April 15), Boys' Day (May 5), Samoan Flag Day (in August), Aloha Festivals (September or October), and Pearl Harbor Day (December 7).

INSURANCE Trip-cancellation insurance helps you get your money back if you have to back out of a trip, if you have to go home early, or if your travel supplier goes bankrupt. Other forms of insurance can help if you miss a flight or cruise or need medical care. For all types of insurance we recommend such marketplace sites as: **Square Mouth.com** and **InsureMyTrip.**

com. You'll key in your age and the details of your trip and receive in return a list of potential policies, all from established insurance companies, in a range of prices. You'll also be able to quickly scan and see what is and isn't covered by each policy.

Although it's not required of travelers, health insurance is highly recommended. Unlike many European countries, the United States does not usually offer free or low-cost medical care to its citizens or visitors. Doctors and hospitals are expensive, and in most cases require advance payment or proof of coverage before they treat patients. Lack of health insurance may prevent you from being admitted to a hospital in non-emergencies, but don't worry about being left on a street corner to die: The American way is to fix you now and bill the living daylights out of you later.

INTERNET ACCESS All hotels and most vacation rentals have Wi-Fi, usually free or included in the resort fee. **Whole Foods** (www.wholefoodsmarket.com/stores/maui) at the Maui Mall in Kahului has free Wi-Fi, as does **Starbucks** (www.starbucks.com/store-locator) with stores in Kahului, Pukalani, Lahaina, and Kihei. If you need a computer, visit a **public library** (for locations, check www.publiclibraries.com/hawaii.htm). A library card gets you free access; purchase a 3-month visitor card for $10.

MAIL & POSTAGE At press time, domestic postage rates were 35¢ for a postcard and 55¢ for a letter. For international mail, a first-class postcard or letter up to 1 ounce costs $1.15. For more information go to **www.usps.com**. To find the nearest post office, call ☎ 800/ASK-USPS [275-8777] or log on to www.usps.gov. In Lahaina the main post office is at the Lahaina Civic Center (1760 Honoapi'ilani Hwy.), in Kahului there's a branch at 138 S. Pu'unene Ave., and in Kihei there's one at 1254 S. Kihei Rd. Mail can be sent to you, in your name, c/o General Delivery, at the post office. Most post offices will hold your mail for up to 1 month.

PASSPORTS Anyone traveling to Hawai'i from outside of the U.S. is required to show a passport. Bring a photocopy of your passport with you and store it separately; if your passport is lost or stolen, the copy will help you get a new one reissued at your consulate. If you are an American citizen flying to Hawai'i from the U.S. mainland, a driver's license or state ID will suffice. ***Note:*** Effective October 1, 2020, all travelers must show identification that complies with the REAL-ID Act: either a passport or an ID/driver's license from a REAL-ID compliant state. Check with the Department of Homeland Security to see if your ID is compliant (www.dhs.gov/real-id; ☎ 202/282-8000).

PHARMACIES **Longs Drugs** (www.cvs.com) has five pharmacies on Maui, two of which are in stores open 24 hours: in Kihei (1215 S. Kihei Rd.; ☎ 808/879-2023), and in Kahului at the Maui Mall Shopping Center (70 E. Kaahumanu Ave.; ☎ 808/877-0068). The Kihei store has the longest pharmacy hours: 8am to 9pm weekdays, 7am to 7pm Saturday, and 9am to 6pm Sunday. See website for hours of other locations.

SAFETY Although Hawai'i is generally a safe tourist destination, visitors have been crime victims, so stay alert. The most common crime against tourists is rental-car break-ins. Never leave any valuables in your car, not even in your trunk. Be especially careful in high-risk areas, such as beaches and trailheads.

Never carry large amounts of cash. Stay in well-lighted areas after dark. Don't hike alone on remote trails or swim solo in the ocean.

SENIOR TRAVELERS Discounts for seniors are available at almost all of Maui's major attractions, and occasionally at hotels and restaurants. The savings tend to be solid for attractions, but for lodgings check Booking.com or another discount hotel site to make sure you're actually getting the best rate with a senior discount. Members of **AARP** (www.aarp.org; ☎ 800/424-3410 or 202/434-2277) are usually eligible for extra discounts. AARP also puts together organized tour packages at moderate rates. Some great, low-cost trips to Hawai'i are offered to people 55 and older through **Road Scholar** (11 Avenue de Lafayette, Boston, MA 02111; www.roadscholar.org; ☎ 800/454-5768), a nonprofit group that arranges travel and study programs around the world.

If you're planning to visit Haleakala National Park, you can save sightseeing dollars if you're 62 or older by picking up a **Senior Pass** from any national park, recreation area, or monument. This lifetime pass has a one-time fee of $80 ($20 for annual pass) and provides free admission to all of the parks in the system, plus 50% savings on camping and some recreation fees.

SPECTATOR SPORTS Maui hosts a slew of professional and amateur sports events that are exciting to watch. Golf fans can witness the annual **PGA Tour's Sentry Tournament of Champions** in Kapalua in January (www.golfatkapalua.com; ☎ 808/669-8044); windsurfing aficionados can catch the **Maui Aloha Classic** competition at Ho'okipa in late fall (www.internationalwindsurfingtour.com); and basketball fans get front row bleacher seats at the annual **Maui Invitational** college basketball tournament in November (www.mauiinvitational.com). There are even rousing **polo** matches to rally behind in Makawao in spring and fall (www.mauipoloclub.com; ☎ 808/877-7744).

TAXES The United States has no value-added tax (VAT) or other indirect tax at the national level. Local taxes, however, are levied on all purchases, including hotel and restaurant checks and airline tickets. These taxes will not appear on price tags. Maui County has a general excise tax of 4.166%, which applies to all items purchased (including hotel rooms). On top of that, the state's Transient Accommodation Tax (TAT) is 10.25%. These taxes, combined with daily resort fees of $25 or more, can add significantly to your room rate. Budget accordingly.

TELEPHONE For directory assistance, dial ☎ 411; for long-distance information, dial 1, then the appropriate area code, and then 555-1212. The area code for all of Hawai'i (not just Maui) is 808. Calls to other islands are considered long distance. For calls to other islands you have to dial 1 + 808 + the 7-digit phone number.

TIPPING Tips are a major part of certain workers' income, and gratuities are the standard way of showing appreciation for services provided. (Tipping is certainly not compulsory if the service is poor!) In hotels, tip bellhops at least $2 per bag and tip the housekeepers $2–$4 per day (more if you've left a disaster area for him or her to clean up). Tip the doorman or concierge only if he or she has provided you with some specific service (for example, calling a cab for you or obtaining difficult-to-get theater tickets). Tip the valet-parking attendant $3–$5 every time you get your car.

In general, tip service staff such as waiters, bartenders, and

hairdressers 18% to 20% of the bill. Tip cab drivers 15% of the fare.

TOILETS You won't find public toilets on the streets in Hawai'i, but you can find them in hotel lobbies, restaurants, museums, department stores, service stations, and at most beach parks (where you'll find showers, too). Large hotels and fast-food restaurants are often the best bet for clean facilities. Restaurants and bars in busy areas may reserve their restrooms for patrons.

TRAVELERS WITH DISABILITIES Travelers with disabilities will feel welcome in Maui. Hotels are usually equipped with wheelchair-accessible rooms and swimming pools, and tour companies provide many special services. Beach wheelchairs are available at Kama'ole I in Kihei (ask lifeguard). For tips on accessible travel in Hawai'i, go to the **Hawai'i Tourism Authority** website (www.gohawaii.com/trip-planning/accessibility). Travelers with disabilities who wish to do their own driving can rent hand-controlled cars from **Avis** (www.avis.com; ☎ 800/331-1212) and **Hertz** (www.hertz.com; ☎ 800/654-3131). The number of hand-controlled cars in Hawai'i is limited, so be sure to book well in advance. Maui recognizes other states' windshield placards indicating that the driver of the car is disabled, so be sure to bring yours with you. Travelers who use a Seeing Eye dog or other kind of service dog will need to present documentation that the dog has been certified as a service animal, is microchipped, and has had rabies shots and flea prevention medication according to a strict timetable. A local veterinarian must be hired to inspect the dog and his papers at Kahului airport. For more information, contact the **Animal Quarantine Facility** (hdoa.hawaii.gov/ai/aqs/aqs-info; ☎ 808/483-7151).

A Brief **History**

BETWEEN A.D. 300 AND 1200 Using the stars and currents as their guides, Polynesian wayfinders sail double-hulled canoes across the sea to Hawai'i. They bring with them everything needed for survival, including tools, medicine, animals, and around 30 different plant species.

AROUND 1300 Transoceanic voyages halt; Hawai'i begins to develop its own culture in earnest. Sailors become farmers and fishermen, and build temples, fishponds, and aqueducts to irrigate *kalo lo'i* (taro paddies). Each island is a separate kingdom, divided into smaller districts called *ahupua'a*. Each wedge-shaped *ahupua'a* runs from the mountain to the sea, granting its residents access to a wide range of natural resources. The *ali'i* (chiefs) create a caste system with numerous *kapu* (restrictions). The arts flourish; Hawaiians develop sophisticated dances, chants, weaving techniques, and *kapa* (barkcloth) patterns.

AROUND 1400 Work begins on a massive *heiau* (temple) later known as Pi'ilanihale in Hana. When complete, it will span 3 acres (1.2ha) with 50-foot-tall (15m) walls.

AROUND 1577 Pi'ilani, a high chief from Hana, is born. He unites Maui under single rule, builds fishponds and irrigation fields,

and begins paving a road of smooth stones 4 to 6 feet (1.2–1.8km) wide around the entire island. His sons and grandson complete the project.

MID-1700S A pregnant woman in Kona craves the eyeball of a man-eating shark, signifying that her unborn son is destined to be a powerful chief. She gives birth to Kamehameha I in North Kohala on Hawai'i Island. Fulfilling many prophecies, the boy grows into a great warrior.

1768 Ka'ahumanu is born, reportedly in a cave at Pu'u Kauiki in Hana. She later becomes the favorite wife of Kamehameha I and an influential figure in the Hawaiian monarchy.

1778 Captain James Cook sails into Waimea Bay on Kaua'i, where he is welcomed as the god Lono. His sailors trade nails for fresh water and pigs, and despite Cook's edict, have sex with Hawaiian women. The foreigners bring syphilis, measles, and other diseases to which the Hawaiians have no natural immunity, thereby unwittingly wreaking havoc on the native population. The captain and four of his crew are killed the following year during a scuffle over a stolen boat in Kealakekua Bay on Hawai'i Island.

1782 Kamehameha I begins his campaign to conquer the Hawaiian Islands.

1790 During the Battle of Kepaniwai (the damming of the waters), Kamehameha thrashes the Maui forces in 'Iao Valley with Western guns and cannons. Maui chiefess Kalola and her granddaughter Keopuolani (Hawai'i's highest-ranking princess) escape through the mountains to Olowalu and continue by canoe to Moloka'i.

1795 Kamehameha I finally conquers Maui. He marries Keopuolani to establish his dominance, and makes Lahaina the capital of his new kingdom.

1801 Kamehameha I stops on Maui with his fleet of war canoes on his way to do battle on O'ahu and Kaua'i. He stays in Lahaina for a year, constructing the Brick Palace, Hawai'i's first Western-style structure.

1810 Kamehameha I unites the Hawaiian Islands under single rule.

1819 Kamehameha I dies; his son Liholiho is proclaimed Kamehameha II. Under the influence of Queen Ka'ahumanu, Kamehameha II orders the destruction of *heiau* and an end to the *kapu* system, thus overthrowing the traditional Hawaiian religion. The first whaling ship, *Bellina*, drops anchor in Lahaina.

1820 Missionaries arrive in Lahaina from New England, bent on converting islanders and combating the drunken licentiousness of visiting sailors. To spread the gospel, missionaries create a Hawaiian alphabet and introduce written language. They establish the first high school and newspaper west of the Rockies. Ka'ahumanu and Keopuolani convert to Christianity, influencing thousands of Hawaiians follow suit.

1845 King Kamehameha III moves the capital of Hawai'i from Lahaina to Honolulu, where the natural harbor can accommodate more commerce.

1849 George Wilfong, a sea captain, builds a mill in Hana and plants some 60 acres of sugar cane, creating Hawai'i's first sugar plantation.

1876 Sugar planters engineer an elaborate ditch system that takes water from rainy Ha'iku and delivers it to the dry plains of Central Maui, cementing the future of sugar in Hawai'i.

JANUARY 17, 1893 A group of American sugar planters and missionary descendants, with the support of U.S. Marines, imprison Queen Lili'uokalani in her palace in Honolulu and illegally overthrow the Hawaiian government.

JUNE 16, 1897 U.S. President McKinley acts to annex the Hawaiian Islands formally. Queen Lili'uokalani travels to Washington in protest and 21,269 Native Hawaiians (more than half the entire population) sign a petition against annexation. The following year, Congress passes McKinley's resolution.

APRIL 30, 1900 Congress passes the Organic Act, establishing the Territory of Hawai'i with Sanford Dole as its first governor.

NOVEMBER 22, 1935 Pan American Airways offers the first commercial flight from the U.S. mainland to Hawai'i—16 hours from Los Angeles to Honolulu.

DECEMBER 7, 1941 Japanese Zeros bomb American warships based at Pearl Harbor and nearby airfields, plunging the U.S. into World War II.

AUGUST 21, 1959 Hawai'i becomes the 50th state of the United States.

1960 Amfac, owner of Pioneer Sugar Company, builds Maui's first destination resort in Ka'anapali.

1967 The state of Hawai'i hosts 1 million tourists.

1975 Maui reaches the 1 million annual tourists mark. Ten years later the number is 2 million.

1990S Hawai'i's economy suffers following a series of events: First, the Gulf War severely curtails air travel to the island; then, Hurricane 'Iniki slams into Kaua'i, crippling its infrastructure; and finally, sugar-cane companies across the state began shutting down, laying off thousands of workers. Maui weathers this turbulent economic storm.

NOVEMBER 4, 2008 Barack Obama, a Punahou School graduate, becomes the first Hawai'i-born President of the United States.

AUGUST 21, 2009 Hawai'i, the 50th state, celebrates 50 years of statehood.

DECEMBER 2016 Hawai'i's oldest and largest sugar plantation, Hawaiian Commercial & Sugar Company, ceases operations, ending 168 years of sugar harvests in the Islands.

The Hawaiian **Language**

Almost everyone in the Islands speaks English. But many folks now speak Hawaiian, the native language, as well. All visitors will hear the words *aloha* (hello/goodbye/love) and *mahalo* (thank you). If you've just arrived, you're a *malihini*. Someone who's been here a long time is a *kama'aina*, child of the land. When you finish a job or your meal, you are *pau* (finished). On Friday it's *pau hana*, work

finished. You eat *pupu* (appetizers) when you go *pau hana*.

The Hawaiian alphabet, created by the New England missionaries, has only 12 letters: the 5 regular vowels (*a, e, i, o,* and *u*) and 7 consonants (*h, k, l, m, n, p,* and *w*). The vowels are pronounced in the Roman fashion, that is, *ah, ay, ee, oh,* and *oo* (as in "too")—not *ay, ee, eye, oh,* and *you*, as in English. For example, *huhu* is pronounced *hoo-hoo*. Most vowels are sounded separately, though some are pronounced together, as in Kalakaua (*Kah-lah-cow-ah*).

Two Hawaiian diacritical marks will help you with pronunciation: The *'okina* is a backward apostrophe that separates vowels and can also appear at the beginning of a word that starts with a vowel. It's pronounced as a pause or glottal stop; some consider it the 8th consonant. *Ho'okipa*, which means hospitality, is pronounced *ho-oh-kee-pah*. The *kahako* is a line above a vowel (macron) that lengthens the vowel and indicates stress on the syllable in which it appears. (It is not used in this guide for typographical reasons.)

Useful Words & Phrases

Here are some basic Hawaiian words that you'll often hear in Hawai'i and see throughout this book. For a more complete list, consult www.wehewehe.org.

ali'i: *Hawaiian royalty*
aloha: *greeting or farewell*
halau: *school*
hale: *house or building*
heiau: *Hawaiian temple or place of worship*
kahuna: *priest or expert*
kama'aina: *island-born or long-time Hawaii resident*
kane: *man, men*
kapa: *barkcloth*
kapu: *taboo, forbidden*
keiki: *child*
lanai: *porch or veranda*
lomilomi: *massage*
mahalo: *thank you*
maika'i: *good*
makai: *a direction, toward the sea*
malama: *to take care of, protect*
mana: *spirit power*
mauka: *a direction, toward the mountains*
mu'umu'u: *loose-fitting gown or dress*
'ono: *delicious*
pali: *cliff*
paniolo: *Hawaiian cowboy(s)*
wahine: *woman, women*
wiki: *quick*

Pidgin: Try Talk Story

If you venture beyond the tourist areas, you might hear another local tongue: Hawaiian Pidgin, a blend of Hawaiian, English, and the languages of the early sugar plantation workers: Chinese, Japanese, Portuguese, etc. "Broke da mouth" (tastes really good) is a favorite phrase you might hear. If you're lucky, you could be invited to hear an elder "talk story" (chat and tell stories).

Eating in Maui

When it comes to dining in Maui, all I can say is: Come hungry and bring a fat wallet. Dining has never been better on the Valley Isle, which is presently producing numerous enterprising and imaginative chefs. The farm-to-table concept has finally taken root on this

bountiful island, where in past years up to 90% of the food had been imported. Today chefs and farmers collaborate on menus, filling plates with tender micro-greens and heirloom tomatoes picked that morning. Fishers reel in glistening *'opakapaka* (pink snapper), and ranchers offer up flavorful cuts of Maui-grown beef.

A new crop of inspired chefs is taking these ripe ingredients to new heights. At **Ka'ana Kitchen** (see p 128), chef Isaac Bancaco nearly outshines his celebrity neighbor, "Iron Chef" Masuhara Morimoto (who brought his high-octane Japanese fusion cuisine to **Morimoto Maui** in Wailea, p 130). Also in Wailea, *Top Chef* fan favorite Sheldon Simeon celebrates his Filipino heritage and Hilo roots at upscale **Lineage** (p 128), and shows equal creativity with lunch fare at his humbler **Tin Roof** in Kahului (p 132). In Napili, former *Iron Chef* sous chef and local award-winner Jojo Vasquez puts an elegant, island-inspired spin on brunch, served daily at his new Fond restaurant.

Good-value plate lunch places and food trucks stand ready to satisfy you as well. The **plate lunch,** like Hawaiian Pidgin, is a gift of the plantation era. You'll find plate lunches served in to-go eateries across the islands. They usually consist of some protein—fried mahimahi, say, or teriyaki beef, shoyu chicken, or chicken or pork cutlets served *katsu* style: breaded, fried, and slathered in tangy sauce—accompanied by "two scoops rice," macaroni salad, and a few leaves of green, typically julienned cabbage. Chili water and soy sauce are the condiments of choice. Like **saimin**—the local version of noodles in broth topped with scrambled eggs, green onions, and sometimes pork—the plate lunch is Hawai'i's version of comfort food.

Because this is Hawai'i, at least a few fingerfuls of **poi**—steamed, pounded taro (the traditional Hawaiian staple crop)—are a must. Mix it with salty *kalua* pig (pork cooked in a Polynesian underground oven known as an *imu*) or *lomi* salmon (salted salmon with tomatoes and green onions). Other tasty Hawaiian foods include ***poke*** (pronounced *po-kay*), a popular appetizer made of cubed raw fish seasoned with onions, seaweed, and roasted *kukui* nuts; ***laulau,*** pork, chicken, or fish steamed in *ti* leaves; **squid *lu'au,*** cooked in coconut milk and taro tops; ***haupia,*** creamy coconut pudding; and ***kulolo,*** a steamed pudding of coconut, brown sugar, and taro.

A Hawaiian Seafood Primer

To help familiarize you with the menu language of Hawaii, here's a basic glossary of island fish:

'ahi: *yellowfin or big-eye tuna*
aku: *skipjack tuna*
hapu'upu'u: *grouper, a sea bass*
hebi: *spearfish*
kumu: *goatfish*
mahimahi: *dolphin fish (the game fish, not the mammal)*
monchong: *bigscale or sickle pomfret*
onaga: *ruby snapper*
ono: *wahoo*
opah: *moonfish*
'opakapaka: *pink snapper*
papio: *jack trevally*
shutome: *broadbill swordfish*
tombo: *albacore tuna*
uhu: *parrotfish*
uku: *gray snapper*
ulua: *large jack trevally*

Airline & Car Rental Websites

Airlines on Maui

AIR CANADA
www.aircanada.com

ALASKA AIRLINES
www.alaskaair.com

AMERICAN AIRLINES
www.aa.com

DELTA AIR LINES
www.delta.com

HAWAIIAN AIRLINES
www.hawaiianair.com

MAKANI KAI AIR
www.makanikaiair.com

MOKULELE AIRLINES
www.mokuleleairlines.com

SOUTHWEST AIRLINES
www.southwest.com

UNITED AIRLINES
www.united.com

WESTJET
www.westjet.com

Car Rental Agencies on Maui

ALAMO
www.goalamo.com

AVIS
www.avis.com

BUDGET
www.budget.com

DOLLAR
www.dollarcar.com

HERTZ
www.hertz.com

MAUI CRUISERS
www.mauicruisers.net

NATIONAL
www.nationalcar.com

ALOHA RENT-A-CAR
www.aloharentacar.com

Index

See also Accommodations and Restaurant indexes, below.

Accommodations

Restaurants

Photo Credits

p i, left: Konrad Mostert; p i, middle: Galyna Andrushko; p i, right: Sheri Swailes; p ii, top: Courtesy of Montage Kapalua Bay Hotel; p ii, second from top: RuthChoi; p ii, middle: Maridav; p ii, second from bottom: Hawaii Tourism Authority (HTA) / Tor Johnson; p ii, bottom: Courtesty of Hawaii Tourism Authority (HTA) / Tor Johnson; p iii, top: Courtesy of Maui Visitors Bureau; p iii, second from top: Courtesy of Maui Girl; p iii, middle: Courtesy of Mill House Restaurant; p iii, second from bottom: Courtesy of Maui Film Festival/ Randy Jay Braun; p iii, bottom: Courtesy of Hotel Wailea/ Glenn Parry; p viii-p 1: EQRoy / Shutterstock.com; p 3: EQRoy / Shutterstock.com; p 4, top: Courtesy of Hotel Wailea/ Quincy Dein; p 4, bottom: Ryan Siphers; p 5: Courtesy of Montage Kapalua Bay Hotel; p 7, top: tdee photo cm; p 7, bottom: Andy Konieczny; p 8: smfato/ Frommers.com Community; p 9: RuthChoi; p 11: Hiroyuki Saita / Shutterstock.com; p 12: Ryan Siphers; p 13: Courtesy of Maui Wine/ Tony Novak-Clifford; p 15: Courtesy of Hawaii Tourism Authority/ Tor Johnson; p 16: Maridav; p 17, top: Chris Howey; p 17, bottom: Courtesy of Hawaii Tourism Authority/ Tor Johnson; p 19: Courtesy of Blue Hawaiian Helicopters/ Karl Weatherly; p 20: Hawaii Tourism Authority (HTA) / Dana Edmunds; p 21, top: Courtesy of Four Seasons; p 21, bottom: Courtesy of Surfing Goat Diary; p 22, top: Chris Allan / Shutterstock.com; p 22, bottom: EQRoy / Shutterstock.com; p 23: Maridav; p 25: Courtesy of Ka'anapali Beach Hotel; p 26, top: Brian Lauer; p 26, bottom: © Courtesy of Maui Ocean Center; p 27: Courtesy of Mill House; p 28, top: Courtesy of Atlantis Submarine Maui; p 28, bottom: © Pacific Whale Foundation; p 31: Pierre Leclerc; p 32, top: Courtesy of Merriman's Hawaii; p 32, bottom: Courtesy of Maui Visitors Bureau; p 33: Courtesy of Pa'ia Bay Coffee; p 35: Courtesy of Lumeria; p 36, top: Ryan Siphers; p 36, bottom: Courtesy of Montage Kapalua Bay; p 39: hin255; p 40: mikeledray; p 41: Courtesy of Maui Wine/ Randy Jay Braun; p 43: Ryan Siphers; p 44: Ryan Siphers; p 45: Ryan Siphers; p 46: Forest and Kim Starr; p 47: Hawaii Tourism Authority (HTA) / Tor Johnson; p 49: Ryan Siphers; p 51: Ryan Siphers; p 52: Ryan Siphers; p 53, top: Ryan Siphers; p 53, bottom: Chris Howey; p 55: Joe West; p 56: Hawaii Tourism Authority (HTA) / Tor Johnson; p 58, top: Forest and Kim Starr; p 58, bottom: © Courtesy of Maui Ocean Center; p 61: Kirt Edblom; p 65: Travis; p 67: Hawaii Tourism Authority (HTA) / Tor Johnson; p 68, top: Ryan Siphers; p 68, bottom: Ryan Siphers; p 69: SaraJane; p 71: Ryan Siphers; p 72: Ryan Siphers; p 73: Ryan Siphers; p 74, top : Lee Prince; p 74, bottom: Ryan Siphers; p 75: Courtesy of Hawaii Tourism Authority (HTA) / Tor Johnson; p 76: Stephanie Coffman; p 78: dejetley; p 79: Courtesy of Hawaii Tourism Authority; p 80: Ryan Siphers; p 81: Circumnavigation; p 82: Hawaii Tourism Authority/Tor Johnson; p 83: Courtesy of Maui Visitors Bureau; p 85: topseller; p 86: Russ Beinder; p 87: Tracy Immordino; p 89: EpicStockMedia; p 91: Shane Myers Photography; p 94: porqpyne/ Aaron Chong Photography; p 95: © Photo by Erica Chan, Courtesy Wailea Golf Club; p 97: idreamphoto; p 98: © UWA/Frommers.com Community; p 101: © Kristin Mills; p 102: Courtesy of Blue Hawaiian Helicopters/Karl Weatherly; p 103: © Courtesy of Skyline Eco-Adventures; p 105: EpicStockMedia; p 107: © Dai Mar Tamarack; p 108, top: Courtesy of Pacific Whale Foundation/ Bryan Berkowitz for Pacific Whale Foundation; p 108, bottom: John Orsbun / Shutterstock.com; p 109: Courtesy of Maui Girl; p 116, top: © Kristin Mills; p 116, bottom: Courtesy of Hui No'eau Visual Arts Center/ BRYAN BERKOWITZ/Hui Douglass Chun; p 117, top: bkkstocker; p 117, bottom: Melissa Doroquez; p 119, top: Courtesy of Native Intelligence; p 119, bottom: © Courtesy of Maui Ocean Center; p 120: CJ Anderson; p 121: Courtesy of Mill House Restaurant; p 122: Travis Jacobs; p 129, top: Courtesy of Lineage; p 129, bottom: Courtesy of Mala/ Debbie Hollman; p 130, top: Courtesy of Merriman's Hawaii/ Tony Novak-Clifford; p 130, bottom: Courtesy of Mill House Restaurant; p 132: Courtesy of Sansei; p 133: Courtesy of Maui Film Festival/ Randy Jay Braun; p 137, top: Ryan Siphers; p 137, bottom: Courtesy of Maui Brewing Co.; p 139, top: Courtesy of Maui Cultural Center / Tony Novak-Clifford; p 139, bottom: Courtesy of Ka'anapali Beach Hotel; p 140: © Courtesy of Hawaiian Slack Key Guitar Productions; p 141: Courtesy of Hotel Wailea/ Glenn Parry; p 142: Courtesy of Aqua-Aston Hospitality; p 147, top: Courtesy of Hamoa Bay; p 147, bottom: Courtesy of Kaanapali Beach Hotel; p 148: Courtesy of Plantation Inn; p 149: Courtesy of Ritz Carlton Kapalua/ Jason Dewey; p 150: Courtesy fo Travaasa Destinations; p 151: Hawaii Tourism Authority/ HTA; p 153, top: Lynn Yeh; p 153, bottom: Joey Riz; p 155, top: Hawaii Tourism Authority (HTA) / Heather Goodman / @hbgoodie; p 155, bottom: Hawaii Tourism Authority (HTA) / Dana Edmunds; p 157: Courtesy of Four Seasons; p 158: Hawaii Tourism Authority (HTA) / Lanai Hospitality Partners; p 159: Courteys of Four Seasons/Don Riddle; p 160: Hawaii Tourism Authority/ Tor Johnson; back cover: DonLand.

Contents

Frommer's

Maui day BY day®

6th Edition

by Jeanne Cooper